DIGNITY OF WORK

John Paul II Speaks To Managers and Workers

Robert G. Kennedy

UNIVERSITY PRESS OF AMERICA

Lanham • New York • London

University Press of America,® Inc.
4720 Boston Way
Lanham, Maryland 20706

3 Henrietta Street
London WC2E 8LU England

Printed in the United States of America
British Cataloging in Publication Information Available

Library of Congress Cataloging-in-Publication Data

John Paul II, Pope, 1920–
Dignity of work : John Paul II speaks to managers and workers / [edited by] Robert G. Kennedy.
p. cm.
Includes bibliographical references and index.
1. Work—Religious aspects—Catholic Church—Papal documents. 2. Economics—Religious aspects—Catholic Church—Papal documents. 3. Business—Religious aspects—Catholic Church—Papal documents. 4. Executives—Conduct of life—Papal documents. 5. Businessmen—Conduct of life—Papal documents. 6. Employees—Conduct of life—Papal documents. 7. Catholic Church—Doctrines—Papal documents. 8. Christian ethics—Catholic authors—Papal documents. I. Kennedy, Robert G. II. Title.
BX1795.W67J64 1994 261.8'5—dc20 94–25526 CIP

ISBN 0–8191–9619–3 (cloth : alk. paper)
ISBN 0–8191–9620–7 (pbk. : alk. paper)

™ The paper used in this publication meets the minimum requirements of American National Standard for Information Sciences—Permanence of Paper for Printed Library Materials, ANSI Z39.48–1984.

TABLE OF CONTENTS

List of Talks with Themes

FOREWORD

The authors of *The Dignity of Work* have done a great service for all who are interested in Catholic social teaching for they have brought together and edited the teachings of Pope John Paul II on the subject of work. This book is a book of record. The Pope's statements on work can now all be found easily in one place. It is a handy reference work and a compendium of Catholic Social Teaching. The editing has been limited to the elimination of duplication. This allows the Pope to speak in his own words.

It is evident that this subject has long been one of interest and great reflection for the Holy Father. He grounds his teaching on labor on the dignity of the human person as revealed from Genesis onward. And while work is the starting point, it does not stand in isolation. It is always seen in a broader context, that is, as related to such topics as solidarity, subsidiarity, democracy, family, unemployment and, above all, human dignity. A constant theme is that the end of all work and enterprise is man, not profit.

Yet profit has a role to play. An important contribution of Pope John Paul II to Catholic social teaching is his emphasis on entrepreneurship. The entrepreneur -- the risk taker and innovator -- is "indispensable." His "task is of the first order in society." The recognition of the role of the managers and leaders of business fills in an area that was missing or underrated in early Catholic social documents.

The Holy Father seeks a healthy balance between labor and labor unions on the one hand and business leaders on the other hand. They need each other and complement each other. Their roles are not inherently adversarial. The Pope speaks of the right to a job as a fundamental right and also of the right of "economic initiative."

A theme that runs throughout the Pope's statement is the essential nature of business ethics. Morality cannot be relegated to one's private life. It must also be in the marketplace and in the public forum. The separation of ethics from public life is a source of many of the problems plaguing society.

The tone of these messages is one of hope. It is positive and encouraging. For work is "an act of love and it turns into joy, the deep joy of giving one's self through work to one's own family and to others, the intimate joyousness of offering one's self to God and of serving one's brothers, even though such giving entails sacrifices. Thus Christian work has a paschal meaning." (*Origins*, Vol. 12, No. 23) What a lofty and enabling view of work!

Rev. Msgr. Terrence J. Murphy
Chancellor
University of St. Thomas
St. Paul, MN

PREFACE

What does a pope know about work and management? Pope John Paul II is recognized as a poet, a philosopher, a playwright, and a theologian, but rarely as a manager or as a worker. Yet, as a laborer in a quarry, as the pastor of several parishes, the archbishop of Cracow, and the head of the largest organization in the world, John Paul has experience with both management and labor. As archbishop, he managed schools, hospitals, parishes and other services in a Communist environment hostile to the Church. Elected to the papacy on October 16, 1978, he has proven to be an extraordinary manager. He has reorganized the Vatican bureaucracy, overseen the revision of canon law (the laws of the Catholic Church), traveled to nearly every country in the world to visit local churches, and managed numerous political and ecclesial conflicts.

John Paul's life is also marked by a spirituality which has enabled him to understand his wide experiences more profoundly. In addition, he was a widely respected scholar in several areas of theology and philosophy. This professional competence is crucial because it provides a vision of human action within which the disciplines of management can be properly understood. As both a practitioner and a theoretician, John Paul is well aware of the objections to bringing faith to the workplace. Nevertheless, he is convinced that a proper understanding of management and work must be founded upon a religious and moral conception of the human person.

The collection of addresses in this volume, given to various audiences around the world, provides an outline for a Christian vision of management and work. This vision is both collaborative and directed toward the common good. John Paul begins with the biblical theme that human persons are created in the image of God. As a result, everyone who works, whether as a security guard, as a chief executive officer, as a teacher, a homemaker, an accountant, a skilled laborer or a mid-level manager, collaborates with God in the work that they do. God has a claim on our work, a claim that invites and challenges us to direct our work toward the common good and our own human fulfillment.

This challenge is especially keen for managers, whether in business, not-for-profit organizations or government. John Paul explains that their role in organizing work for the common good is irreplaceable. Their work is not merely technical; like all workers they should view their activity "in the light of collaboration with God." More particularly, business managers have been given an abundance of gifts, both intellectual and monetary, which are essential to a sound economy. This heritage of gifts has a divine purpose. It should be administered with technical competence and guided by the principles of human dignity, the common good, the universal destination of goods as well as the virtues of prudence, solidarity, justice and charity.

In developing this Christian vision of management and work, John Paul is concerned with those who would restrict its real meaning to the maximization of economic utility, and see it merely as another tool for increasing profits. This view of management reduces the business enterprise "to a complex of structures resting exclusively on technical and economic values." It also sets aside the principles and virtues mentioned above. John Paul does not deny the economic value of managerial work. Managers can never abdicate the economic responsibility that comes with their role as stewards for the owners of businesses. However, neither can the model of the Christian manager, described so richly in the following addresses, be restricted to economic values. The Christian understanding of work entails a model of a deeply human manager "who is aware of his duties, honest, competent, and imbued with a profound social sense, that makes him capable of rejecting the inclination to selfishness." It is a model that calls business people to be architects of a more just and participative economy; in other words, to use their talents and skills for the common good.

A note about the addresses themselves. John Paul has given over 10,000 addresses and homilies in his pontificate. Over 300 of them have been given on topics related to work and management. We have selected the addresses, given between 1978 and mid-1992, that we think are representative of the best of his thought in these areas. We have edited them by removing most of the opening greetings and closing remarks so that the reader could more easily get to the substance of his message. Each address is preceded by a list of themes which are stressed in the text. A list of these themes with a brief description appears at the end of the volume. The chapters are divided according to the audiences. Chapter 1: Managers, Entrepreneurs and Professionals; Chapter 2: Managers and Workers; Chapter 3: Workers; Chapter 4: General Audiences. It is important to note that although many of the addresses are directed toward those in the business sector, the messages are applicable to other sectors of the economy.

On a more personal level, we want to say that we have found this material to be edifying for our roles as teachers and scholars. We have been moved to take our own vocations more seriously and in a more Christ-like direction. The danger of cynicism exists for each profession, where the professional loses sight of the moral and spiritual meaning of his or her work. In these addresses, John Paul makes it very clear that all work has nobility, purpose and value, and that cynicism in the workplace undermines Christian vocation. We hope that readers of this collection will also find in these addresses a moral and spiritual renewal of their own professional lives.

Finally, we must acknowledge the help we have received from many people. The president of the University of St Thomas, Fr Dennis Dease, approved the formation of the Center for Christian Social Thought and Management, under whose auspices this work was done. Mr John Murray provided both financial assistance and helped us to understand more clearly the Christian vision of management. Msgr Terrence Murphy, chancellor of the University of St Thomas, also helped fund our work through the Aquinas Foundation. The late Dr John Nemo, Dean of the undergraduate college at St Thomas, also provided funding and, more importantly, moral support and encouragement. Dr Helen Alford, Visiting Scholar at the Center, assisted with the final editing and wrote the introduction. Sue Moro edited and formatted the text and produced it into final form, all with great patience and professionalism. Jeff Ward patiently entered corrections and helped to bring the material to its final form. We also owe a special thanks to Joseph McLean, who typed, edited and researched the material, and whose humor, dedication, generosity and friendship brought a sense of community to the project.

Gary Atkinson
Robert G Kennedy
Michael Naughton

1 May 1994 — Feast of St Joseph the Worker

Introduction to the Thought of John Paul on Work and Management

"With work then it begins: the growing in the heart and mind, great events, a multitude of men are drawn in"[1]
Karol Wojtyla (John Paul II), 1956

Work is the Starting Point

"Work is the key to the social question," wrote John Paul in his encyclical, Laborem Exercens.[2] By this, he means more than just questions to do with economics; for him, the whole moral order to some extent depends on human beings working together for the common good. Without a doubt, in characterizing the background to John Paul's talks to workers and managers, one needs to begin with the idea of work. But, if one begins with work, almost immediately, as a key opens a door, an examination of work leads into much broader issues of business, economy and social responsibility. John Paul's poetical language says this concisely; through work, there is a "growing in the heart and mind"; as a result, "great events" are possible, involving a "multitude." In this short account, we can only highlight the main outlines of John Paul's thought.

His background

The world of work was important to John Paul long before he became Pope. Shortly after his ordination, November 1st 1946, the Archbishop of Cracow gave him money to travel around Western Europe to get some idea of pastoral practice there. It was during this trip that he met Cardijn's Young Christian Workers movement and became attracted by the worker priest movement in France as an example of an effective means of evangelization in the modern world.[3] Thus, he could see the importance of Christian workers witnessing to their faith in their workplace as one of the most important means for Christianizing the world today. Throughout his talks as Pope, this theme of the need to witness to one's faith at work is one that is often repeated.[4] Later, as a Cardinal himself in Cracow, his diary was filled with meetings with scientists, gardeners, doctors, ex-service personnel, teachers and nurses. Most important of all, as a young man in Poland during the Second World War, he worked at the Solvay factory in Cracow, while caring for his ailing father and pursuing his studies and his interest in theater. This work experience was to be a most formative influence on his life.[5] Some of his poems indicate the impact that this experience had on him, as the opening quotation shows. Similarly, as the pontiff, he has said on numerous occasions that he learned the gospel anew during his period of labor.[6] Through it, he was able to gain an appreciation of the "Gospel of Work," and began to see how important it was that God has revealed himself to us as a creator/worker, both in creating the world and in becoming incarnate among us, working with us, and finally suffering and dying for us as the culmination of his work in the world. The full implications for theology of this viewpoint of God, revealing himself first of all as an active, creative worker, have perhaps yet to be properly fathomed.

His academic formation

Not only is his life experience of work important to know in order to understand his writings, but his thought also needs to be understood because of the profound way in which he is able to interpret his experiences. His interest in phenomenology means that he treats his work experience as a point of departure for exploring work from many perspectives. In his major philosophical work, published in English as *The Acting Person,* he sets up a conceptual scheme which forms the matrix in which his thought on work in his encyclicals and talks takes shape. The need to work is seen as a special case of the general human need to act purposively. In acting one unites mind and body through interpreting information from one's senses and setting an objective or intention in one's mind which then one accomplishes through one's body. In acting, one experiences one's mastery over oneself and over material things, as well as the limitedness of one's being. In part, because of this emphasis in his thought on the need to act purposively, John Paul can see unemployment as a fundamental evil that deprives a human being of the normal and healthy channels of human development. One is not able to act purposively and experience mastery over creation through working for one's living. This approach to human action is also behind his outright condemnation of any work system that makes the worker subservient to the machine, taking away from that person the possibility to act purposively and thus corrupting the true nature of work.

Core ideas in the teaching of John Paul on work and management

In one sense, it is very easy to summarize John Paul's teaching on these issues. The one point he makes consistently, in every talk he gives to many different groups in different contexts, is the primacy of the human person. This primacy comes from the heart of his theology, which he expressed in the opening line of his first encyclical after becoming Pope: "The centre of nature and history is Jesus Christ, the Redeemer of Man. . . Man is the special road of the Church."[7] In all areas of life, then, John Paul wishes to emphasize that the first duty of work and business is to serve the human being, to "make life more human."[8] Thus, he does not allow for an instrumentalization of the producer for the sake of the consumer; the needs and rights of a human person must be respected at all times, in the workplace no less than the marketplace. It is fundamentally opposed to the common good to play the human person as worker off against the human person as customer. We are always and in every place human (physical, spiritual, moral) beings and that integrity of the human person must be respected at all times.[9] This provides a radical critique of our capitalist work structures, where to a greater or lesser extent, the worker is instrumentalized for the sake of the customer. While it is true that in *Centesimus Annus*, John Paul does see that the market can play a useful role in economics, in the context of his other writings, it can be seen that his approbation is not absolute and is limited by his prior concern with the dignity of the human person. As Schall says, the Church maintains a "critical realism" in relation to economic and political structures.[10] John Paul is being realistic in recognising that capitalistic markets are the best form of economic order that we have so far conceived, while at the same time realizing that the system contains some fundamental flaws.

Within the structure of his primary concern with the human person, John Paul makes a number of important points, of which the following are especially important:[11]

- the need to develop virtues in the workplace, especially solidarity, so as to build a "civillization of work."[12]
- the need to integrate work and family life, which concerns issues such as a just wage and appropriate working arrangements for parents with children.[13]
- the need to see and use technology as an "ally" in the development of human work and the family. This fundamentally positive attitude to technology contrasts with other thinkers in the Christian tradition who see technology as opposed to the good of the human person.[14]
- the role of unions in promoting the common good of society by representing workers in just claims for remuneration or participation at work.[15]
- the need for a spirituality of work, in which the whole person unites his or her labor with the labor of the Creator and the Redeemer.[16]

These areas indicate the breadth and detail of his thought, and also that he cannot be classed either as a liberal, free market economist, nor as a socialist. At the same time, one could see weaknesses in his thought, despite its richness. Throughout his pontificate, his primary concern is with those typically termed "workers," even though he takes every opportunity to meet with a wide number of businesspeople. He could do well to develop a more differentiated approach to "managers," who are a very diverse group. The problems of, say, a foreman or supervisor might be more like those of a "worker," whereas the situation of an entrepreneur or a CEO of a large corporation would usually be quite different. Added to this, his theory of virtues in the workplace is rather rudimentary; the virtue of solidarity is certainly central to running a business well, but what about the virtues needed in particular situations? Again, his use of the concept the "indirect" employer points towards something very important, but is not analytically very useful, since it covers such a wide and diverse set of actors (government, customers, competitors, suppliers, funders and investors). He could say more about the nature of the product as part of working well.[17] Finally, we could mention that his concern is largely with paid employment; volunteer work is not considered in the same light. The one exception to this is his concern for work in the home, and the role of the mother in caring for children. He does clearly indicate that this is work as important and creative as any other, and that it should be recognized as such. Even here, however, there is some ambivalence; curiously, when he speaks of the Holy Family, he never refers to Mary's work as contributing to the support of the family in this way.

Despite these weaknesses, John Paul represents one of the most important thinkers on the question of work and management in our time. His constant concern to remind us of the basics, of what working is *for*, and his concern to meet with and understand businesspeople from many different industries and countries, makes a knowledge of his thought essential for anyone serious about understanding and improving our world of work and economics.

Helen Alford

Notes

[1] From "Inspiration," one of the poems in the cycle "The Quarry," from J. Peterkiewicz, trans., *Collected Poems* (New York: Random House, 1979).

[2] *Laborem Exercens,* n.3.

[3] He had already met Cardijn in Rome, where he had attended some of his lectures at the Gregorian University. See M. Malinski, *Pope John Paul II: The Life of Karol Wojtyla,* Translated by P.S. Falla, (New York: Seabury, 1979).

[4] See the index entry under "Christian Witness/ Mission" which has one of the highest number of references.

[5] See talk 63 of this collection, he speaks of his work in the factory as "one of the most interesting and formative periods of my life."

[6] See entry in the index for "Gospel of Work" to find references to the particular talks in which John Paul makes this point.

[7] *Redemptor Hominis,* n.1.

[8] *Laborem Exercens*, n.3.

[9] This approach could be seen as analogous to the "consistent life ethic" developed in particular by Cardinal Bernardin; a consistent application of the primacy of the person throughout an area of human existence, in this case, the sphere of work and economics. See J. Bernardin, *Consistent Ethic of Life,* (Kansas City: Sheed and Ward, 1988).

[10] James V. Schall, "Capitalism, Business and Human Priorities," in J.W. Houck and O.F. Williams, eds., *The Judeo-Christian Vision of the Modern*

Corporation, (Notre Dame, IN: University of Notre Dame Press, 1982), p. 109.

[11]The glossary lists 37 ideas used in the thought of John Paul. The index indicates where these ideas appear throughout the talks.

[12]See, for example, talks 60 and 61.

[13]See, for instance, talk 59 for a discusion of the fundamental, ontological relation between work and the family; they are both ways of filling and subduing the earth and need each other in order to do so.

[14] See the index for references. Two alternative views are expressed by Gill and von Balthasar, for instance; See E. Gill, *Sacred and Secular,* (London: J. M. Dent, 1940); H.U. von Balthasar, *Science, Religion and Christianity,* (London: Burns and Oates, 1958).

[15] See, for example, talk 63.

[16]For instance, see his prayer for workers, p. 15

[17]However, in his poetry, he does consider some of these problems. See "The Car Factory Worker" and "The Armaments Factory Worker," in J. Peterkiewicz, trans., *Collected Poems* (New York: Random House, 1979).

CHAPTER 1: ADDRESSES TO MANAGERS, ENTREPRENEURS AND PROFESSIONALS

1. The Entrepreneur and Manager Have a Responsibility to Promote Non-Economic Values[1]

Common Good, Community of Persons, Dialogue and Cooperation, Economic Laws and Profits, Entrepreneurship, Human Development/Progress, Human Rights/Dignity, Humanization/Dehumanization, Professional Training/Responsibility, Universal Destination of Goods, Work and the Worker.

[An address on November 24, 1979 in Rome, to the Christian Union of Entrepreneurs and Managers.]

My first thought for you, today, cannot but be one of esteem, approval, and encouragement for the significant presence that you, avoiding all ostentation, really make felt in society. Yours is a task in which I see the outlines of a real and proper civil and social "service": a service for all those employed in the various fields of entrepreneurial activity. Of course, I am not able to go into the specifically technical characteristics of this activity; nor do you, I think, expect this of me, to whom the Lord has entrusted the pastoral office of indicating in all active forms of human life the supreme norm to reach eternal salvation.

Service of the Entrepreneur to Society

You consider it your duty also to try to meet the legitimate claims that come from the workers in your firms. The entrepreneur and managerial staff must do everything in their power to give a hearing, a due hearing, to the voice of the worker in their employment and to understand his legitimate demands for justice and fairness, overcoming all selfish temptations to make the economic factor a law unto itself. You know and wish to remind everyone that any lack of attention in this sector is culpable, any delay fatal. So many conflicts and antagonisms between workers and employers often have their roots in the unproductive soil of the refusal to listen, rejection of dialogue or undue postponement of it. Time spent meeting your employees personally, making your relations with them more human and giving your firms a dimension more fit for man, is not time wasted.

Dehumanization Caused by "Productivism"

You are not unaware of the situation of so many factory workers who, if obliged to live fenced off, as it were, in an artificial structure, run the risk of feeling atrophied in their interior spontaneity. Machines, with their rigid automatism, are unrewarding and offer little satisfaction. The very relations between fellow workers, when they become depersonalized, cannot give the necessary comfort or support; and the machinery of production, distribution and consumption often forces workers to live in a "standardized" way, without initiatives, without choices.

This level of dehumanization is reached when the scale of values is reversed and "productivism" becomes the only parameter of the industrial phenomenon, when the interior dimension of values is neglected, when the aim pursued is rather the perfection of the work than the perfection of the one who carries it out, giving preference in this way to the work as compared with the worker, the object as compared with the subject.

Respect for Human Rights

Here the discourse, which moreover is familiar to you, would tend to widen and would lead to speaking of the more general and universal question of human rights. But it would take us far away; so I will merely recall a short passage from my first Encyclical in which I affirmed that violation of fundamental human rights "can in no way be reconciled with any program that describes itself as 'humanistic.' And what social, economic, political or cultural program could renounce this description?"[2]

Discovery of Superior Values

You are quite certain that it is only in this perspective that man – every man, whether he is an entrepreneur or executive, or a collaborator in the various sectors of the clerical class and workers – can find again his own deep meaning, thus being enabled to express his talents, collaborate, participate and cooperate in the smooth operation of the enterprise, of which all are, together, collaborators and architects.

In this way the time allotted for work also recovers its important meaning, no less than that reserved for rest. They both allow man to discover himself again and at the same time those superior values of love and solidarity which allow him to reach complete development, freeing him of possible and ever imminent frustrations.

Created Goods Destined for All

Here are some indications, dear brothers, which may be useful to you in carrying out your difficult and responsible activity as entrepreneurs and executives. In conclusion, I am happy to make my own the wish that my great predecessor, Paul VI, addressed to you in his last discourse, left to you as a testament: "May your Christian testimony really contribute to spreading in the environment of enterprise the conviction that created goods are destined for all men so that they 'would be shared fairly by all mankind under the guidance of justice tempered by charity.'[3] May your example stimulate a use of the income available that is not arbitrary or selfish; above all, may the approach you have taken to activity in the enterprise make the latter a community of persons, in which each one will feel appreciated in his own dignity, through responsible participation in the common work."[4]

2. *Professionals Have Special Responsibilities to Their Society and Their Church*[5]

Christian Witness/Mission, Common Good, Human Rights/Dignity, Professional Training/Responsibility, Service, Work and Prayer, Work and Society.

[An address on February 18, 1981 at the Aranete Coliseum, Philippines, to representatives of various professions.]

It is a joy for me to be able to greet the representatives of various professions from different parts of the Philippines: lawyers, doctors, nurses, engineers, educators, and members of other professions as well. Many of you are in positions of leadership or community service in the world, or lay leaders in the Church – you are people who have had the benefit of education and training. Permit me to go immediately to the heart of my message. It is this: Jesus Christ needs you for the building up of his Kingdom on earth. And the Church needs your special gifts, individually and collectively, to fulfill her mission of communicating Christ. Moreover, millions of your fellow men and women count on your services in order to live worthy lives in accordance with their human and Christian dignity.

You can see then that this meeting emphasizes the Church's great interest in you, and her desire to consult, to listen to and to bring together all those who play a responsible part in the different fields of culture, and who exercise this responsibility in a Christian spirit of service. As representatives of professions that require greater educational attainment, and as creators and spreaders of culture, you share the Church's life and mission in a specific way.

This present meeting also emphasizes the need to go beyond an individualistic way of life. It is up to you to create ever more effective forms of association and collaboration between Catholics belonging to the professions in general and within each profession in particular, so that you can reflect upon your responsibilities as Christians in the light of faith and the Church's social teaching.

Personal and Social Effort

You are people who have reached your present positions as a result of hard and serious efforts, both personal and collective: personal efforts, in the sense that the studies which you undertook in order to obtain your professional qualifications certainly demanded of you sacrifice, self-discipline and intellectual rigor. It is only after you have reached the goal that you can properly appreciate the path that has led to it. One only reaps the fruits of what was well sown in the first place. But you are also the result of a great effort on the collective level, for your families and your nation have had to invest great material and spiritual resources in order to train and perfect ever more numerous builders of society, with a solid intellectual and technical education.

Calling to Serve Family and Society

You have a twofold calling. In the first place, you have to meet your personal needs and those of your families, through the exercise of your professions. In this you have sometimes experienced difficulties and frustrations and perhaps even discouragement. And yet you must not give up, knowing as you do that you are also called upon to make your contribution to the service of the common good. When things are going well, never shut yourselves off from society for the sake of making money, gaining power or acquiring more knowledge, do not retreat into a position of privilege. May you put your talents to good use by serving ever more generously the needs and the aspirations of all your brothers and sisters in the Philippines. I am thinking in particular of that great number of people who, as a result of different circumstances – injustice, poverty, the need to make a bare living, the lack of cultural stimulus – have been unable to attain the levels of university training and education that you have enjoyed.

Thus there is a close link between your demanding professional activities and the hard toil of the factory worker, the life of the worker on the land, the self-denial of the housewife in her home. This is why your sensitivity to human and Christian values will be the source of a creative energy that will help you to place your skills and your activity really and effectively at the service of your people, in response to their needs.

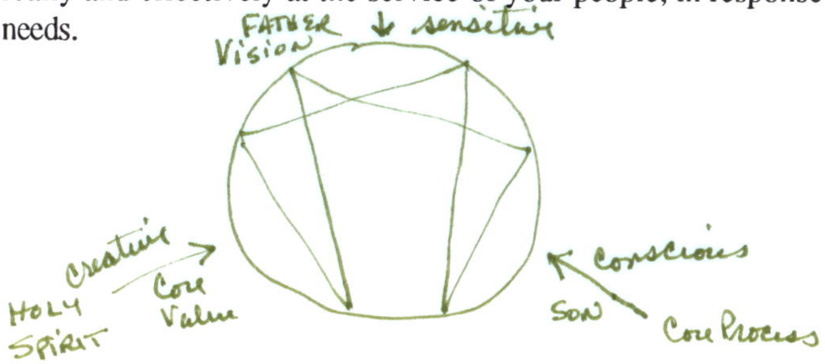

Social Goals

The complete development of the people of your country, and the satisfaction of their spiritual and material needs, call for much effort on your part: health-care for everyone; the defense of the sacred nature of human life and its promotion; the affirmation of the role of law in social and political relations if true order and real freedom are to be ensured; the building of worthy housing, properly adapted to every family and every individual; the education of youth by teaching directed towards the search for truth and its affirmation; the balanced and fruitful management of natural resources in order to ensure that everyone has a fair share of their benefits – all these are matters that concern you directly.

Apostolate of Professional Witness

It is often the case that the great percentage of the lay people who are zealously endeavoring as organized groups to permeate temporal affairs with the spirit of the Gospel and to build genuine Christian communities come mostly from non-professional groups. Thus an unfortunate impression is created that the leader/professional groups are not deeply interested in religious activities. In a country where the vast majority of people look up to the leaders and are easily encouraged by example, this apostolate of witness and example has great effectiveness and should be increasingly adopted. I sincerely hope that you can offer more and more of your talent and time in the service of the Church, in the lay apostolate of building up an authentic Christian community. Those, for example, who are recognized leaders in the field of health can do much to promote the Catholic principles regarding the intrinsic value of life in all its stages. Similarly, in the other professions, true Christian leadership is most effective.

Integrity, Love and Personal Piety

May your efforts in this direction always be sustained by inflexible integrity of conduct, in the midst of the professional problems that you meet. But even more, may they be inspired by a desire to help those who are most in need, so that your service will be ruled by the criteria of justice and truth, of freedom and integrity, and be crowned with love. Remember always that as Christians you are called to love in accordance with the principles that you have learned from Christ and his

Church. You are called to live upright lives consistent with your Gospel principles.

Everyone is aware that the disciplines that you exercise call for constant renewal, in order that you may keep up with the rapid pace of new discoveries. Your capacity to adapt yourselves and to keep abreast of these developments will depend on your constant study of the basic principles underlying these disciplines. And may your Catholic faith also be constantly renewed; may it grow deeper and develop, through the radical dynamism of constant conversion to Christ, a conversion animated by a life lived according to the Gospel and in harmony with the Magisterium, nourished by a life of personal piety based upon prayer and the reception of the sacraments. May the testimony of your faith shine brightly in your professional lives, as well as in your personal and family lives.

Specialization Versus Culture

You are aware of the present-day risks involved in shutting oneself up within the narrow limits of a "specialization." Such specializations can narrow one's horizons, fragment one's personal life and obscure the right nature of life in general. It is very clear that professional specialization must be considered within the wider setting of what is called general culture. It is in this context that I urge you to take as your fundamental points of reference the religious and ethical values that are the powerful promoters of culture, by shedding their light on man's different problems and deepest aspirations, and by transforming his whole life and all his knowledge. Your professional experience will thus gain in depth, perspective and fruitfulness.

A Life-Giving Wisdom

As Catholics with greater attainment and as representatives of the professions, you are called upon to show how your knowledge and the professional work blend with the wealth and resources of the culture of the people of the Philippines. That culture is rooted in the Christian tradition, and is therefore imbued with liberating and life-giving wisdom concerning the being and dignity of the human person, concerning the meaning of his life, his death and his final destiny.

3. The Mission of the Holy See Entails Special Responsibilities and Rights for its Workers[6]

Community of Persons, Fair Wage, Gospel of Work, Service, Work and the Worker.

[From a letter dated November 20, 1982 to Cardinal Agostino Casaroli, Secretary of State for the Vatican.]

In the exercise of its mission the Apostolic See has recourse to the valuable and precious work of the particular community made up of all those – men and women, priests, religious and laity – who spend themselves in its departments and offices at the service of the universal Church.

To the members of this community there are assigned tasks and duties, each one of which has its own purpose and dignity either because of its subjective content and the value of the work itself, or because of the person who carries it out.

This concept of community, applied to those who help the Bishop of Rome in his ministry as Pastor of the universal Church, permits us first of all to indicate the unified character of the tasks, however different. All the persons, in fact, who are called to perform them participate really in the unique and unceasing activity of the Apostolic See, and therefore in that "anxiety for all the Churches"[7] which from the earliest times inspired the service of the Apostles, and which today in large measure is the prerogative of St. Peter's successors in the Roman See. It is very important that all those who are associated in whatever way with the activities of the Apostolic See should be aware of this specific character of their duties: an awareness indeed which has always been the tradition and boast of those who wish to dedicate themselves to the noble service.

This consideration applies both to ecclesiastics and religious as well as the laity; it applies to those who occupy posts of high responsibility as well as office workers and those who carry out manual labor, to whom are assigned subsidiary functions. It regards both those assigned directly to the service of the Apostolic See, inasmuch as they work for those organisms which in their ensemble come under the name of the "Holy See," and also those in the service of the Vatican City State, which is so closely linked with the Apostolic See.

In the recent encyclical *Laborem Exercens* I recalled the principal truths of the "Gospel of Work," and of the Catholic doctrine on human labor, always very much alive in the tradition of the Church. It is necessary that the life of the unique community which works under the shadow of Peter, in such immediate contact with the Apostolic See, should be in conformity with these truths.

Responsibility and Loyalty

In the face of those who by their help express a solidarity with the Holy See and share to some extent in its pastoral care, responsibility and loyalty are manifested by scrupulous fidelity to all tasks and duties assigned as also by the zeal, industry and professionalism which should distinguish those who participate in the activities of the same Apostolic See. Besides, it is necessary always to have the right intention so as to administer prudently, by reason of their purpose, both the material goods which are offered, as well as what is acquired or preserved by means of such goods, including the safeguarding and improvement of the precious inheritance of the See of Peter.

In the use of the means destined for these purposes the Apostolic See and those who directly collaborate with it should be distinguished not only by a spirit of thrift, but also by a readiness to bear always in mind the actual, limited financial resources of the Holy See and their origin. Obviously such interior attitudes will be quite connatural, by formation, in the minds of the religious and ecclesiastics; but they should not be wanting in those lay people who by free choice undertake to work for and with the Apostolic See.

Moreover, all those who have particular responsibilities in directing departments, offices and services of the Apostolic See, as well as those assigned to definite functions, will be able to unite this spirit of thrift with a constant commitment to render ever more effective the different activities, by means of labor organization based, on the one hand, on full respect for persons and for the valuable contribution that each one makes according to his own proper competence and function; and, on the other hand, on the use of appropriate structures and technical instruments so that the activity carried out may correspond in an ever better way to the needs of the service of the universal Church. Having recourse to everything learned from experience, science and technology, one will do one's best so that human and financial resources will be used with greater efficiency, by avoiding waste, the seeking of particular interests or of unjustified privileges, and by promoting at the same time good human relationships in every sector and the true and just interests of the Apostolic See.

Just Wage

Among those who work for the Apostolic See there are many ecclesiastics who, living in celibacy, have not the responsibilities of a family. They are due a remuneration proportionate to the tasks carried out and such as to ensure a fitting sustenance and to permit them to carry out the duties of their state, including also those responsibilities which they may have in certain cases to come to the help of their parents or other members of the family dependent upon them. Nor should there be overlooked the demands of their regular social relationships, in particular and above all, the obligation which, because of their evangelical vocation, is more binding for ecclesiastics and religious than for the laity.

Moreover, the remuneration of the lay workers of the Holy See should correspond to the work done, at the same time bearing in mind the responsibility they have to support their families. In a spirit of deep concern and of justice one must then take into consideration what are their objective material needs and those of their families, including those pertaining to the education of the children and to suitable insurance for their old age, for the purpose of making due provision for them. The basic directives in this sector are to be found in the Catholic teaching of remuneration for work. These directives are immediately available in the examination of the experiences and programs of society and especially in those of Italian society to which, in fact, nearly all of the lay employees of the Apostolic See belong.

Associations for Workers

To promote such a spirit of concern and justice on behalf of those who work for the Apostolic See, an important contribution can be made by associations of workers, such as the Association of the Vatican Lay Employees recently established. Similar organizations which assume a specific character within the Apostolic See constitute an initiative in conformity with the social doctrine of the Church, which sees in them one of the apt instruments to guarantee in a better way social justice in relations between worker and employer. However, it is not in accord with the social doctrine of the Church if this type of organization should become an instrument of out and out conflict or of class struggle; nor should they have a political character or serve, openly or secretly, the interests of a party or of others aiming at objectives of a very different nature.

I am confident that associations such as that already existing and above mentioned, inspired by the principles of the Church's social teaching, will discharge a fruitful function in the community of workers in solidarity and harmony with the Apostolic See. I am also certain that in approaching the problems of work and in the development of constructive and continuous dialogue with the competent bodies, they will never fail to bear in mind in every case the special character of the Apostolic See as indicated in the first part of this letter.

In regard to all that has been herein set out, your Eminence shall prepare the requisite executive documents to ensure, by means of suitable norms and structures, the promotion of a work community in accordance with the principles stated.

Personal Involvement in Work

In the encyclical *Laborem Exercens* I mentioned that the worker's personal dignity requires to be expressed in a particular relationship with the work entrusted to him.

This relationship, which can be objectively realized in different ways according to the kind of work undertaken, will be subjectively achieved when the worker, even though performing a work for which he is paid, nevertheless carries it out as if he were working "on his own." Since we are speaking here of a work carried out in the context of the Apostolic See, and therefore characterized by the fundamental specific nature above referred to, this relationship demands a deeply felt participation in that "anxiety for all the Churches" proper to the See of Peter.

The employees of the Holy See should, therefore, have a profound conviction that their work involves, above all, an ecclesial responsibility to live in a spirit of authentic faith, and that the juridical-administrative aspects of the relationship with the Apostolic See are to be viewed in a special light.

The Second Vatican Council has offered us copious teachings on the way in which all Christians, ecclesiastical, religious and lay, can – and should – make this ecclesial concern their own.

It therefore seems necessary, especially for those who work for the Apostolic See, to review in depth, first of all, their personal awareness of the universal apostolic commitment of Christians and of that resulting from the specific vocation of each one: of the bishop, the priest, the religious and the layman. Indeed, the answers to the present day difficulties in the field of human labor are to be sought in the sphere of social justice; but they are to be sought also in the area of the interior relationship with the work which each one is called upon to do. It seems evident that work, whatever it may be, which is carried out for the Holy See requires this in a very special way.

Mutual Respect

Over and above a deepened interior relationship, this work, in order to be advantageous and peaceful, requires mutual respect based upon human and Christian brotherhood on the part of all and for all those who are awaiting it. Only when it is joined to such a brotherhood (that is, with the love of man in truth), can justice be manifested as real justice. We must seek to know "of what spirit we are."[8]

These final questions, briefly referred to, cannot be adequately formulated in administrative-juridical terms. However, that does not exempt one from the search and effort necessary to render operative, within the ambit of the Apostolic See, that spirit of human work which comes from our Lord Jesus Christ.

4. Economics Must Always Be Directed to the Good of the Person[9]

Community of Persons, Dialogue and Cooperation, Economic Laws and Profits, Human Development/Progress, Meaning of Work, Work and Society, Worker Participation, World Community.

[An address on May 22, 1983 in Milan, to business leaders and economic managers of Italy.]

To all I address my greetings, which are not only for this occasion, but come from sincere sentiments of deep consideration, since I well know of how great a part of the economic and social life of beloved Italy you are promoters and leaders. The degree of well-being which society enjoys today would be unthinkable without the dynamic figure of the business man, whose function consists of organizing human labor and the means of production so as to give rise to the goods and services necessary for the prosperity and progress of the community.

Dynamic Role of Business People

My affectionate thought is intended to embrace also the tradesmen and artisans, whose profession bears genuine human values, and who I know are represented here.

During my visits in Italy I have often met the workers, but this is the first time I have had the occasion to address my words to economic managers.

The occasion invites me to express to you several considerations on the specific activity which commits you in the various sectors of economic life and on the ethical values connected with enterprise.

Worker Participation

The starting point is offered to me by a particularly rich text of the Second Vatican Council. It is a part drawn from the *Pastoral Constitution on the Church in the Modern World*: "In economic enterprises it is persons who work together, that is, free and independent human beings created in the image of God. Therefore the active participation of everyone in the running of an enterprise should be promoted. This participation should be exercised in appropriately determined ways. It should take into account each person's function, whether it be one of ownership, hiring, management, or labor. It should provide for the necessary unity of operations."[10] Reflecting on this conciliar text, it appears immediately evident that there are two fundamental ethical principles in which the Church's social thought regarding enterprise and its inner life is summarized: enterprise unites and associates human persons, who are treated as such; the work of the person requires his initiative and responsibility in the life of the same enterprise.

Community of Persons

In the encyclical *Mater et Magistra*, my predecessor of venerated memory John XXIII gave expression to this profound social and human ideal of enterprise: "One must aim," he wrote, "that enterprise become a community of persons in the relationships, the functions and the positions of all its subjects."[11]

This concept of enterprise as a community of persons constitutes the source of the exacting ethical requirements of all those who, directly or indirectly, have to do with the social and economic life of the community. As you well know, in a truly human economy, enterprise cannot be identified only with the holders of capital, since it is fundamentally a community of persons characterized by the unity of labor, in which personal services and capital serve for the production of goods.

In my encyclical *Laborem Exercens* I spoke of the conflict between capital and labor, which is experienced in industrialized countries which have already entered into the phase of post-industrial society through the development of high technologies. In several sectors, these technologies reduce the need for manual labor, accentuating, together with other factors, the serious phenomenon of unemployment, with the danger of subtracting from enterprise that profound ethical and social element of a community of persons which ought to be proper to it.

In this meeting with you, businessmen of various sectors of the economy and production in an industrialized country like Italy, a meeting which takes place during a difficult moment for the economy, I want to refer to several phenomena and problems which particularly affect the strengthening or the loss of the true ethical significance of enterprise.

Labor and Capital

In the context of production and its organization there meet, on the one hand, the businessmen or employers, both direct and indirect, and on the other, the workers with their talents, the possibilities to utilize them in the commitment of their services, and their rights.

The Church faces the conflict between capital and labor by trying to defend man in his rights, denounce injustices and contribute positively to the solution of problems.[12] The social doctrine which she proposes always orients itself more towards an organization of labor and the process of industrial production which responds fully to the true dignity of the human person, the principal and irreplaceable ethical value in economic activity, since the economy and production are for the good of man and not man for the accumulation of capital. An economy oriented solely to profit would not create a community of persons, nor would it generate a true social culture of responsible participation of all the subjects of enterprise.

In the encyclical *Laborem Exercens*[13] I offered a means of solution to this risk, which is inspired by the ethical value of enterprise as a community of persons; "by associating labor with the ownership of capital, as far as possible, and by producing a wide range of intermediate bodies with economic, social and cultural purposes." This ethical response to the conflict does not permit that absolute autonomy and independence of capital precisely from which arise the alienation and violation of the dignity of the human person in enterprise.

Economics for the Sake of the Human Person

In order to be able to look confidently to the future of the world of work, it is necessary that the focal point of economic activity always be the interest for every human being: man and his values must always be the principle and aim of economics.

Even in moments of major crisis, the over-evaluation of profit can never be the criterion which governs enterprise's choices. If one really wants to create a community of persons at work, it is necessary to keep in mind man in the concrete and the tragedies, not only for the individual but also for the family, to which the recourse of dismissal would inexorably lead. Certainly this praxis, as much as it might be suggested by circumstances, does not favor the dignity of individuals and of the labor community as a whole.

To you illustrious representatives of private and public industry, agriculture, commerce, services or artisan activity, I address my heartfelt appeal that the efforts in the positions of work be united and increased. These will allow young people to find work and will allow everyone to count on a secure means of support for themselves and their dear ones. The general situation of economic inflation and recession must never hinder seeking with every effort and with tenacious perseverance how to prevent both the causes which provoke the situation and the distressing human situations which result from it.

What are the ways which the Church proposes to create some enterprises that would be true communities of work in order to unite labor and capital? In the aforementioned encyclical I wrote that "the means of production cannot be possessed against labor, they cannot even be possessed for possession's sake, because the only legitimate title to their possession – whether in the form of private ownership or in the form of public or collective ownership – is that they should serve labor."[14]

Joint Ownership of the Means of Labor

The proposals of the social teaching of the Church refer to the joint ownership of the means of labor, to the workers' participation in the management and in the profits of enterprises, to the so-called "shareholding" of labor, and other similar forms of participation. All the subjects of enterprise, just as all the living forces of society, must together seek the forms and the concrete structures to realize this primordial objective of collaboration between capital and labor in the just hierarchy of values. To this end, the Church does not propose uniform technical solutions, but encourages the search for solutions based on the dignity and capabilities of the workers and which at the same time respect the economic and social function of enterprise.

In this context the trade union also enters as a dynamic factor in the social organization. In an industrial society like the Italian one, not to mention Milan's, a city so vivacious and pulsating with activity, these organizations are indispensable and irreplaceable elements of social life and of the enterprise community, notwithstanding the influences which try to distort their true ethical value in the promotion of social justice or to obstruct the relations within the enterprise which conform most to the principle of the priority of the person over capital.

True Interdependence

Between the opposed philosophies – the one of sole economic competition and that of participation – the community enterprise demands that in the process of production and in the social relations one opts for the application of the second, participation, creating among all the members of enterprise a true and effective interdependence. Such a personal correlation between the direct and indirect leaders of enterprise and labor, sustained by the social policies of the state, is a necessary condition for bringing into harmony with one another members of the working world in enterprise, to promote the personal and community dynamism of the life of enterprise and to overcome conflicts.

International Social Justice

In saying this my thought also extends to the field on international relations, where it is also necessary to be committed so that social justice can be affirmed. Last year, speaking at the inaugural session of the International Symposium on *Laborem Exercens*, I observed: "New possibilities are sighted on the horizon, which can now no longer be conceived in restricted, uniquely national terms. If the problems which modern man must face cannot be understood except by realizing their world dimension, it will also be on the international scale, in many cases, that solutions will have to be sought. Rightly, therefore, a new international economic order is ever more frequently hoped for today. This order, overcoming the insufficient and inadequate models of the past, will assure making a just sharing in the goods of creation, with particular sensitivity for peoples in the process of development."[15]

The putting forth of this gigantic effort, as it is proposed by the Church's social teaching, requires a high dose of availability to sincere dialogue and generosity in facing sacrifice in every sector, in a way that the result is not so much the safeguarding of the interests of one or the other party, but rather a situation in which the worker is always more "man" in his work, and enterprise is the dynamic expression of the participation of all.

The Church's dialogue with the modern world about ethico-community values is its way of being present, under the action of the Holy Spirit, in temporal realities. The Church recognizes the development of these values in the individual conscience and in interpersonal relationships of the man of today. Wherever there is dependence on complex economic factors and on technological development, true progress consists in the "interpersonal" community.

Overcoming An Individualistic Ethic

The action of the Holy Spirit and the power of the Eucharist, this divine Reality to which today's Solemnity of Pentecost and the conclusion of the National Eucharistic Congress recall us, push us ahead toward overcoming every individualistic ethic; toward the constant return to the primary value of the human person, widening the horizons of love; toward the achievement of social justice in respect for the equality of all men; toward the development of the sense of responsibility, of common commitment and of participation.[16]

5. *Genesis Reveals the Meaning of Work*[17]

Christian Witness/Mission, Collaboration with God, Dignity of Work, Dominion over the Earth, Humanization/Dehumanization, Gospel of Work, Meaning of Work, St. Joseph, Technology, Universal Destination of Goods, Work and Family.

[From a homily on January 29, 1985 in Ciudad Guayana, Venezuela, to South American managers, professionals and workers.]

I greet in a special way all the world of labor, come not only from Venezuela but also from other countries of Latin America, because of the development of the industry of iron and steel, of aluminum and the hydroelectric industry, which has made this city one of the most important industrial nuclei of Venezuela. For this reason, the problem of work, of human work, occupies the center of this eucharistic liturgy.

The Meaning of Work from Genesis

To speak of this problem obliges us to go back to the origin of the creation of man, as we have heard it in the book of Genesis. God is the creator of all things, and of man. This is the basis that lets us call man a person: because he is the image and likeness of God, created with intelligence, will and the power to dominate the earth. This distinguishes him from the rest of creation, because he is called further to communion with God through the grace of Jesus Christ.

Man works because he is like God. Among all the creatures of the world, only man works consciously. The animals are very active, but none works in the sense of human work. In fact, to work means to make the earth subject or dominate it, as we have read in the book of Genesis. Every work, independent of its particular characteristics, has this end. We may say that in God's plan, work is a domination using power and authority received from God, even when it has the most servile character in its human aspect. Work, every work, even when man administers and directs the work of others, in a word, every activity of man has this prerogative: physical work like your work in industry, in the countryside and in the ancillary services, intellectual work, artistic work, the work of pure and applied research, etc.

The book of Genesis says that the Creator has given all the earth, in a certain sense all the visible world, to man and has put it under his domination. As the image and likeness of God, man domesticates the earth, makes it his own by humanizing it in a responsible manner. At the same time, God has given this world to man as a task for his work. The lower creatures have been put under man, and at the same time he has been given the resources contained in the created world, beginning from the visible riches which are found, so to speak, on the surface, and going as far as the riches hidden deeply in the structure of matter, which man's genius gradually discovers.

The book of Genesis speaks of dominion over all the earth, i.e., of its visible riches and of those it hides: "And God said, 'Let us make man according to our image, in our likeness, and let him have dominion over the fish of the sea and over the birds of the sky, over the cattle and over all the earth.' "[18]

Ethics Must Guide Technology

Man makes the earth subject, or dominates it, by means of work, the vocation which God has given him to collaborate in the work of creation. For this, to obtain personal fulfillment in work, man makes use of technology. We are witnesses today of the transformations caused by the sciences and technologies put into effect by man's intelligence. Nevertheless, although the technical instrument has a positive value, since it helps in the intelligent and responsible exercise of man's dominion over the earth, serious doubts and questions arise too: for technology in fact can become – and has become – alienating and manipulative; and finally we must reject, morally speaking, a certain ideology of technology, because it has imposed the primacy of matter over spirit, of things over the person, of technology over morality.

This dehumanizing and depersonalizing tendency explains why the Church does not tire of calling for a radical revision of the notions of progress and development: Pope Paul VI did this in his encyclical *Populorum Progressio* almost twenty years ago now; and I have done this from the See of Peter and on my pastoral pilgrimages.

How long must man, and the people of the Third World, unjustly support the primacy of the economic processes over the inviolable human rights and, in particular, over the rights of the workers and of their families? It is here, in the inviolable and sacred human values and rights of the person, that it is necessary to think and define anew the notions of development and of progress.

The book of Genesis says that the Creator has united human work to the necessity of rest and of festival: "Then God, on the seventh day, brought to its close the work that he had done ... and God blessed the seventh day and consecrated it."[19] We see clearly in God's intention that work is for man, and not man for work; that work is for the realization of his humanity, of his vocation as person and son of God.

Dignity of the Worker Guides the Economy and Organizational Structures

It is this principle of the dignity of the person of the worker that must determine the possible structures of the industrial systems and of every economic, political and social process, unless we wish to continue with the terrifying imbalance of a minimal percentage that enjoys the wealth, alongside a high percentage that has nothing – especially in the countries of the Third World. The great differences of social position and of the privilege of income between the one group and the other are disproportionate. Work is a good for man, but a good that belongs to all, despite the effort it involves, and not just for a few.

This becomes clearer when we consider the fact that "God created man ... male and female he created them,"[20] thus beginning the family. "Be fruitful and multiply."[21] Work is subordinate to the ends proper to man and to humanity, with the family always in a primary position as the interpersonal community of a man and a woman, called to transmit life to their children; to the new persons, created like them in the image and likeness of God. This is why the Church tirelessly affirms that work is for the family, and not the family for work.

I desire that this fundamental and eternal image of human work be imprinted in the conscience of all those who form or create a new, growing and prosperous milieu of work in this region of Venezuela.

The Doctrine of Creation Gives Us the Priority of Labor

The key idea of the whole encyclical *Laborem Exercens* is the "basic problems of work,"[22] which leads to the affirmation that "at the very origin of human work lies the mystery of creation."[23] In this perspective, and bearing in mind the "diverse experiences of history," the problem of work appears as "a great reality ... closely bound to man as to its proper subject and to his rational activity."

Despite the effort and the endeavor that it demands, "work does not cease to be a good." "This characteristic of human work, totally positive and creative, educative and meritorious, must be the basis of the evaluations and the decisions made today concerning work, including those that refer to the subjective rights of man." And thus it is necessary to give first place constantly to "the principle of the priority of labor over capital."[24]

In the light of this principle it is necessary to study the "great conflict" which has been manifest, and continues to manifest itself for two centuries now, between the "world of capital" and the "world of labor."[25] Admitting that labor and capital are inseparable components of the process of production, it is absolutely necessary to bring the legitimate interests and aspirations into a permanent harmony in order to overcome the antagonism between the one and the other – a harmony between those who control the means of production and the workers. But "the just endeavors to assure the rights of the workers must always take into account the limits imposed by the general economic situation of the country. The demands of the trade unions may not turn into a kind of 'egoism' of the group or class, but must rather aim to correct – looking to the common good of the society as a whole – whatever is defective in the system of ownership of the means of production or in the manner of administering or controlling them."[26]

In the age of mechanized labor, like the work done here in Ciudad Guayana, man may not lose his privileged position given by the Creator: he is the subject of the work, not the slave of the machine, of technology. Technology, understood "as a whole set of instruments which man uses in his work, is undoubtedly man's ally. It facilitates his work, perfects, accelerates and augments it. ... However ... technology can cease to be man's ally and become almost his enemy, as when the mechanization of work 'supplants' him, taking away all personal satisfaction and the incentive to creativity and responsibility, when it deprives many workers of their previous employment, or when through exalting the machine, it reduces man to the status of its slave."[27]

The Gospel of Work: The Redemption of Work

This is why the "Gospel of Work" must be brought into the concrete work of everyday, living the message of Jesus in work and knowing that Christ is close to the worker in his everyday life, that he belongs to the world of labor and that work too bears that sign of his Cross, suffering, effort, frustration and pain. This too is the Church's path, to be very close to the world of labor today.

This image of work, which the social teaching of the Church inherits in the Word of the living God, taking account always of the living experiences of the world of human work, has yet another central point of reference. In today's Gospel, we have heard the words about "the son of the carpenter."[28] Jesus Christ, Son of the Living God, of the same Living God, of the same substance as the Father, became man as the Eternal Word. And as man, for the many years of His hidden life at Nazareth, he worked beside St. Joseph, whom men took to be His father. For this reason he was called "the son of the carpenter," because Joseph was an artisan, a carpenter. Jesus of Nazareth, whose whole life was the messianic mission, spent many years in manual labor.

In this way he united human work to the work of the Redemption of the world, and also confirmed the dignity of man's work which has its beginning in God. Workers, therefore, and especially manual workers, rightly look to St. Joseph and to the "son of the carpenter," seeking in them the confirmation of the essential values of work and of this dignity which belongs to the man who works.

6. *Tourism Fosters Important Social, Spiritual and Religious Values*[29]

Human Rights/Dignity, Service, Solidarity, World Community, Work and Leisure.

[An address on November 14, 1985 in Rome, to members of the World Travel Congress of the American Society of Travel Agents.]

There are many authentic human values which are encouraged and enhanced by tourism, and I wish to speak of some of these today. Yet, as I begin, I cannot overlook certain negative factors also connected with this phenomenon. I refer to those practices which demean the tourists themselves or serve to exploit the countries visited. What is important is that the basic dignity of every person be respected, both the dignity of the visitors and that of the people being visited.

Unifying the World

In considering the positive developments that have taken place during the last several decades, we can see in many cases how tourism has strengthened unity and fraternal solidarity between individuals and between nations. The world is becoming a global village in which people from different continents are made to feel like next-door neighbors. Modern transportation has removed many of the obstacles formerly imposed by geographical distances. It has enabled people to appreciate each other better and to engage in fruitful dialogue and mutual exchange. In facilitating more authentic social relationships between individuals, tourism can help overcome many real prejudices, and foster new bonds of fraternity. In this sense, tourism can be a real force for world peace.

Spiritual and Religious Values

Through the recreation and leisure made possible by travel, people are restored and renewed, body and spirit. They return home to family and work with a new perspective and enthusiasm for life. The Church also attaches importance to the phenomenon of tourism because of the cultural enrichment that it offers. This corresponds to the deep longings of the human heart and can counterbalance certain dehumanizing tendencies in our highly technological society. The spirit is uplifted and refreshed in the contemplation of what is beautiful, whether it is embodied in the wonders of creation or expressed in works of art.

When tourism truly fosters this contemplation of beauty, it elevates and invigorates, and favors a dialogue with the Creator, for God is the source of all that is truly beautiful in nature as well as in the arts. Not only for Christians but for all who believe in God, the contemplation of beauty is a way to inner harmony and joy.

The Church likewise appreciates the complex reality of tourism as a means of furthering certain religious values. A clear example of this is the common practice of making a pilgrimage, that is, a journey to a sacred place or sanctuary for a religious motive. This practice is not restricted to any one people or religion. The spiritual value of going on pilgrimage has long been present in the Judeo-Christian tradition, and it is found to penetrate all the aspects of the pilgrim's life.

Christians and Service

The Christian message has always emphasized the service of others. As travel agents and tour operators, you indeed are people who serve. You are so often in a position to offer counsel and assistance to others. You help those who routinely make business trips. You assist individuals and families during their vacations and holidays. Some of you are in a position to offer a helping hand to the aged and the handicapped. You may, at times, be able to give particular attention to young people, helping them to appreciate the wonderful opportunity of discovering different cultures and broadening their horizons. As you give assistance to travelers in their journeys, may you know that special joy that God grants to those who place themselves at the disposal of others. In this context, I would like to express my gratitude for all that your colleagues throughout the world have done for me during my various apostolic journeys.

By way of conclusion I wish you to know that I very much appreciate your efforts to cultivate human understanding and cultural enrichment through tourism. As people of good will, strive to eliminate injustice and discrimination and seek to transform the world into a civilization of love. The encounters engendered among peoples through travel are not only a condition for the realization of peace but a positive contribution toward peace.

---

7. The Responsibility of Entrepreneurs Is to Develop a Community of Work[30]

Collaboration with God, Entrepreneurship, Meaning of Work, Participation, Technology, Universal Destination of Goods.

[An address on December 14, 1985 in Rome, to members of the Union of Christian Executive Entrepreneurs.]

The UCID [Union of Christian Executive Entrepreneurs] was born following the sad experience of the Second World War, at a singularly critical and delicate moment not only for Italy but for all of Europe. It was a moment and a time of reconstruction and lively recovery, in which the new economic and political structures appeared and put down their roots. You recall how, on the social scene of the country at that time, models of life and ideologies which were to leave a very deep mark upon subsequent years presented and rapidly affirmed themselves.

At the center of that social dynamism and as a basic structure of economic rebirth, the business firm was proposed, and with it the determining role of the leaders of this form of work organization, your role as entrepreneurs and executives, assisted by the necessary collaborators, the technicians, administrators, researchers, study and programming teams. In this way there was being realized the peaceful and organic – so to speak – socio-economic revolution of our times, still rapidly developing.

The Influence of the Gospel in the Business Enterprise

However, within that lively context there very quickly appeared the risk that the world of business enterprise might be reduced to a complex of structures resting exclusively on technical and economic values, thus losing contact not only with that higher sphere of values which is proper to human beings elevated to the dignity of children of God, but also with those values that belong to man by the simple fact of being man. It was then that, with an idea that was new and daring for those years but right, some of you – first in the major industrial centers of Genoa and Milan, then in other parts of Italy – asked yourselves what light could be shed upon the complex world of business enterprise by the teachings of the Gospel, and what might be, as a consequence, the ethical commitment which would impose itself upon the Christian conscience of the entrepreneurs and executives faced with the appeals of the day. They understood that with regard to these questions it was necessary to reflect and search not in an isolated but in a communitarian way, and from a specifically Christian point of view.

Thus began the UCID, and with it a long journey of commitment and responsibility that was able constantly to nourish itself with a suitable catechesis, to which particularly prepared ecclesiastics made their contribution. ... Those were not easy years; in a time of contrasts, in which opposing ideologies sought to take hold of the working world, the members of the UCID assumed the burden of overcoming forms of fatalism and rigidity by accepting a social discourse inspired by the teachings of the Gospel. Forty years later it is possible to comprehend the usefulness of such an effort, carried out in the heart of a society profoundly marked by the industrial phenomenon, and in which Catholic entrepreneurs and executives have occupied such an eminent position of orientation and formation in the light of Christian principles.

New Developments for Promoting the Dignity of Workers

I wish to acknowledge this and congratulate you on the mission carried out by UCID; but I desire just as much to encourage you for the future. The future, as you know, is full of questions and acute problems for your world of business enterprise.

The fortieth anniversary of your association occurs, in fact, at a time of prelude to a new industrial phase, full of changes and innovations for the entire working world.

Yesterday's economic theories are showing their limitations in various respects. New proposals are being advanced in an attempt to formulate better relations between capital and labor, giving greater attention to the personal dignity of all who participate in the process of production. One notes the need to involve workers, too, in the process of the formation of capital and in the decisions which regard the firm, according to a "participatory" conception of the economy which opens upon exceptionally stimulating prospects for those who are interested in overcoming the various ills suffered by the world in which you find yourselves working.

Furthermore, the development of so-called "informatics," while it progressively lightens the load of manual labor, offers to each individual even greater possibilities for providing his own responsible contribution to the formation process of the firm's plan and to the working out of the choices through which the firm's life is expressed.

The Vocation of the Executive

Along with this growing importance of the individual component of that complex world which is the firm, a renewed appreciation of the role of the entrepreneur and of the executive is being affirmed very significantly. After years of open or subtle controversy, ever greater segments of the population are rediscovering the indispensable contribution that enterprising risk and executive professionalism are called to make to social progress. People are becoming aware of the fact that without you, entrepreneurs and executives, a modern organization of the business firm is unthinkable. Nor is it possible to realize that constant adjustment among market needs, worker expectations and the demands of correct business management upon which the health of the economic social system depends.

This situation has restored space and credibility to you in public opinion, entrepreneurs and executives, favoring attitudes of greater willingness to dialogue on the part of other social components. It is your task to correspond to the changed climate with a renewed sense of personal and communitarian responsibility, working in your respective areas with that spirit of service that has been inculcated in the members of the Union from the beginning.

Facing New Challenges

This will allow you, even at this time of profound structural changes, to assume that "active and forward-looking position in ordering the social aspect of the firms according to the requirements of Christian thought," which is one of the institutional goals established in the Union's statutes.[31]

That the present moment in history marks a sort of epochal transition as far as the organization of work is concerned is a reality that is apparent to everyone. Automation is producing instruments capable of substituting for man in vast sectors hitherto covered by the direct activity of laborers, technicians, employees. On the other hand, this process – which tends to extend itself – while it offers tremendous experiences for the growth of the firm, also produces situations and problems which have not yet been resolved. In fact, the phenomenon which today disturbs the progress of the most thriving complexes is precisely that of growing unemployment. When it reaches certain proportions, it can become a true social calamity; but also, where it begins to swell, it shows itself to be a phenomenon that demands enormous expenditures, and it risks turning against the productive structures themselves, rendering vain the advantage realized with the new technologies. We must say sincerely that with regard to this point there is still a long road ahead of us, analogous to what took place when the birth of industry transformed the productive system.

The Fundamental Principle of Human Dignity

Once again the Church asks you to keep before you, in this context, the great principle of social justice, without which the entire economic system is exposed to the risk of dangerous degeneration. This principle, as you know, affirms that man is the subject of work, and the end of the whole economy is not profit, but the promotion of the person. In this regard, here is what Vatican Council II says: "Human work which is exercised in the production and exchange of goods or in the provision of economic services, surpasses all other elements of economic life," because it "proceeds from the human person, who as it were impresses his seal on the things of nature. Since economic activity is, for the most part, the fruit of the collaboration of many men, it is unjust and inhuman to organize and direct it in such a way that some of the workers are exploited."[32] It is necessary, then, to provide for man, to guarantee the good of the person, of every person, even in the midst of the new technological revolution. As I affirmed in the encyclical *Laborem Exercens*, "it is respect for the objective rights of the worker – every kind of worker, manual or intellectual, industrial or agricultural, etc. – that must constitute the adequate and fundamental criterion for shaping the whole economy, both on the level of the individual society and state and within the whole of the world economic policy and of the systems of international relationships that derive from it."[33]

Certainly, the Church does not claim to dictate the appropriate techniques for resolving these problems. Yet she feels that she cannot neglect the duty of recalling to your consciences – and to the consciences of all who have responsibility in these fields – the moral principles which must oversee every decision in such matters.

The Universal Destination of Material Goods

Fundamental among these is the principle that the goods of the universe have been created for all men in order that, through work, they might serve toward the complete development of all. From this universal destination of goods, private property receives its functions, its contents and its limits. It is thus necessary that each individual, without letting himself be dominated by the craving to win greater power, open himself to dialogue and collaboration, with the competent participation of the organs of the political community as well.

Collaboration Versus Exploitation

This theme of collaboration, which your statutes want "effective and equitable between the subjects of production,"[34] is one which today broadens out upon international horizons. In production, as in all work activities, interdependence among states becomes more multiform and intense from one day to the next. Often, these dependencies have been seen or interpreted as forms and occasions for exploitation, especially at the expense of the poorer populations. We must ask ourselves today if this reciprocal possibility and requirement of relations at the world level might not become instead, with the good will of all, a positive occasion for finding ways toward a greater use of human work forces, in a context not of competition but of collaboration between peoples. The task of entrepreneurs and executives in this regard will have to include the study of ways of illuminating, explaining and inventing the strategies of action that may save man, orient choices and find remedies for the possible negative aspects, in order to ensure that human beings always be the privileged users and conscious architects of development.

Free Response of Christian Lay People

Just as the rapid evolution of technology demands urgent changes and new projects for business firms, so the attention toward man requires just as much wisdom, inventiveness and diligent generosity, so that the profound values upon which rests the moral order of the work culture are not inverted. The Church must put her trust in the conscientious responsibility of committed lay persons like yourselves in order to see her message realized, knowing well that you are not conditioned by almost mechanistic or fatalistic conceptions of economic development. Indeed, you are convinced that in the last analysis it is always the human person who directs the fortunes of development and measures their consequences. Economic and social questions always depend on choices and on the qualities of the persons who operate within them; on their good will as well as their ability and skill in dealing with problems – in a word, on their "responsibility." The Church, therefore, is near to you; she is firmly convinced that you, like laborers and technicians, are a necessary component of the work structure, and she particularly trusts in you for the development and the improvement that you can contribute to the civilization of work.

I hope that you will be able to be true protagonists of hope for new times, the workers of positive, peaceful and encouraging signs in the world of business enterprise, under the guidance of the fundamental inspiration of a lively and generous Christianity.

8. Respect for Human Dignity Should Govern All Economic Activity[35]

Common Good, Human Rights/Dignity, World Community.

[An address on April 12, 1986 in Rome, to members of the United States' Commission on Executive Exchange.]

It is a pleasure for me to welcome you to the Vatican today as members of the President's Commission on Executive Exchange. I wish to congratulate you, for in being designated to this position you represent America's most important business corporations and federal government agencies. You have a wealth of experience in both the private and public sectors of your nation's life, and your mutual exchange provides a basis for more effective cooperation between business and the agencies of government.

I am happy that you have come to Rome in the course of this year's International Seminar, which is enabling you to meet business executives throughout Europe. It is my hope that your talks will be fruitful and provide you with a better understanding of the economic and social issues of the day.

Concern for the Welfare of All

I would encourage you always to look beyond the immediate concerns of your own country, and to make the welfare of the people of all nations a primary concern. The true dignity of every human person should be the basic ethical principle governing economic activity, since the economy and production are for the good of the human person and not vice versa.

May God grant you wisdom in your decisions, prudence in your words and actions, and concern for the dignity and equality of every individual, so that you will always render true service to humanity.

9. *Direct Your Energies to the Wealth of Love, Not the Love of Wealth*[36]

Christian Witness/Mission, Common Good, Economic Laws and Profits, Human Rights/Dignity, Humanization/Dehumanization, Private Property/Co-ownership, Service, Solidarity, Universal Destination of Goods.

[An address on April 11, 1987 in Buenos Aires, to Argentinean entrepreneurs.]

In the course of my pastoral visit to your country, I am pleased to be able to meet you today, who are here as representatives of the world of enterprise, finance, economics, industry and commerce. I am aware that you are a group of specially qualified persons, on whose important activity depends a considerable part of the economic life and, consequently, the welfare of many families.

Abundance Carries Special Duties and Gratitude

During these days in which I have travelled the length and breadth of your country, I have been able to see for myself how much God has blessed the Argentinean people. Hence, I would like to point out, before anything else, your first and foremost duty as persons on whom a good part of the abundant resources of this country depends, your duty to be grateful to God for the gifts he has placed in your hands.

It is that you give thanks to God for the fertility of your fields, for the abundance of your livestock and many other natural resources and products of labor; above all, give thanks for the enterprising spirit and the capacity for work with which he has endowed you, so that, together with the many men and women who help in the realization of your enterprises and projects, you may serve the common good in the vast and complex area of the production of goods and services. If you did not fulfill this first obligation of justice to God, the Father of all, neither would you be just with people, who are your brothers, nor could you bring to completion with a human and Christian spirit the great tasks in which you are daily engaged.

Economic Problems

I am also aware that, together with this abundance of resources, in recent years you have suffered economic and financial difficulties, which were sometimes critical. I am referring particularly to the serious problems concerning the foreign market for the products of your agricultural and livestock industries, as well as the repercussions of that situation on your economy. You have seen to what extent the progress of nations depends greatly on the international order, which demands the search for solutions expressive of true solidarity and cooperation among different peoples, and based on the consciousness of universal brotherhood.

It is in times of difficulty that your enterprising spirit is put to a test. At these times there is a need for greater effort and creativity, more sacrifice and determination not to abandon the search for ways to overcome such situations, but to use all the legitimate means at your disposal and make all the timely requests. As your activity always has a profound dimension of service to individuals and society and, in a special way, to your workers and their families, you can understand why I am encouraging you to be particularly magnanimous in those difficult circumstances. In fact, the survival and growth of your businesses or investments are of interest to the whole labor community which constitutes the enterprise, and to the whole society. For this reason, times of crisis suppose an economic yet still more ethical challenge which everyone must face, overcoming the selfish interests of individuals, groups or nations.

Respect for "Human Capital"

You know very well that the mission of the Church and of the Pope is not to give technical solutions to socio-economic problems. However, it is a part of their mission to enlighten the consciences of people so that their activities may be truly human; to help lead them to oppose any degradation of the person, so that he is not treated or does not see himself as a mere means of production. I understand that this message is particularly relevant for you under the present circumstances. In fact, it is intended to strengthen that human disposition which, as I said, is being put to the test among you today, as well as to evaluate the "human capital," which is the most important source of the country's riches.

In this same context, when I was speaking once to men and women who are engaged in business enterprises, banking and commerce, I pointed out to them that "the degree of well-being that society enjoys today would have been impossible without the dynamic figure of the entrepreneur, whose function consists in organizing human labor and the means of production in order to produce goods and services."[37] Without any doubt, your task is of the first order of society.

That reality is based on your having received the "inheritance" of a twofold patrimony, that is, the natural resources of the country and the fruits of the work of those who have preceded you.[38] Independently of who the present title-holders may be, this refers to the heritage of all the Argentineans, which nobody should squander or misuse. These resources should be administered not only with technical competence and the capacity of initiative, but above all with a well-formed Christian conscience in all the demands of justice and charity inherent in your mission.

Entrepreneur as Steward

The work of the entrepreneur can very well be compared to that of the steward whom the Gospel speaks of, and from whom his Master asks an accounting of his work. These words are also addressed to you: "Draw me up an account of your stewardship" (Lk 16:2). Together with the Lord, people, your brothers, also ask you; they have also been called to have a share in the inheritance that God has placed, above all, in your hands. Therefore, feel the great moral responsibility that belongs to you. Consider that all those goods are jobs for so many men and women, they are the future of many families, they are the talents that you have to make productive for the good of the community.

The resources of capital, the goods which constitute the heritage of the country, regardless of who their title-holders may be, are a source of livelihood for the people; they "cannot be possessed against labor, they cannot even be possessed for possession's sake, because the only legitimate title to their possession . . . is that they should serve labor, and thus, by serving labor, that they should make possible the achievement of the first principle of this order, namely, the universal destination of goods and the right to common use of them."[39] In this sense, you are to contribute to the increase of productive investments and jobs, the promotion of adequate forms of workers' participation in the administration and uses of the enterprise, and the opening of opportunities that will allow more people to own property, as the basis of a just and unified society.

You have in your hands an inheritance that should bear fruit for the good of all, and with the collaboration of all. You need much daring, which is also a consequence of true Christian prudence, to pass on to the next generations the heritage you have received, but improved both in quality and in quantity. Have the healthy pride of bequeathing a better future to your children, to the children of all Argentineans! However, it should be a future that will also include the example of your generous dedication to work.

Workers in a Common Task

In assuming that responsibility you have a strong element at your disposal, business. In it the owners, managers, employees and workers work together in a common task. They are not enemies, but brothers and sisters. As the Second Vatican Council has said: "In business enterprises it is persons who associate together, that is, men who are free and autonomous, created in the image of God. Therefore, while taking into account the role of every person concerned, owners, employers, management and employees, and without weakening the necessary executive unity, the active participation of everybody in administration is to be encouraged."[40]

Business: A Human Vocation

Thus understood, businesses are legitimate expressions of freedom. They belong to the vocation of man, to his creative initiative, to the needs of the community and to the possibilities which the riches of creation entrusted to the human being offer.

To the unified understanding of the business community is certainly joined the subsidiary function of the State, which should always see in it a faithful and necessary cooperation directed to the common good.

Promotion of the Common Good

In my meeting with the businessmen and laborers of Spain in Barcelona, I told them that "business is called to fulfill, under your influence, a social function, which is profoundly ethical: that of contributing to the perfection of man without discrimination, by creating conditions that will make it possible for work not only to develop the capacities of the person, but also at the same time to achieve an effective and reasonable production of goods and services, and will make the worker aware of working on something that is really his own."[41]

In this way, business is not only increasing material wealth and the great promoter of socio-economic development, but also the cause of personal progress which allows the creation of more humane living conditions. Its activity is inserted within the framework of the common good, which embraces "the sum total of all those conditions of social life which enable individuals, families, and organizations to achieve complete and efficacious fulfillment."[42]

In synthesis, the fundamental law of all economic activities is the service of man, of all men and of the whole man, in his complete totality – material, intellectual, moral, spiritual and religious. Consequently, profit should not only be used to increase capital, but it should also be destined, with a social sense, to the raising of the wages, providing social services and opportunities for technical training, research and cultural promotion along the path of distributive justice.

A business that respects these social goals evidently requires a model of a deeply human entrepreneur, who is aware of his duties, honest, competent, and imbued with a profound social sense, that makes him capable of rejecting the inclination to selfishness, of preferring the wealth of love to the love of wealth. We can see certain biblical similarity between the businessman and the Shepherd. It is an analogy.

Spiritual Problems Take Priority over Economic Ones

Beloved businessmen and women, we have already spoken about the highly complex and delicate environment in which you exercise your professional activity. Likewise, I also know the various kinds of difficulties that hinder your work, problems that are related to trade cycles, the sometimes difficult relations with your collaborators and workers, misunderstandings and accusations that sometimes make you their favorite target.

I insist that I am aware of the existence of these problems, which are often objectively most serious. However, permit me to remind you that the great concern, the great business affair that you must conduct in your life, is to conquer heaven, eternal life. The Lord says to you: "What gain is it for a man to have won the whole world and to have lost or ruined his very self?"[43] This reference has to be made. This has to be made at least when the one who speaks to you is a Bishop a

Pope, a Pastor, one who is responsible for a higher economy, the divine economy.

Never forget that the real dangers are the temptations that can lead your consciences and activity astray, namely, the insatiable thirst for profit, easy and immoral gains, waste, the temptation of power and pleasure, limitless ambitions, uncontrolled selfishness, dishonesty in business affairs and injustice towards your workers.

Carefully watch yourselves for these snares. Never kneel before the golden calf! Never abandon the narrow path of business integrity, which alone, together with a worthily earned material well-being, can offer peace and serenity to you and your families.

Association with God as Co-Workers

Businessmen and women who are by majority Christians, you should be the architects of a more just, peaceful and fraternal society. Be men and women of dynamic ideas, creative initiatives, generous sacrifices and a firm and sure hope. Remember, with the force of Christian love you will achieve important goals. Be encouraged to follow the example of the pioneers who, with nothing but their determination and faith in God, began what have developed into many of your big enterprises today – the people who, working alone, even with their bare hands and with practically no technical knowledge, laid the foundations of the future economic development of the country.

Observe solidarity among yourselves, as well as with the other sectors of the community which share in your problems, your sacrifices and your hopes; and do this for the welfare of your beloved country.

Should there be anyone who has lost all hope in the construction of that more just society which we all desire, let us tell him forcefully yet lovingly that there is a system for the solution for the difficult problems that affect man. It is to return to God the Creator who through his Providence continues working in the great enterprise of the world; he has chosen you to be associated with his Providence as his co-workers.

Thus, no matter how great the difficulties, no matter how fruitless your efforts may seem, always go forward, accepting the challenge of the times; and beyond the confidence you have in your ability and efforts, remember the saying of the Lord: "Seek first the kingdom of God and his justice, and all these other things will be given you as well."[44]

God's Love Experienced in One's Work

Yes, even in the midst of difficulties, if you know how to give generously of yourselves for the common welfare through the exercise of your profession, if you show love for God and your brothers in the administration of your businesses, you will certainly experience God's love for you. As St. Paul writes, he "will provide you with all the seed you want and make the harvest of your good deeds a larger one."[45] God accepts human activity and rewards it with new blessings, with fruits that will be revealed not only in heaven but also in your land.

I conclude by offering for your consideration other words of St. Paul in his first Letter to the Christians of Corinth, an important commercial port of his time; "Neither the planter nor the waterer matters; only God, who makes things grow."[46] Before the panorama of your extensive and fertile fields, it is easy to raise the heart to God in thanksgiving with the help of the Pauline text, recognizing that is he who makes things grow. The words of the Apostle also help us understand that you will not be able to attain the true progress of this great country of Argentina without God. He alone can give the true dimension to your work and your initiatives, the dimension which fosters authentic growth, expressed not only in economic terms, but above all in fruits of peace, concord and human and Christian solidarity.

10. The Communications Media Must Be Directed towards the Common Good[47]

Christian Witness/Mission, Collaboration With God, Common Good, Human Rights/Dignity, Justice, Environment, Fair Wage, Materialism and Consumerism, Meaning of Work, Service, Solidarity.

[An address on September 9, 1987 in Los Angeles, to executive leaders of the communications industry.]

I am very pleased to be here with you. I would like to be able to greet each one of you personally and to express my regard for you individually. Although this is not possible, I wish to express my sincere respect for all the categories of the media that you represent – the film industry, the music and recording industry, radio, electronic news, television and all those which inform the world through the written word – and for the diverse functions that you perform as workers, writers, editors, managers and executives. I greet you in the full range of your activities, from the very visible to the relatively hidden.

My visit to Los Angeles, and indeed to the United States, would seem incomplete without this meeting, since you represent one of the most important American influences on the world today. You do this in every area of social communications and contribute thereby to the development of a mass popular culture. Humanity is profoundly influenced by what you do. Your activities affect communication itself: supplying information, influencing public opinion, offering entertainment. The consequences of these activities are numerous and diverse. You help your fellow citizens to enjoy leisure, to appreciate art and to profit from culture. You often provide the stories they tell and the songs they sing. You give them news of current events, a vision of humanity and motives for hope. Yours is indeed a profound influence on society. Hundreds of millions of people see your films and television programs, listen to your voices, sing your songs and reflect your opinions. It is a fact that your smallest decisions can have global impact.

A Force for Great Good or Ill

Your work can be a force for great good or great evil. You yourselves know the dangers as well as the splendid opportunities open to you. Communication products can be works of great beauty, revealing what is noble and uplifting in humanity and promoting what is just and fair and true. On the other hand communications can appeal to and promote what is debased in people: dehumanized sex through pornography or through a casual attitude towards sex and human life; greed through materialism and consumerism or irresponsible individualism; anger and vengefulness through violence or self-righteousness. All the media of popular culture which you represent can build or destroy, uplift or cast down. You have untold possibilities for good, ominous possibilities for destruction. It is the difference between death and life – the death or life of the spirit. And it is a matter of choice. The challenge of Moses to the people of Israel is applicable to all of us today: "I set before you life and death. Choose life."[48]

Responsibility to Communicate the Truth

There is something of great interest for all of us in the Constitution of the United States. The same amendment that guarantees freedom of speech and freedom of the press also guarantees freedom of religious practice. The link between the art of human expression and the exercise of religion is profound. Social communications in fact provide an important first step in uniting human beings in mutual love, and this first step is also a step to God, "for God is love."[49] Religious practice, for its part, fosters communication with God. It also fosters human communication, since human communication is part of that relationship of love for neighbor that is mandated in both the Old and New Testaments.

It is easy to see why the Church has recognized and taught that people have a right to communicate. Linked to this right is the right to information about which the Second Vatican Council speaks in these words: "Because of the progress of modern society and the increasing interdependence of its members, it is clear that information has become very useful and generally necessary. ... There exists therefore in human society a right to information on the subjects that are of concern to people."[50]

In this way, then, the Church recognizes the need for freedom of speech and freedom of the press, just as does your constitution. But she goes further. Rights imply corresponding duties. The proper exercise of the right to information demands that the content of what is communicated be true and – within the limits set by justice and charity – complete.[51] Your very profession invites you to reflect on this obligation to truth and its completeness. Included here is the obligation to avoid any manipulation of truth for any reason. This manipulation in fact takes place when certain issues are deliberately passed over in silence, in order that others may be unduly emphasized. It also occurs when information is altered or withheld so that society will be less able to resist the imposition of given ideology.

The obligation to truth and its completeness applies not only to the coverage of news, but to all your work. Truth and completeness should characterize the content of artistic expression and entertainment. You find a real meaning in your work when you exercise your role as collaborators of truth – collaborators of truth in the service of justice, fairness and love.

Mass Communication Can Bring Solidarity

Your industry not only speaks to people and for people: it makes communication possible among them. In this we see how your activities transcend the categories of both rights and duties and confer upon you inestimable privileges. Just before joining you this afternoon, I met young people in several cities by using satellite links. For me this is just one example of how your industry can help foster communication and unite people in fraternal love. It is within your power to use technology to promote what is deeply human and to direct it to the work of peace. You have marvelous tools which others lack. They must be employed in the service of people's right to communicate.

In today's modern world there is always the danger of communication becoming exclusively one-way, depriving audiences of the opportunity to participate in the communication process. Should that happen with you, you would no longer be communicators in the full, human sense. The people themselves, the general public whom you serve, should not be excluded from having the opportunity for public dialogue.

In order to foster such a dialogue, you yourselves, as communicators, must listen as well as speak. You must seek to communicate with people, and not just speak to them. This involves learning about people's needs, being aware of their struggles and presenting all forms of communications with the sensitivity that human dignity requires – your human dignity and theirs. This applies especially to all audio-visual programs.

Human Dignity in the Image of God

At the basis of all human rights is the dignity of the human person created in the image and likeness of God.[52] A recognition of this human dignity is also a part of your civil tradition in the United States, and is expressed in the declaration of your nation's independence: all people are created equal in their human dignity and are endowed by their Creator with inalienable rights to life, liberty and the pursuit of happiness. All other rights too are rooted in human dignity, including the right to maintain one's privacy and not to be exploited in the intimacy of one's family.

The fundamental dignity of the human person is still more strongly proclaimed by the Church. She raises her voice on behalf of people everywhere, declaring the dignity of every human being, every man, woman and child. None is excluded because all bear the image of God. Physical and mental handicaps, spiritual weaknesses and human aberrations cannot obliterate the dignity of man. You will understand why the Church attaches such importance to this principle found on the first page of the Bible: it will later become the basis of the teaching of Jesus Christ as he says: "Always treat others as you would like them to treat you."[53]

Respect What Is Human and Recognize What Is Good

In particular, social communications must support human dignity because the world is constantly tempted to forget it. Whether in news or in drama, whether in song or in story, you are challenged to respect what is human and to recognize what is good. Human beings must never be despised because of limitations, flaws, disorders, or even sins.

Twenty years ago, my predecessor Pope Paul VI, speaking to a gathering much like this one, told that creative community in Rome: "It is a fact that when, as writers and artists, you are able to reveal in the human condition, however lowly or sad it may be, a spark of goodness, at that very instant a glow of beauty pervades your whole work. We are not asking that you should play the part of moralists, but we are expressing confidence in your mysterious power of opening up the glorious regions of light that lie behind the mystery of human life."[54]

The World Is at Your Mercy

As you do precisely this – open up the glorious regions of light that lie behind the mystery of human life – you must ask yourselves if what you communicate is consistent with the full measure of human dignity. How do the weakest and the most defenseless in society appear in your words and images: the most severely handicapped, the very old, foreigners and the undocumented, the unattractive and the lonely, the sick and the infirm? Whom do you depict as having – or not having – human worth?

Certainly your profession subjects you to a great measure of accountability – accountability to God, to the community and before the witness of history. And yet at times it seems that everything is left in your hands. Precisely because your responsibility is so great and your accountability to the community is not easily rendered juridically, society relies so much on your good will. In a sense the world is at your mercy. Errors in judgement, mistakes in evaluating the propriety and justice of what is transmitted, and wrong criteria in art can offend and wound consciences and human dignity. They can encroach on sacred fundamental rights. The confidence that the community has in you honors you deeply and challenges you mightily.

Respect Your Own Dignity

I would encourage you in yet another way: to respect also your own dignity. All that I have said about the dignity of human beings applies to you.

Daily cares oppress you in ways different from those arising in other kinds of work. Your industry reflects the fast pace of the news and changing tastes. It deals with vast amounts of money that bring with them their own problems. It places you under extreme pressure to be successful without telling you what "success" really is. Working constantly with images, you face the temptation of seeing them as reality. Seeking to satisfy the dreams of millions, you can become lost in a world of fantasy.

At this point, you must cultivate the integrity consistent with your own human dignity. You are more important than success, more valuable than any budget. Do not let your work drive you blindly, for if your work enslaves you, you will soon enslave your art. Who you are and what you do are too important for that to happen. Do not let money be your sole concern, for it too is capable of enslaving art as well as souls. In your life there must also be room for your families and for leisure. You need time to rest and be recreated, for only in quiet can you absorb the peace of God.

You yourselves are called to what is noble and lofty in human living, and you must study the highest expressions of the human spirit. You have a great part in sharing the culture of this nation and the other nations. To you is entrusted an important portion of the vast heritage of the human race. In fulfilling your mission you must always be aware of how your activities affect the world community, how they serve the cause of universal solidarity.

Nobility of Communication

The Church wishes you to know that she is on your side. For a long time she has been a patron and defender of the arts; she has promoted the media and been in the forefront of the use of new technology. The first book for the printing press of Johannes Guttenberg, the inventor of movable type, was the inspired work of God, the Bible. Vatican Radio was established under the direction of the inventor of radio, Guglielmo Marconi.

Today, too, the Church stands ready to help you by her encouragement and to support you in all your worthy aims. She offers you her challenge and her praise. I pray that you will welcome that help and never be afraid to accept it.

Ladies and gentlemen of the communications industry, I have set before you the broad outlines of a choice for good within the framework of your profession. I ask you to choose the common good. It means honoring the dignity of every human being.

I am convinced that to a great extent we can share a common hope, rooted in a vision of the human race harmoniously united through communication. I am sure too that all of you, whether Christian or not, will permit me to allude to the great fascination that surrounds the mystery of the communicating word. For Christians, the communicating word is the explanation of all reality as expressed by Saint John: "In the beginning was the Word; the Word was in God's presence, and the Word was God."[55] And for all those who hold the Judeo-Christian tradition, the nobility of communication is linked to the wisdom of God and expressed in his loving revelation. Thus the Book of Deuteronomy records God's communication to Israel: "You shall love the Lord your God with all your heart, and with all your soul, and with all your strength. Take to heart these words which I enjoin on you today."[56]

Ladies and gentlemen, as communicators of the human word you are the stewards and administrators of an immense spiritual power that belongs to the patrimony of mankind and is meant to enrich the whole of the human community. The challenge that opens up before you truly requires generosity, service and love. I am sure that you will strive to meet it. And, as you do, I pray that you will experience in your own lives a deep satisfaction and joy. And may the peace of God dwell in your hearts.

11. The Virtue of Solidarity Is Important for Business Leaders[57]

Christian Witness/Mission, Collaboration with God, Common Good, Community of Persons, Dialogue and Cooperation, Humanization/Dehumanization, Solidarity.

[An address on May 12, 1988 in Santa Cruz, Bolivia, to Bolivian intellectuals and business leaders.]

It is a source of great joy and satisfaction for me to be able to share these moments of my visit in this beloved land of Bolivia with you, the men and women who in a very special way represent the culture and animating force behind so many of the activities that are such an important element in the development of your nation. These two sectors, so intimately related, are, I would say, complementary because the productive activity, which is a cultural expression, in itself, should be inspired by and for humanity and should create everything necessary to satisfy basic needs and create the conditions that will promote all the human dimensions of every member of society.

In my travels I have always tried to give special emphasis to these encounters, since I am well aware of the important responsibilities that you bear in your society. I have not come here to speak with you about matters that are better left to you who are experts in the field. I come to you as pastor and as a brother, desirous of sharing with you our common patrimony of faith, to evaluate with you the enormous possibilities offered by the Christian message that is the inspiration for your work and for all your activities, and that is summed up as the Catholic social doctrine, which is simply a contemplation of humanity and the various ways people relate to one another in the world as seen in the light of revelation. This doctrine seeks to lead people to respond, with the support also of rational reflection and of the human sciences, to their vocation as responsible builders of earthly society.[58]

Responsible Leadership

Responsible builders! No one can doubt that this is a responsibility and task which faces each one of us. Therefore, as we already know from experience, in a society activities and tasks should be distributed among all according to their individual abilities, with everyone without exception collaborating in the search for the common good. What is needed, then, is a functional division of labor that will not give rise to factions nor to discrimination of any kind, and which will lead to certain persons assuming leadership, not as an egotistical privilege, but in the full consciousness of the grave responsibility that coordinating human activity involves. These activities include: intelligent planning of the various phases of social development, investment programs, allocating sufficient funds – in other words, organizing the complex network of activities that indicates the existence of a society that is wise and efficiently organized in all its aspects.

Constructing a Just Society

The just society to which we all aspire is constructed day by day through the collaboration of all its members, fulfilling in this way the loving vocation with which God entrusted human beings when creating them. To construct a city, we might say, is to construct humanity; that is, taking the complete and integral human being as the measure and goal of all social activity, we create the necessary conditions so that each and every member of the human community can realize his full potential.

At this point we could ask ourselves, who truly builds humanity's dwelling place? The beautiful words of the Psalmist come to my mind: "Unless the Lord build the house, they labor in vain who build it."[59] Yes, dear participants of this meeting, a true concern for the person, for his rights, respect for his inalienable and fundamental dignity, will never be completely expressed unless we open our hearts to this truth. Alone, we could never overcome the structures of injustice, the effects of sin, that constitute a real obstacle to growth and to the inspiration necessary to fulfill the most delicate task of guiding the destiny of your nation.

The Virtue of Solidarity

My latest encyclical, in which I wanted once again to emphasize the continued concern of the Church for social matters, is a call for solidarity on all levels. Being a political, cultural or any kind of leader, far from excluding, demands the virtue of solidarity. The modern managerial concept is based on active participation while excluding every form of coercion or violation of human dignity. It requires a knowledge of what the real needs are as well as a burning desire to seek out the best paths leading to solutions of basic problems and to the establishment of a hierarchy in programming activities oriented toward the common good, without resorting to personal or corporate concessions and privileges or granting favors for selfish reasons. Solidarity requires the firm and persistent determination to work for the common good in such a way that we might all be truly responsible for everyone. This determination is based on the solid conviction that what is hindering full development is the desire for profit and the thirst for power, which are temptations that we must look out for and avoid, since many times they masquerade as worthy enterprises.[60]

The Bolivian people have a right to look to the future with hearts full of hope, because you are the repositories of right values that are a mixture of the indigenous traditions and new values that have shaped your identity as a nation throughout your history. The profoundly human nature of Bolivians, your well known hospitality, your firmness in overcoming a wild and often hostile natural environment, your great spirit of solidarity, your resistance in facing misfortune, your tenacious conservation of deep-rooted local customs, all enriched by the Christian values realized through the great work of evangelization whose fifth centenary we are getting ready to commemorate, form a foundation full of promise upon which to build the new society: a more stable Bolivia where all can live in security, strengthened by a more concrete hope for present and future generations.

Faith Makes Ethical Demands

Those of you who are presently engaged in carrying out responsibilities ... in the field of politics or economics, arts or letters, in this beloved Bolivia, must make every effort to integrate the values of your skills or of your assigned task with the truths of the faith that you inherited from your ancestors, and remain open, without reservations or subterfuges, to dialogue and struggle, to participation in all those initiatives that might ennoble your people: in culture, in the development of its natural resources, in building a productive society in which everyone is united and everyone participates, where each person who works to improve it receives just compensation.

The common objective of the challenge facing you should be to serve the pressing needs of the Bolivian people and to prevent future deprivations from arising; to fight against poverty and hunger, unemployment and ignorance; to convert potential natural resources with intelligence, application, responsibility, consistency and honest leadership, into valuable goods and services for Bolivians – for all

Bolivians, without unjust differences offensive to their status as brothers and sisters, as children of the same Father and co-recipients of the gifts the Creator put into the hands of all people.

You must see that this is a service that faith imposes on you. You are called to this work by your fellow citizens, especially those who still suffer unjustly from neglect and poverty in the country, cities and suburbs, by the handicapped who are unable to work for a living, by those needing medical care, by the unemployed, by those not covered by adequate social and legal programs. And these brothers and sisters – even though it might be painful it must be said – make up the greater part of your population.

Raising the level of an entire society requires the infrastructures that make it possible; but it depends in a broad sense on the human qualities of educators and business leaders. Only by living and transmitting fully these moral and human values will you give Bolivia the binding element needed for a cohesive society and for the progress that will liberate it from the difficult socio-economic problems afflicting it and all the great Latin American family today.

Community of Persons

What is needed is a cultural synthesis which is in perfect symbiosis with life, which invites participation in the dialogue between people and communities, and which uses all of its resources to harmonize the riches of its traditional cultures while remaining sensitive to modern needs; a culture which, using the roots of the land itself and its history as a starting point, seeks a common patriotic objective opening out toward new horizons and uniting all peoples in a fraternal embrace.

In this way we will be building a civilization of love, which calls for the virtue of solidarity that "helps us to see the 'other' – whether a person, people or a nation – not just as some kind of instrument with a work capacity and physical strength at low cost and then discarded when no longer useful, but as our 'neighbor,' a 'helper,'[61] to be made a sharer on a par with ourselves in the banquet of life to which all are equally invited by God."[62]

12. Business and Culture Must Collaborate for the Common Good[63]

Christian Witness/Mission, Common Good, Economic Laws and Profits, Entrepreneurship, Human Development/Progress, Materialism and Consumerism, Solidarity, Spirituality, Worker Participation.

[An address on May 15, 1988 in Lima, Peru, to Peruvian leaders of business and culture.]

I would like my first words this evening to express my deep satisfaction in meeting you, the representatives of the business world and the world of culture. During my last visit to Peru you were present in my thoughts. Indeed, when in these lands I thanked God for the evangelization of the new world, I was thinking not only of the work of the missionaries but also of the men and women of culture who helped to shape the identity of these countries in the light of faith. Similarly, in talking about work, I was referring not only to the fundamental role of campesinos and workers, but also to the activities of business people who, through their commitment and dedication, organize production and foster development.

Both worlds are truly expressions of the same reality which can be understood as cultural development in the broadest terms.

Reflection on culture has a long history in the life and thinking of the Church. In fact, it has been a constant concern, which has been emphasized especially at crucial points in the history of humanity. Hence we are dealing with a central theme in the lives of people and of the Church.

Business, for its part, is an important aspect of the broad horizon of culture, all the more so in countries such as your own that are on the way to development, where economic differences are significant. As a result, there is a need for a great effort on the part of the community to reach an economic development sufficient to permit the building of a culture that is genuinely human and truly oriented towards God.

Culture and Christian Faith

The origins of the culture of your country are imbued with the Christian message. The history of Peru has been forged in the fire of faith which has both inspired and left its own mark on the life and customs of the country. In the light of this faith a new synthesis of a mixed culture developed, one which binds together the indigenous American heritage and the European contribution.

However, the endurance of structures which are the source of serious imbalances in society may give rise to a certain diffidence when the time comes to evaluate the underlying faith of the first evangelization, leading to the belief that either it had not penetrated with sufficient force in the criteria and decisions of the leaders of culture and society,[64] or it was weakened through the aggression of extraneous ideologies.

Individualist and Collectivist Ideologies

There are ideologies of an individualistic nature which do not remedy the unjust distribution of wealth, and regard the human person as a self-sufficient individual, inclined towards the satisfaction of his own interests in the enjoyment of earthly goods, without any consideration for the rights of others. On the other hand, there are ideologies of collectivist persuasion, which deny the transcendent vocation of the human person and ascribe to him a destiny that is entirely of this world.[65]

Faced by these concepts inconsistent with your traditional Christian culture, I would like to reiterate to you the invitation which I issued in Santo Domingo to all the peoples of Latin America. By being faithful to the values of human dignity and fraternal solidarity which the people of Peru have in their hearts, as a gospel imperative, resist the temptation of those who would have you forget your undeniable Christian vocation.[66]

Culture Must Serve the Human Person

An interest in culture is first of all an interest in the human person and in the meaning of his existence. These were my words some years ago, addressed to UNESCO: "To create culture, it is necessary to consider, to its ultimate consequences and entirely, man as a particular and autonomous value, as the subject bearing the transcendency of the person. Man must be affirmed for himself, and not for any other motive or reason: solely for himself! What is more, man must be loved because he is man; love must be claimed for man by reason of the particular dignity he possesses."[67] Culture should be the space and means for making life ever more human,[68] and for allowing the person to live a life in conformity with the divine plan. Any culture which is not at the service of the human person is not a true culture.

The Evangelization of Culture

The Church, therefore, makes a radical option for the person in proposing the evangelization of culture. This option, therefore, is for an integral and true humanism which raises the dignity of the person to the true and inalienable dimension of being a child of God. Christ reveals man to man himself.[69] He restores to him his proper grandeur and dignity, enabling him to rediscover the value of his humanity which had been obscured by sin. How great a value the person must possess in the eyes of God to have merited so great a Redeemer!

Hence, the Church can never be at home with those "humanisms" which are limited to exclusively economic, biological or psychic viewpoints. The Christian understanding of life is always open to God's love. In fidelity to this vocation, it tries to remain removed from the different ideologies in order to opt solely for the human person, starting from the liberating Christian message. "The Church," as I pointed out in my recent encyclical *Sollicitudo Rei Socialis*, "does not propose economic and political systems or programs, nor does she show preference for one or the other, provided that human dignity is properly respected and promoted, and provided she herself is allowed the room she needs to exercise her ministry in the world."[70]

The Truth about the Human Person

From the Christian point of view this humanistic option presupposes, like all options, the clear living out of a scale of values, since they are the mainstay of every society. Without values there is no real possibility of building a society that is truly human. They determine not only the meaning of personal life but also the policies and strategies of public life. A culture which has lost its foundation in the supreme values must necessarily turn against the person.

The great problems affecting culture today originate in the desire to separate public and private life from a true scale of values. No economic or political model will fully serve the common good if it is not based on the fundamental values which correspond to the truth about the human person, a "truth that is revealed to us in its fullness and depth in Christ."[71] Systems which raise economic concerns to the level of being the sole determining factor in society are destined, through their own internal dynamism, to turn against the human person.

What is certain is that only by looking to the moral and spiritual capacity of the human person will changes in culture, economy and society occur that are truly at the service of the person. Indeed, sin which is at the root of unjust situations, is, in its proper and primordial meaning, a voluntary act originating in the freedom of the person. For that reason, the rectitude of customs is a condition for the good health of the whole of society.[72]

Evangelizing Culture Touches Every Aspect of the Person

Within the great mission of evangelization to which we are called as a Church, the evangelization of culture holds a special place.[73] It must reach every part of the person and his every manifestation, reaching even to the very root of his being, customs and traditions.[74]

Evangelization demands the effort to move out to meet contemporary man, and searching with him for the ways of dialogue and closeness so that he may improve his condition. It means understanding the mentalities and attitudes of the modern world and bringing the light of the gospel to bear on them. It comes from a desire to reach every level of human life and to make it more worthy. Thus, added value is given to patterns of behavior, criteria of judgement, dominant values, the larger interests, habits and customs which are characteristic of work, family, social, economic and political life.

Faith Contributes to Authentic Culture

Evangelizing culture means fostering humanity in its deepest dimensions. In order to do that, it will sometimes be necessary to illuminate with the light of the gospel all that threatens the dignity of the human person. Moreover, faith helps to produce an authentic culture because it works towards a cultural synthesis within a balanced vision, which can be achieved only in terms of the clearer light which is found in faith. Faith gives the answer from the wisdom which is "ever old and ever new," a wisdom which can help the person to adapt, on the basis of truth, the means to the end, projects to ideals, actions to moral guidelines. This will help to restore a balance of values in today's world. To put it briefly, faith, far from being an obstacle, is an effective force in the creation of culture.

The evangelization of culture in Peru today and in the future must start from an historical premise: the first evangelization – which began almost five hundred years ago – shaped the historical and cultural identity of your people;[75] and the Catholic cultural substrata, appealing particularly to heart and intuition, is expressed in the artistic heritage which is to be seen in your churches, your traditional paintings, your popular art. Frequently its expression in popular piety is very moving.

Faith Becomes Culture

Even if it can be said that faith transcends culture because it finds its origin in God and not in the person, that does not mean that it is set apart from culture. There is an intimate bond between the gospel and human achievement: this bond helps to create culture.

In the same way that culture needs an integral and superior vision of the human person, faith needs to become culture, to be inculturated. "A faith which does not become culture is a faith which has not been fully received, not thoroughly thought through, not faithfully lived out."[76]

Christian Mission Should Not Be Reduced to a Political Program

Hence it is the mission of every Christian to be dedicated to the progressive inculturation of the Gospel message in the variety of cultural expressions that are so deeply rooted in your country. In all of these, faith has played a unifying role. In this way you too will contribute to this endeavor by strengthening the necessary cohesion and unity in your country.

It would not be out of place to draw your attention to the danger that may exist in the process of integrating faith and culture, namely, the danger of temporalism as a reductionist criterion in relation to the Christian message. Among people who are earnestly looking for a greater practice of justice, where social and economic inequalities are great and living conditions for many are often subhuman, there is a frequent temptation to reduce the Church's mission simply to the search for a temporal project or a political program. It is not hard to see where this would lead: the Christian message would be emptied of its essential content, the faith would be adulterated and the Gospel would be betrayed.

Be Real Servants of the Common Good

This evening I would like to address in a special way all those who are involved in creating and promoting culture. Yours is a serious responsibility. Whether culture is fully at the service of mankind or turned against him will depend on the choices you make.

You, the thinkers, are the ones who with a Christian understanding of life, will be able to show that science and faith are not opposed to one another. Indeed, human intelligence with the passage of the centuries has uncovered more and more of the natural mysteries which have intrigued mankind and has taken the veil away from the logical interrelationship which exists between theology and the temporal sciences. The grandeur of intellectual pursuit, as you well know, is seen in the search for the truth. That is how I spoke about it in my encyclical *Redemptor Hominis*: "In this creative restlessness beats and pulsates what is most deeply human – the search for truth, the insatiable need for the good, the hunger for freedom, the nostalgia for the beautiful and the voice of conscience."[77]

What God asks of you is your service to the truth; it must be sought always in research institutes and taught at all times in centers of education; it must govern the work of the mass media, politics, economics, art in all its varied and rich expressions; and it must resist all temptations to manipulate or be manipulated.

In this regard I would like to encourage the professionals in the area of information to be real servants of the common good, something that corresponds to their exalted occupation, one which I might even be so bold as to define as a mission of service to the community. This same society which you are called to serve begs you not to be carried away by vested interests or convenient arrangements in such a way that, by distorting the facts, the peace of the people is jeopardized and the essential values at the heart of democratic stability and constitutional order are undermined.

The Vocation of the Christian Manager Is to Promote the Common Good

I would like to turn my attention to the role of the business person in the present-day world. The task before you, ladies and gentlemen, is to inject the world of work and economics with the ideals of the gospel, as is indicated in the Church's social teaching. In carrying out that arduous task you need to remember that, in spite of the fundamental importance of the means, it is your attitudes which you must first of all examine in the light of faith, in order to change whatever needs to be changed, in accordance with the demands of that same faith.

On occasion your role has been badly interpreted or misunderstood, as if it were necessarily in opposition to workers or bound up with major foreign interests. It is sometimes forgotten that workers and managers together work for the achievement of a common objective. People often forget that you are people of initiative, who take risks, invent new methods, contribute to technological progress and contribute to your community with the fruits of your activities.

The business person who is a Christian cannot but see business as embracing the people who are to grow and be perfected through the work that they do. The ideal of the human and humanizing community must enlighten the concrete reality of business in the midst of a society that is open and pluralistic, by offering a more open and responsible creative force through which effective and rational production of services and goods can be achieved.

Nonetheless, one cannot but lament the fact that there are a number of employers – in different areas of business – who do not respond to the gifts they have received and who appear to ignore their responsibility towards those who work in the company and towards the whole of society. Some seem to forget that they should indeed be the organizers of wealth, but always people who have the common good as their goal; they should not be carried away by the sole desire for what is useful to themselves alone.

Always remember that solidarity and subsidiarity are sure guides for the Christian development of business and society.[78] Business is not only a productive activity, but it is also intended to be a means in which the human person finds fulfillment through work.[79] Always remember that the worker has no capital but himself, and that for him, in the right understanding of business as ordered for the common good, work has priority.[80]

The Problem of International Debt

In addressing employers I cannot avoid thinking of one of the most serious economic problems which plague so many nations in Latin America and particularly Peru.

As I said in my recent encyclical *Sollicitudo Rei Socialis*: "the means intended for the development of peoples has turned instead into a brake upon development and indeed, in some cases, has even aggravated underdevelopment."[81]

Indeed the flow of capital from one country to another, or the existence of public and private credit institutions for regions or nations who need it in order to set up infrastructures or to meet the basic necessities of the people, can be a sign of world solidarity. The criterion which will make this a reality is precisely the sense of solidarity with which it is done. On the part of the country which asks for credit, there must be a close examination of its real priorities, the cost of the loan in terms of finance and human resources, as well as the direct and indirect consequences of delays in payment or default of the debt. Otherwise, the mechanism of credit and loans may be an obstacle and a burden that is too heavy to bear.

As expressed in the document from the Pontifical Commission *Iustitia et Pax*, the problem of the international debt is not only a question of finances and economy, nor is it simply a political question. It is first of all an ethical and moral question. It must be considered and directed towards a solution in the light of the principle of solidarity among peoples and nations, rich and poor, developed and developing, so that no one drowns in the whirlpools of egoism, or profit at any price, or the narrow and strictly materialistic understanding of development.

The Responsibilities of Culture and Business

All of you, representatives of culture and business in this country, bear a great responsibility: to make Peru a place where people not only survive but where, most of all, the citizens are able to live in a way that respects their human dignity in both material and spiritual terms.

May your country continue to be in the future a place of welcome, where the fundamental rights of every person are respected, where selfishness and political antagonism are overcome, where exploitation, violence, and terrorism no longer leave a trail of oppression and death, where civil liberties and the creative power of Peruvians produce a greater cohesion in society as the pledge of a better future when children and young people are no longer the innocent victims of vested interests, party enmities, destabilizing strategies. In short, a society in which Christian values reign supreme and where the noble ideal of solidarity is stronger than the fallen ideal of domination.[82]

Mobilize the Living Resources of Your Nation

In order to carry out this difficult task, your country can count on a wealth of natural resources; but above all, it can count on the treasure of a people with profound Christian roots, whose qualities have to be re-enlivened and empowered to face the challenge of the present moment.

In that plan of solidarity we can all be hopeful about being able to mobilize the living resources of the nation. Both you and I are convinced that through the convergence of so many hearts in solidarity, it will be possible to produce a unified economic plan in which the public authority, without abdicating any of its responsibilities as leaders, may create the peace sufficient to allow private initiative to exercise its decisive influence on the economic development of the whole region.

Challenge to Business and Culture

As Christian employers your country expects much from you, especially in the present economic difficulties, which, even though they affect everybody, affect the poor most of all. Work together with generous dedication and commitment to build an economy that is based on the proper hierarchy of values. Always be attentive to the demands of justice, mercy and solidarity.

I wish to invite you to make an active contribution to the construction and defense of a more human culture. I urge you to become apostles and champions of a culture of life which will be realized in solidarity and development, will reconcile the various elements which appear to be divided, will be based on love and truth and will show in its daily life the importance of goodness and beauty.

13. A Just Society Must Be Founded upon the Truth[83]

Christian Witness/Mission, Gospel of Work, Human Rights/ Dignity, Professional Training/Responsibility, Solidarity, Work and Society.

[An address on May 17, 1988 in Asuncion, Paraguay, to political, cultural, educational and business leaders.]

Not only is the Church in communication with the world; faithful to the mission entrusted to her by the Founder, she is part of the world, of humanity, and thus walks side by side with humanity towards the final destiny which even now is beginning to take form. She is no enemy, as some might think, of authentic development at all levels of human life. On the contrary, she sees in the humanizing progress of the sciences, technology and social organization manifestations of the original will of the Creator who gave to humanity the wonderful work of his hands for the happiness of all. We Christians are convinced that "the achievements of the human race are signs of God's greatness."[84] Even more, we recognize all that is good and noble in the workings of society. The Second Vatican Council teaches that "there is no question of the Christian message inhibiting men from building up the world or making them disinterested in the good of their fellows; on the contrary it is an incentive to do these very things."[85] It encourages its members and all people of good will to take on their responsibilities and fulfil their tasks in society, keeping the common good always before their eyes. This presupposes the creation of the conditions necessary to allow all citizens, without exception, to develop fully as persons. For this delicate task Christians find inspiration in the spirit of the gospel, lived out in the community of the Church under the guidance of the pastors.

The Role of Social Doctrine

The Church not only exhorts people to do good, but by her social doctrine she endeavors to enlighten people in order to direct them in their legitimate quest for happiness and in discovering the truth in the midst of the continuous proposals of dominant ideologies. The

Christian message is marked by optimism and hope because it is based on man. Beginning from a healthy humanism it seeks to have its voice heard in the social, political and economic institutions. The Church has confidence in people, and considers them to be the agents for the construction of society. However, we are talking here about people who are created in the image and likeness of the Creator and are called to give shape and form to that image in their personal and community lives; this is something which must always be kept in mind.

In all this we are talking about a realistic hope and not a utopian one; it is a hope conscious of the ever pernicious existence of sin, which is manifest also in structures which instead of serving the good of man are turned against him. Precisely because of this we find an ambivalence which gives all reality the possibility of being an instrument to carry out God's plan or, on the contrary, to oppose it, as the result of selfishness and the presence of evil.

The Dignity of the Person

In the face of views which are individualistic or set in closed forms of materialism, this doctrine presents an ideal of a society that is united and built on the human person who is open to the transcendent.

The community is the place where man is fulfilled fully as a person in communion with others. The social nature of the human person, life in society, does not come from a "social agreement" as some might think, but rather from the very plan of God who at the beginning said: "It is not good that man should be alone."[86] For this reason we can state that "it should not be thought that reference to the truth about man and to the unconditioned requirement flowing from it has little impact on the solution of the daily and concrete problems raised by society. On the contrary every social relationship, in its ethical substance, consists precisely in the recognition of the dignity of every man, in recognizing that everyone is – really – a person. If the Christian, therefore, does not let himself be guided in this social activity by this view of man, although he will be able to work out partial and technical solutions of individual problems, he will not, in the last analysis, have made society more human, but only, at most, he will have made social organizations more efficient."[87]

The Truth about Man Is the Cornerstone of Society

The Pope wishes to set before you, the builders of society, the certainty that truth has to be the cornerstone, the solid foundation of the whole of society. Pope John XXIII in his great encyclical on peace has said to us: "A civic society is to be considered well-ordered, beneficial, and in keeping with human dignity if it is grounded on truth. As the Apostle Paul exhorts us: 'Away with falsehood then; let everyone speak out the truth to his neighbor; membership of the body binds us to one another.'[88] This will be accomplished when each one duly recognizes both his rights and his obligations towards others."[89]

Clearly, it is not a question of reflecting on the truth in a sterile fashion but of accepting it as the criterion which should influence people in their social relationships and everyday life. It falls to you, not exclusively but in great measure and with a particular responsibility, to make of the web of social, political and economic relations an area of truth in which all members of society may find the fullness of humanity in both its temporal and transcendent dimensions.

Public Morality

A society founded on truth is opposed to all forms of corruption. Hence your bishops, in carrying out their mission as pastors, have called for a "moral renewal of the nation"; indeed, when the public morality is in crisis it not only creates serious difficulties for the members of society, but it also puts their future salvation in jeopardy.

However, what is public morality but the principle which makes it possible in political society for the ideals of justice, peace, freedom and participation to exist? On the contrary, where morality is absent, not only is the achievement of these ideals hindered but also confidence in the institutions is lost; thus passivity and the loss of social initiative are generated. In the Old Testament God called again and again for the practice of virtue, urging mankind to put all its effort into the achievement of the common good, in the knowledge that at the end it will be God himself who will bring the promise of the Kingdom to fulfillment. As we read in the Prophet Isaiah: "Observe what is right, do what is just; for my salvation is about to come, my justice about to be revealed."[90]

Conditions for True Democracy

Values such as peace, freedom, justice and participation, practiced simultaneously and in solidarity, are essential requirements for an authentically democratic society, based on the free consent of all the citizens. Therefore it will not be possible to speak of true freedom, and much less of democracy, where there is no real participation of all citizens in the great decisions affecting the life and future of the nation. In an attitude of harmony and dialogue it is necessary to search for the forms of participation most suited to the expression of the deepest aspirations of all citizens. Order and peace imply a common endeavor; they demand effective respect for the inalienable rights of the human person. Peace is not compatible with the kind of society in which "a small group of individuals set up for their own exclusive advantage a principle of discrimination whereby the rights and even the lives of others are made dependent on the whim of those who are stronger."[91]

We can never lose sight, therefore, of the ethical impulse towards the absolute values, which do not depend on the juridical order or on popular consent. Hence, a true democracy can never in any way be opposed to the values which are seen as fundamental rights, "especially, the right to life at every stage of its existence; the rights of the family, as the basic social community or cell of society; justice in employment relationships; the rights inherent in the life of the political community as such; the rights based on the transcendent vocation of the human being, beginning with the right of freedom to profess and practice one's own religious belief."[92]

Christians and Class Struggle

There is an opposition between the great good of living together in peace and those forces which try to sow violence and hatred as a dialectic solution of conflicts. Hence, the Christian lay person cannot forget that the struggle for justice must not be confused in any way with the program which sees in class struggle the only way to eliminate class injustices in society and to eliminate the classes themselves."[93]

Cultural Originality

Every society also has the right to develop those values which are the expression of the cultural originality of the people. Indeed, the people of Paraguay have enriched Christian culture with a particular way of living in solidarity, of showing hospitality, of displaying courage in the face of adversities. A singularly dramatic history has produced heroic virtues in difficult moments.

Cultural Education

Therefore, education must follow a process of personalization, beginning from the subject himself; it should serve to introduce him to his own culture with all the values and traditions that are proper to it. It should help the person to be familiar with, and to understand, other cultures without in any way lessening his appreciation for what is his own and constitutes his identity.

Education means accompanying the person in his growth, in self-knowledge, in freedom and autonomy and in responsibility. Similarly, it will help him to be the agent of his own growth and to cooperate in the growth of the whole of society. There is a need to educate towards solidarity, by helping the person to overcome all forms of selfishness which generate poverty and take from the fabric of society and public morality.

Obligation to the Poor

Committing oneself to this solidarity presupposes that you will stand on the side of the most needy in your country, in order to defend their rights and hear their just claims. "Every individual is called upon to play his or her own part in this peaceful campaign, a campaign to be conducted by peaceful means in order to secure development in peace, in order to safeguard nature itself and the world about us."[94] The situations of poverty which exist extensively in some countries, including your own, cry out to heaven; they are a hotbed of civil conflict. Therefore, as well as the call to dedicate all your energies and to use your position of leadership to foster integral development in your country for the benefit of all the citizens, I want to remind you of the call from your bishops for more constructive dialogue capable of building bridges of understanding out of mutual respect and freedom.

Christian Roots and Values

Let the words of the prophet ring once more in our ears: "cease doing evil; learn to do good. Make justice your aim: redress the wronged, hear the orphan's plea, defend the widow."[95] In order to reach the desired objectives of justice and peace, freedom and integrity at all levels, you can count on the greatest wealth that a people may possess: the solid Christian values which have been part of your life and customs and which have given life to your nation on its passage through history.

The Christian roots of your people, joined to the hope that comes from your human and spiritual resources, will make each one desire solidarity, generous commitment, mutual respect, ongoing dialogue. Thus, Paraguay may advance more and more towards its objectives of progress through peace, concord and equality among its citizens, without any distinction of origin or social condition.

Trust in Humanity

The Church, in fidelity to the mission which she received from Christ, places her trust in mankind. Indeed, she believes that man can find the path. Even more, she believes that in Jesus we are already on the way to a new humanity, which will really be a community of brothers and sisters.

The Church, however, does not possess "technical solutions." As I said in my last encyclical *Sollicitudo Rei Socialis*, she "does not propose economic and political systems or programs, nor does she show preference for one or the other, provided that human dignity is properly respected and promoted and provided that she herself is allowed the room she needs to exercise her ministry in the world."[96]

---

14. Faith Gives a Perspective to All Human Activity[97]

Collaboration with God, Dominion over the Earth, Solidarity, World Community.

[An address on May 18, 1989 in Rome, to representatives of the Quaker Oats Company.]

The Quaker Oats Company which you represent has a long tradition of growth, not only in corporate or economic terms, but also in regard to humanitarian efforts. During the Great depression of the 1930's, your company showed genuine concern for those who were suffering hardship, and sought to provide for the financial stability of its many employees. In more recent years, the Quaker Oats Foundation has given generous support to various programs which seek to meet people's needs, including many which have been sponsored by Catholic institutions – churches, schools, hospitals and other agencies. I wish to express my appreciation of this clear sense of social solidarity.

Faith and Business

This humanitarian service reminds us that business enterprises have an important role to play in society, and in fostering those spiritual and moral values which lie at its foundation. Those of you who are here today come from various Christian denominations and from Judaism. You are aware of the rich spiritual heritage which we have received from the Judeo-Christian tradition. That tradition calls us to reflect deeply upon the spiritual and moral aspects of all human activity. As men and women made in the image and likeness of God,[98] we have been called to a responsible stewardship over all creation. Our faith in God not only provides us with a source of personal strength and integrity, but also challenges us to cooperate with the Creator in the development of a better world. Faith forms our conscience, and makes us realize that any success, in business or elsewhere, is God's free gift. As the Psalmist once put it: "Unless the Lord builds the house, those who build it labor in vain."[99]

Faith thus gives us a perspective for all our activity. From our spiritual roots, too, come the strength and determination to confront the moral issues and crises of our time. Your work makes you sensitive to the tragic problem of world hunger, which in some places has reached catastrophic proportions. "In the modern world ... starvation claims so many victims, especially among the very young."[100]

The Interdependence of Individuals and Nations

The past record of the Quaker Oats Company in meeting many human needs is in itself a stimulus and a challenge to future efforts. The growing awareness of the interdependence that unites individuals and nations in our time requires "a firm and persevering determination to commit oneself to the common good, that is ... to the good of all and of each individual, because we are all really responsible for all."[101] None of us can close our eyes to the conditions of the poor. None of us can close our ears to the cry of those who are innocent victims of economic disasters.

Dear friends; for the blessings we have received from the hand of God, let us be thankful. And let us pray that we may continue to share all that we have received with those in need.

15. Business People Should Collaborate in Transforming Society according to God's Plan[102]

Collaboration with God, Common Good, Dialogue and Cooperation, Economic Laws and Profit, Environment, Fair Wage, Human Rights/Dignity, Justice, Materialism and Consumerism, Professional Training/Responsibility, Selfishness, Solidarity, Universal Destination of Goods, Work and Family, Work and Society.

[An address on May 9, 1990 in Durango, Mexico, to members of the Durango business community.]

On my apostolic journeys I have always been very interested in meeting men and women in the business world. For me these meetings are an occasion for communicating more directly and openly the spirit behind the papal magisterium in social questions, and for you it is an opportunity to demonstrate your understanding and acceptance of the church's social doctrine.

You truly occupy a most important place in the overall shape of society. Your decisions have a multiplier effect, and they impact especially on the fabric of society and the economy. That is why I place a great deal of hope in you.

From this beloved city of Durango we also feel united with those Mexican business people who have not been able to come to this meeting as they might have wished. Indeed, our gaze extends to all those responsible for economic activity in Latin America. The present circumstances, after the most recent events that took place at the close of last year, demand that we widen the framework of these considerations so as to encompass all the countries of Latin America, although with a variety of nuances.

Human Collaboration with the Divine Plan

The main thread of our reflection will get the figure of the businessperson and the role he or she is called to play in the present circumstances of your continent.

Beyond a technical consideration of this topic, we must contemplate human activity in the light of the collaboration with God that every human being is called to offer.[103] Our world today, including Mexico and all of Latin America as well, must also become an echo of this divine design and collaborate with the Creator in the transformation of the world according to God's plan.

Christ issues a call for the transformation of the world in every age. Christ makes his call from within the needs of each age. He calls out from the hungry and thirsty, from those who have no house in which to dwell nor clothes to put on, from the sick and those deprived of their legitimate freedom.[104] There he stands: in all of them can be recognized the voice and face of Christ.

Making itself an interpreter of this voice of the Lord, the Church continually awakens the conscience of its children and of all people of good will. It is precisely from this angle that I want to share with you some reflections of the figure and role of the Latin American businessperson. The voice of the Lord must reverberate powerfully in Latin America, for the existing deep social differences are there for all to see, and they constitute a huge challenge to those who bear notable responsibility in the socioeconomic sphere.

Need for a Critique of Liberal Capitalism

The events of recent history to which I referred earlier have been interpreted, sometimes superficially, as the triumph or failure of one system vis-a-vis another: namely, as the triumph of the liberal capitalist system. Particular interests would like to carry the analysis to the extreme of presenting the system they regard as the winner as the only path for our world on the basis of the experience of the setbacks suffered by contemporary socialism, and shunning the critical judgement required toward the effects liberal capitalism has produced in the countries of the so-called Third World, at least until the present.

It is not right to claim – as some seek to do – that the social doctrine of the Church flatly condemns an economic theory. The truth is that, while respecting the proper autonomy of science, that teaching offers a judgement of the effects of such a theory's application in history, when the dignity of the person is in some fashion violated or jeopardized. In exercising its prophetic mission, the church wants to encourage critical reflection on social processes, always with a view toward overcoming situations that are not fully in accord with the goals traced by the Lord of Creation. It would be wrong for the Church to remain on the level of mere social critique. It is up to its members, who are experts in various fields of knowledge, to carry on the search for valid and lasting solutions that may guide human processes toward the ideals proposed by the revealed word.

Poverty's Causes Require Careful Analysis

In the specific case of Mexico, it must be acknowledged that despite the vast resources with which the Creator has endowed this country, the ideal of justice is still a long way off. Alongside great wealth and lifestyles similar to those of the most prosperous countries – and sometimes even greater – stands the vast majority without even the most basic resources. In recent years the currency's buying power has declined more, and phenomena that reflect the way the economy is organized, like inflation, have produced painful effects on all levels. It must be repeated once more: it is always the weakest who suffer the worst consequences as they find themselves encased in a circle of increasing poverty. Why not cry out, with the Bible, that the misery of the weakest cries out to the Most High?[105]

Foreign indebtedness has unquestionably worsened the situation, but it would be unjust to seek in it the only explanation, thereby casting the blame on factors weighing on the country from outside. The present situation is the result of systems and decisions that go back a long way; they are extremely complex and therefore require a careful analysis so as to try to detect the causes, understand the complicated mechanisms and creatively propose new strategies that can assure not only that there is bread on every table, but also that the conditions for the development of each and every one of the citizens are met.

Universal Destination of Goods

The search for real solutions assumes sacrifices on the part of all, but we must not forget that often it is the poor who are compelled to make sacrifices while the owners of great fortunes show no willingness to give up their privileges for the sake of others. The science of economics makes it clear that material goods are scarce and hence ought to be administered rationally. For his part, the Creator has destined the totality of the goods of creation for the benefit of all human beings, as revelation and Christian tradition marvelously instruct us. Hence it is that the excessive cornering of goods by some deprives the majority of those goods, and thus is accumulated a wealth that produces poverty. This principle is likewise applicable to the international community.

In its social teaching, the Church has offered to humankind sufficient principles which a just economy would have to put into practice. The magisterium has fulfilled its mission, and now it is up to you, the experts, who are also members of the Church, to make a serious effort to find real, courageous, practical solutions. New and complex situations inside and outside the cultural realms demand with renewed vigor the activity of the lay faithful.[106] Your country, ladies and gentlemen, needs the collaboration of each and every one of you. Each one, in accordance with his or her specialty, is called to accept with humility and generosity the challenge posed by the present situation of injustice so as to dedicate the best of his or her experience and professional training in the service of a great, just and fraternal homeland, above and beyond any selfishness of class or party.

Solidarity

Work and economic activity constitute one of the most important burning issues in Latin America. And it is up to you to raise that issue deeply and seriously not by focusing only on the purely technical level, but keeping before you a much broader horizon, namely that of people. Latin America must move ahead with the work of its men and women, thanks to a current of real and effective solidarity.

Many efforts have been made on this continent so that it might be free and worthy of the human being. Do not allow that generosity of the past to be spoiled. Dire poverty causes slavery; it is itself a lack of freedom. Increasing impoverishment undermines human dignity and stability. Hence, the future of the freedom and dignity of Latin America demands that a very special battle be waged starting now, not with weapons, but by means of the ingenuity and work of its peoples; and in that endeavor you occupy a prominent place.

Going beyond Mere Humanitarianism

In view of these demands, there begins to take shape, as it were, a new characteristic profile of the business man or woman. I am referring especially to the attitude of service to the common good that ought to typify your activity. This is something that goes beyond mere humanitarianism, that is, a readiness to help out in occasional emergencies. Rather, it consists of a constant readiness, of a way of conceiving one's function as a businessperson, of a style marking one's way of acting.

It is ultimately a matter of accepting responsibility for activities with all their consequences. Such responsibility revolves around three basic coordinates: the persons who make up business enterprises, society and the environment. You have in fact a grave responsibility toward the persons work in your companies.

Creation of Jobs and Fair Wages

Fortunately, there has been a growing awareness that human work cannot be viewed from the merely commercial perspective as a "commodity" that is bought and sold.[107] There is something inseparable from work of the utmost importance: the dignity of the person.[108] On the other hand, do not forget that the only legitimate title for owning the means of production is that they serve labor.[109] Hence, one of your greatest responsibilities must be that of creating jobs.

Closely connected with what has been said is the question of the just wage. As I have written in the encyclical *Laborem Exercens*: "In the context of the present there is no more important way for securing a just relationship between the worker and the employer than that constituted by remuneration for work."[110]

Openness to Just Demands of the Common Good

A second aspect of the businessperson's attitude of service is manifested in his or her responsibility toward society. It is well to recall that the progress of society ought to be oriented toward the common good of all citizens, that is, avoiding the temptation to turn the national community into something that is at the service of the particular interests of the company. In fact, it is not at all uncommon to observe that certain campaigns against birth or that promote consumer culture have their origin in the economic interests in the business or financial world. Unfortunately, examples of this sort of thing could be multiplied. On the contrary, what must characterize the businessperson is loyal openness to the just demands of the common good. That is a matter of wanting to make the company a factor of genuine growth in society.

In this same framework of considerations we must also highlight the economic solidarity that is so necessary in Latin America. The undeniable problems common to the whole continent can be confronted jointly.[111] The isolation of the various economies serves none of the countries involved. Hence, in economic projections the national perspective must be overcome so as to give life to a continental economic project capable of presenting itself as a valid interlocutor on the international and world scene. The scope of your vision discerns this demand, and there have been constant striving and the sense of responsibility crown these efforts with success.

Responsibility for the Environment

Even though it is mentioned last, responsibility toward the environment is not the least important. This issue affects humankind as a whole, and lately it has forced all to pay attention. In fact, the ecological deterioration of the environment has been increasing rapidly. Indeed, the way resources are exploited must change as soon as possible. In this respect we can observe forms of inertia that are dangerous today and are causing an understandable alarm.

The preservation of environmental conditions for the sake of a better kind of development and human life in common is a moral duty and a new challenge to the creativity and responsibility of every businessperson.

The Danger of Consumerism in the Family

Before concluding I would like to briefly reflect on your responsibility toward yourselves and toward your families. It is true that many of you here present are motivated in your work by a sincere desire to serve. But it is equally true that a grave danger may be lying in wait for you: subjection to earthly goods, the all-consuming desire for profit – normally connected to the thirst for power – "at any price."[112] When people succumb to this temptation, the result is a crass materialism and, at the same time, a radical dissatisfaction that humans feel when they seek to quench their thirst for Infinite Good with material creatures.[113]

Moreover, it sometimes happens that this unchecked ambition also translates into a certain neglect of family life and the education of one's children. If this is not recognized or is not resolved, there can be real crises in marriage and in the lives of children. Thus we have here a new call from Christ. Your family demands something more than the high living standard you may be able to provide; it demands your presence, your affection, your sincere interest as husband and father or as wife and mother.

Seek First the Kingdom of God

I want to conclude our meeting with the words of the Lord: "Seek first his kingship over you, his way of holiness, and all these things will be given you besides."[114] The awareness of being builders of a more just, peaceful and fraternal society will more than repay your work and self-denial on behalf of those most in need.

I invoke over you, and over your families and co-workers, the protection of Our Lady of Guadalupe, so that this great nation may advance toward a new stage of solidarity and justice, of honesty and welfare for all.

16. Business Leaders Have a Responsibility to Promote the Common Good in the Face of Social Difficulties[115]

Common Good, Dignity of Work, Economic Laws and Profits, Entrepreneurship, Human Development/Progress, Human Rights/Dignity, Meaning of Work, Professional Training/Responsibility, Service, Solidarity, Unemployment.

[An address on November 11, 1990 in Naples, Italy, to Neapolitan business leaders.]

Although it is one of Italy's largest industrial zones, Naples is among those in greatest crisis. The metropolitan area is largely in a fragile, disconnected and potentially worsening situation; its process of change is hindered by urban imbalances, lack of a transportation system and other essential public services. Unemployment tends to be concentrated within the least protected parts of the population: young people and women. Progress in the labor market is slowed down by the phenomenon of the workers who are technically employed, but in reality are stalled in the ranks of those who are laid off. In some cases people take recourse in "cottage industries" or in illegal employment or elements of the "shadow economy." I am also aware of the significant burden represented by child labor which stems from, among other reasons, the troublesome phenomenon of school truancy. To all these ills are added the spread of drugs and the renewed growth of organized violence.

Dare to Be Creative

Ladies and Gentlemen, I feel personally involved in your concerns. I also know that these many social problems, including the worrisome growth of organized crime, certainly do not promote the growth of private enterprise. Be brave! Your task is precisely not to stop in the face of difficulties, but rather to dare, to be creative, for the sake of your legitimate profit and for the good of the entire society. Taking on the task of changing the current situation is the responsibility, first of all, of political leaders and administrators, who have the obligation to assure law and order in daily life, respect for rights and for the rules of society. Each person, however, must be ready to make his or her own contribution. I invite you, therefore, to mobilize your best resources to that purpose. Indeed, great responsibilities fall to you, and they are all the more delicate to the extent that they affect those characteristics of the economic development of Southern Italy and Naples. There can be no development without the involvement and the will of the local people. The development of Italy's south will take place when local energies are released. Your business leaders must be in the front lines in this effort.

I ask you, who possess an ancient industrial tradition, great intellect and professional skills, as can be seen by your many fellow citizens in other parts of Italy and the world, not to assume attitudes of resignation or discouragement, but rather to have the courage to risk going the extra mile for the good of the community. For this I particularly appeal to those who profess to be believers. No one can call himself or herself a Christian and remain indifferent in the face of a brother or sister in difficulty, in the face of growing unemployment, the lack of housing, or insecurity and injustice. Justice demands that; charity requires it.

St. John warns us: "One who has no love for the brother he has seen cannot love the God he has not seen."[116]

True Development Respects the Dignity of the Person

In order to be authentic and integral, society's development must first of all take into account respect for the dignity of the human person. The human person must never be sacrificed to it. However, development can be conceived and achieved to the detriment of the human person. The adequate solution to society's complex problems comes about first of all from the careful examination of their structural and functional causes. It comes about not only through technological and economic planning, but also, and above all, through a vigorous ethical and spiritual response. This demands each person's readiness to face matters and change them, and to honestly seek truth, serious professional preparedness and constant attention to the interests of the entire community. Ultimately that implies a different life style, one marked by service and solidarity. The inadequacies of the urban social system, which everyone complains about, are not accidental.

Mobilization of Conscience

Therefore, we must be aware that the limitations of Naples and the South are the result of specific causes which require the involvement of the entire nation in opting for solidarity with a consistent development plan.

In their recent document *Development in Solidarity: the Italian Church and the South*, the Italian bishops, affirming the need for ethical openness on the part of the government and citizens, have called everyone to an authentic mobilization of consciences against the various pollutants within society, which in practice represent a denial of human dignity.

Mentioning the moral question in reference to the problems of the South is an invitation to reflect on the problems of labor and business and on the interaction of the economic and ethical dimensions in light of the basic moral and spiritual values which the Church never ceases to propose.

Christian Conception of Work

The Christian concept of work has its roots in the biblical passage on creation, in God's original command: "Fill the earth and subdue it."[117]

The fact that the one who works is a person gives a specific ethical value to that activity, a value which is independent of the type of work done and the way in which it is done.

As the Second Vatican Council emphasizes, "by offering his or her work to God a person becomes associated with the redemptive work itself of Jesus Christ, who conferred an eminent dignity on labor when at Nazareth he worked with his own hands."[118] If such is the dignity of work, one can better understand the negative consequences deriving from unemployment, from the other problems connected with it, and more generally, from the economic crisis which you are undergoing. Various social ills, such as crime, narcotics consumption and trafficking, corruption and organized violence, can flourish more easily precisely because of such situations. Therefore, we can never give them enough attention.

Authentic Development Possible only through Solidarity

Among the many ways in which the Church feels the need to serve mankind, there is also her effort to enlighten it and reflect on the authentic meaning of development. Our current technological development certainly plays a positive role in the progress of human history. However, economic aspects alone cannot be considered without touching upon the intrinsic connection between authentic development and respect for the values of the person.

In the encyclical *Sollicitudo Rei Socialis*, I emphasized that authentic development can come about only through solidarity,[119] that is, "the firm and lasting determination to commit oneself to the common good."

Moral Criteria for Profits

The principle of solidarity is especially to be applied to the business world. There are moral criteria, not only economic ones, at the root of concrete business decisions. Among these, the primary one is certainly the principle of the common good. Pursuing profit as such is certainly not unjust if the profit is obtained by licit means and through proper management of the business. The search for a reasonable profit is also linked with the right of "economic initiative," which I defend in the aforementioned encyclical. Profit, however, cannot be held up as an absolute; it is only a working norm and is subordinate to the duties deriving from the principle of solidarity.

Today we are witnessing the growing separation between the economic and ethical dimensions when instead they should be in constant interaction.

In relation to events and phenomena within society, more and more we are seeing cases where the economy defends decisions which it makes without any reference to ethics.

The Church, which teaches the "truth about humankind," knows the greatness of the person and his or her limitations as a creature. She knows the human thirst for well-being and the difficulties which cause people to become wrapped up in selfish interests. Likewise, she is quite aware that no system created by human beings, even though it may tend to improve continually, could ever achieve the fullness of justice upon this earth; in every system there will always be the need to correct aspects which work against human dignity and everybody's participation and the common good.

Service and Solidarity

Dear Friends, I would like to conclude these reflections with a reference to an essential aspect of the Christian vocation, the aspect of "service," which gives meaning and value to every human endeavor. The directions for the route to follow are given to us directly by Christ the Lord, who, although He was God, became a man among humans, "not to be served, but to serve."[120] The Church's social doctrine, which has assimilated this supreme example, teaches that the person can fully find himself or herself only though generous self-giving.[121] The Church feels it is her duty to tell all of you that the most authentic force for development is love which is expressed in effective solidarity. It is in this light that I invite you to live and carry on with your activity.

17. European Business Leaders Should Employ the Spiritual and Cultural Resources of Europe for the Well-Being of All[122]

Economic Laws and Profits, Human Development/Progress, Human Rights/Dignity, Materialism and Consumerism, Private Property/ Co-ownership, Professional Training/Responsibility, Spirituality, Universal Destination of Goods.

[An address on December 6, 1990 in Rome, to Presidents of European Industrial Confederations.]

As business leaders, you have come together to sign and publicize a Common Declaration in the framework of the so called "new European architecture," the new situation of Europe resulting from the extraordinary political and institutional transformations which have been taking place internationally. When you met in Paris in December 1988 you stated that Europe was your "common enterprise," and you committed yourselves to greater cooperation in industry and to solidarity with the Governments and peoples of Europe in the construction of a better future for this continent. No approach to European development in prosperity and peace is possible without taking into account the specific contribution of business leaders to the present and future well-being of society.

Right of Economic Initiative and Its Limits

The Church, in her social teaching, respects and defends the right of economic initiative as an expression of the subjective creativity of individuals and groups.[123] But she emphasizes strongly that the economic process, which has a decisive influence on the life of almost every inhabitant of the earth, does not end in the production of wealth and material goods. Economic activity has an intrinsic social and moral function stemming from the inalienable dignity of the people involved and from the principle of the prior universal destination of goods.[124] Fortunately, a too narrow concept of development is giving way to a growing consciousness of the need to place economic growth at the service of the human, social, cultural and political advancement of peoples.

It is against the background of these general principles that I am pleased to note your concern to work for a development that improves standards of living in Europe, that respects the environment, that takes into account the special needs of less developed regions, that seeks to strengthen freedom and democracy, solidarity and peace. For this you intend to promote respect for the human aspects of all strategies and programs.

Role of the Spiritual and Cultural Dimensions of Europe

Europe is your common enterprise. You are therefore committed to the advancement of the single European market, with all that it entails of freedom of movement for people, capital and goods. But you are also aware that Europe is not merely or primarily an economic reality: it is above all a sublimely rich and intense cultural and spiritual experience. Likewise, European integration cannot be envisioned except as embracing the whole extension of the continent, which is determined by geography but even more so by the common religious heritage shared by its peoples, almost all of whom were baptized at one stage or another into the Christian faith.

Europe has the historical foundations and the spiritual and cultural resources necessary to build a way of life based on a humanism capable of correcting the materialistic and technological excesses present in other models of development. Business and industry will contribute to the achievement of this goal in the measure that they pursue objectives that are not merely economic but truly human. The members of your Association have a significant role to play in the growth of a society that takes full account of the spiritual dimension of its people, overcoming outdated contrasts between faith and science, between religion and "progress." In this respect, the only worthy goal of all our efforts is the realization of a European continent which is ever more the expression of the highest values of the human spirit.

The Church has surely been the single most important factor in the formation of the "character" of Europe. From the Church's two-thousand-year experience, allow me to draw the certain conclusion that no model of progress that does not take into account the ethical and moral dimensions of economic activity will succeed in winning the hearts of Europe's peoples. The primacy of the "spiritual" in the widest sense of this term is a principle from which the peoples of Europe cannot depart without doing violence to their constitutive historical genesis and development.

Moreover, Europe has always been distinguished by its openness to the rest of the world. Without ulterior motives of domination, it now has a calling to be open to the so-called "South" of the world: those vast sectors of humanity which are in need of Europe's help in order to be able to take charge of their own destiny. It is my hope that as business leaders you will always be convinced that poverty and the economic dependence of poorer nations is a moral category which makes serious ethical demands on the decisions to be made concerning the ownership and the use of the world's wealth and goods.[125]

Stewards of the World's Goods

Distinguished Ladies and Gentlemen, I appeal to you to work in your "common enterprise" for the well-being of the millions of human beings in Europe and elsewhere who stand to benefit from the realization of an authentically human development and progress. Recall the Gospel parable of the "faithful and wise steward" who gives the members of the household their portion of food at the proper time.[126] We are all administrators, not absolute owners, of the world that God has placed in our hands in order to make it bear fruit for the greatest benefit of all, and ultimately for His own glory. That glory is reflected not only in the beauty of nature but in the dignity of every human being, the image of God, and in the beauty of peace and brotherhood between all the members of the one human family. May He who is the Father of all give you the wisdom and courage to use your resources to direct your economic, civic and political influence towards the construction of a world of justice, peace and solidarity.

18. Christian Managers Have International Responsibilities to Overcome Economic Divisions[127]

Economic Laws and Profits, Human Rights/Dignity, Justice, Professional Training/Responsibility, Solidarity, World Community.

[An address on March 9, 1991 in Rome, to members of International Christian Union of Business Directors.]

You are not looking for an easy way out by bringing a Christian aspect to your jobs as business managers. You must reconcile demands which often can be considered contradictory: those which regard the rules and constraints of economic life, sometimes hard and even implacable; those which refer to technological development, which is always changing and costlier; and, on the other hand, those that proclaim the human and Christian conscience, those moral laws which are essential for our dignity as creatures made in the image of God. You find yourselves at the point of convergence of several series of laws – natural, technical, civil, and finally moral and evangelical.

Aim of a Just Society

I will go no further in this analysis. I simply want to encourage you in your common research which will aid you to respond better to what I may call your vocation. You must seek to act with the best professional skill in order to develop the best relations among all the personnel of your businesses, with those who use your products or services, with the various social agents or authorities responsible for the common good, all of this without ever losing sight of the primary objective, which is the construction of a just society in which the whole ensemble of people can achieve true social balance. I also note that business constitutes one of the intermediary bodies called to allow those who participate in its activity not only to earn a living for themselves and their family, but allow to develop a large part of their capacities.

Social Problems

There will be no lack of obstacles on your path. Our era seems to multiply them in its own way. Throughout the world disparities in the treatment of workers between one place and another appear more clearly than ever before, and that affects the conditions of production and the market. Certain lucrative activities are in question which must be purified or renounced: I am thinking particularly of all that runs counter to human life and nature, from the exploitation of the environment to the development of weapons of unprecedented concept or the trafficking in drugs, which is also deadly; I am thinking too of the deviations and excesses of the many forms of financial manipulation. In order to safeguard the morality of the economic activity, you need a clear philosophy and a courageous desire to remain faithful to the enlightening demands of the word of God and the Church's teaching. I know that your movement is working in that direction and calls you ceaselessly to renew your adherence to Christ in the faith, to live as his disciples in love for mankind, and to effectively put it to work in all your activities.

"New Things"

You yourselves emphasize that 100 years after the "new things" which provided Leo XIII's reflections, our own age is in turn rich in "new things," in political, social, economic and technological changes.

A sizable part of the world is being liberated from ideological constraints of a collectivism which seriously fettered whole peoples, reduced their creativity, prevented their healthy social and economic development. You have weighed the importance of these changes. You know, from your own fields of study, that the passage to new forms of the market economy cannot come about, especially in central Europe, without the costly reconstruction of whole economies, exacting a human price that is sometimes at the extremes of what is bearable.

International Support

You have wasted no time in taking the initiative to meet your counterparts in the nations faced with such changes in order to share with them the fruit of your experience, and offer them support so that they may organize and help one another in the area of Christian reflection on economic life, with a clear evaluation of what is at stake in their countries' accession to forms of enterprise and systems of exchange which are rather new to them. In this regard, I hope that the important discussions which you had with them in Prague last October will bear lasting results.

This reference to a new situation which more directly concerns Europe does not allow me to neglect the other parts of the world. UNIAPAC carries out part of its activity in the regional or continental context. It seems to me that this corresponds to the real needs, as I have said many times during the course of my pastoral visits. Even when we speak of the globalization of the economy, one cannot face its demands nor lessen its defects and injustices without holding trusting dialogues between partners who practice a constructive solidarity in their own region. Christians must work seriously among themselves and with all their partners so that some day we can overcome that division of the world which ranges from a first, second, third and even a fourth world! Can we accept that the terms North and South mean that people in one part enjoy more of the earth's goods while they are deprived of them in the other? On your level, do not stop acting against this unworthy division of the human family, far from the Creator's will, and which, as you know well, constitutes an obstacle to social and international peace.

19. Christian Business Leaders Possess a Mission to Provide Christian Witness[128]

Christian Witness/Mission, Community of Persons, Justice, Professional Training/Responsibility, Service, Solidarity, Spirituality.

[An address on April 12, 1991 in Rome,
to Italian Catholic business leaders.]

I thank you for your visit and bid you a cordial welcome. Your association, which takes its inspiration from the perennial Gospel values, has its aim to promote in industry and labor a climate of true solidarity in order to stimulate an effective, just collaboration among all who participate in the production process. Spreading and fulfilling the principles of the Church's social doctrine, you want to put the Christian concept of work into practice. I heartily encourage you to work always with expertise and responsibility. I thank the president of your association who expressed your sentiments to me and interpreted your hopes and intentions.

New Conditions

The encyclical *Rerum Novarum* faced with clarity the "conditions of the workers" which were, as you know, rather precarious at that time, not infrequently lacking legal and juridical protection and subject to pernicious forms of exploitation and abuse.

Fortunately times have changed. Social evolution has also affected the world of labor, and today business is more sensitive to the just demands of workers, overcoming the mentality of the absolute and unlimited profit which was dominant at that time. You are business leaders, and Catholic at that. Your attitude and behavior in regard to the conditions of the workers in your businesses cannot help but be inspired by the Church's social Magisterium.

Business Is a Community of Persons

In the light of Christian social doctrine today a business is understood as a "community of persons" who work together to produce a service to offer society.

Indeed, it is a matter of a productive entity whose foundation and development must deal with the complex rules of the economy. You are quite aware of this, as you also know the demands, or rather the urgent needs, that it has of investment, technological renewal and continuous links with financial agencies.

Managers Need Spiritual Virtues

You are called to respond through your operations to the shareholders, employees and workers and, in a certain sense, to all of society. An executive, a manager, an assistant administrator, must have good technical and administrative training. They should have broad natural abilities and professional skill. In reality, they should have authentic human and spiritual virtues.

Therefore, even if a business is an economic entity, even if it is one of the things that are essential for an area's prosperity, it cannot be reduced to that alone. Inasmuch as it is a community of persons, it is basically a human structure whose activity and economic and technological involvement must be inspired by and oriented to the ethical and moral values of justice and social solidarity.

Justice

First of all, *justice*: justice in regard to your own workers, and in regard to the society to which are offered goods and services which can be truly useful according to a hierarchy of priorities which are themselves enlightened by criteria of the moral order.

Social Solidarity

At justice's side there is *social solidarity* which urges economic workers not to look on the company as an unlimited resource to exploit for their own good. Solidarity, furthermore, is not limited to the immediate context in which the business is located. It is rather a constant reminder of a broader vision which looks for that interdependence which today characterizes and defines human relationships, especially economic ones.[129] It is quite fitting that the congress you are holding is devoting a great deal of its study to those aspects and problems.

Justice and solidarity invite us to consider the use of natural resources and commit us to a responsible protection of the environment. Indeed, it is necessary, in the name of justice and solidarity, to take into close consideration the quality of the habitat and life, both within and around every productive entity.

Professional Tasks for Christians

These are some highlights and observations upon which you, especially as Catholic business leaders, have taken the opportunity to reflect. You must often make decisions which affect the company's economic progress, and therefore its morality and solidarity. Therefore, besides your managerial and entrepreneurial ability, you must also have a profound knowledge of your function, which is enlightened by the supreme values which must guide the Christian's professional activity.

Prayer and Holiness

The task which has been entrusted to you is certainly not easy, and there are many difficulties which can create serious obstacles. However, do not forget that the Lord's grace is with you if you faithfully and perseveringly seek to walk the road mapped out by the Gospel. For this you need to ask daily for his help in prayer and listening to his word. You need to strengthen more and more your knowledge of Christian social principles. The call to holiness is also addressed to you who, as a living part of the People of God, have received "a message of salvation intended for all people."[130]

Mission of Christian Business Leaders

In this centennial year of *Rerum Novarum*, the year of the Church's social teaching, I therefore exhort you to improve your mission as Christian business leaders in order to make the human and Christian virtues shine forth in the complex world of economic activity, the virtues which make that world respect the dignity of the person and be open to mutual solidarity.

Notes

1 The translation was taken from *L'Osservatore Romano*, December 24, 1979, p. 3.

2 *Redemptor Hominis*, n. 17.

3 *Gaudium et Spes*, n. 69.

4 Address to UCID, 12 February 1977.

5 The translation was taken from *L'Osservatore Romano*, February 23, 1981, pp. 10, 11.

6 The translation was taken from *L'Osservatore Romano*, December 6, 1982, pp. 2-4.

7 2 Cor 11:28.

8 Lk 9:55 (Vulgate).

9 The translation was taken from *L'Osservatore Romano*, June 20, 1983, pp. 9, 11.

10 *Gaudium et Spes*, n. 68.

11 *Mater et Magistra*, n. 78.

12 *Laborem Exercens*, n. 1.

13 *Laborem Exercens*, n. 14.

14 *Laborem Exercens*, n. 14.

15 *Insegnamenti*, 1982, 1, p. 1096.

16 *Gaudium et Spes*, nn. 25-37.

17 The translation was taken from *The Pope Speaks*, Summer 1984, pp. 130-135.

18 Gen 1:26.

19 Gen 2:2-3.
20 Gen 1:27.
21 Gen 1:28.
22 *Laborem Exercens*, n. 11.
23 *Laborem Exercens*, n. 12.
24 *Laborem Exercens*, n. 12.
25 *Laborem Exercens*, n. 11.
26 *Laborem Exercens*, n. 20.
27 *Laborem Exercens*, n. 5.
28 Mt 13:55.
29 The translation was taken from *The Pope Speaks*, Spring 1986, pp. 45-47.
30 The translation was taken from *L'Osservatore Romano*, January 13, 1986, p. 10.
31 Art. 5, b.
32 *Gaudium et Spes*, n. 67.
33 *Laborem Exercens*, n. 17.
34 Art. 5, c.
35 The translation was taken from *L'Osservatore Romano*, April 21, 1986, p. 2.
36 The translation was taken from *L'Osservatore Romano,* May 18, 1987, pp. 12-13.
37 Speech to the entrepreneurs of Milan, May 22, 1983.
38 *Laborem Exercens,* n. 13.
39 *Laborem Exercens*, n. 14.
40 *Gaudium et Spes,* n. 68.
41 Discourse of November 7, 1982.
42 *Gaudium et Spes*, n. 74.
43 Lk 9:25.
44 Mt 6:33.
45 2 Cor 9:10.
46 1 Cor 3:7.
47 The translation was taken from *L'Osservatore Romano*, September 28, 1987, p. 1.
48 Dt 30:19.
49 1 Jn 4:8.
50 *Inter Mirifica*, n. 5.
51 *Inter Mirifica*, n. 5.
52 Gen 1:27.
53 Mt 7:12.

54 Allocution of May 6, 1967.
55 Jn 1:1.
56 Dt 6:6.
57 The translation was taken from *Origins*, May 26, 1988, p. 27.
58 *Sollicitudo Rei Socialis*, n. 1.
59 Ps 127:1.
60 *Sollicitudo Rei Socialis*, n. 38.
61 Gen 2:18-20.
62 *Sollicitudo Rei Socialis*, n. 39.
63 The translation was taken from *L'Osservatore Romano*, June 20, 1988, pp. 20-22.
64 *Puebla*, n. 437.
65 *Instruction on Christian Freedom*, n. 13.
66 Address in Santo Domingo, October 12, 1984.
67 Address to UNESCO, June 2, 1980.
68 *Redemptor Hominis*, n.14; *Gaudium et Spes*, n. 38.
69 *Gaudium et Spes*, n. 22.
70 *Sollicitudo Rei Socialis*, n. 41.
71 *Dives in Misericordia*, n. I, 2.
72 *Instruction on Christian Freedom and Liberation*, n. 75.
73 *Puebla*, n. 365ff.
74 *Evangelii Nuntiandi*, n. 20.
75 *Puebla*, nn. 412, 445-446; Address to the bishops of CELAM in Santo Domingo, December 10, 1984.
76 Letter constituting the Pontifical Commission for Culture, May 20, 1982.
77 *Redemptor Hominis*, n. 18.
78 *Sollicitudo Rei Socialis*, n. 32.
79 *Laborem Exercens*, n. 14.
80 *Laborem Exercens*, n. 2.
81 *Sollicitudo Rei Socialis*, n. 19.
82 *Sollicitudo Rei Socialis*, n. 46.
83 The translation was taken from *L'Osservatore Romano*, June 27, 1988, pp. 16-17.
84 *Gaudium et Spes*, n. 34.
85 *Gaudium et Spes*, n. 34.
86 Gen 2:18.
87 Address to meeting sponsored by the conference of Italian Bishops, October 31, 1981.
88 Eph 4:25.

89 *Pacem in Terris*, n. 35.
90 Is 56:1.
91 Message for the World Day of Peace, 1982.
92 *Sollicitudo Rei Socialis*, n. 33.
93 *Laborem Exercens*, n. 11.
94 *Sollicitudo Rei Socialis*, n. 47.
95 Is 1:16-17.
96 *Sollicitudo Rei Socialis*, n. 41.
97 The translation was taken from *L'Osservatore Romano*, May 15, 1989, p. 4.
98 Gen 1:26-27.
99 Ps 127:1.
100 *Sollicitudo Rei Socialis*, n. 44.
101 *Sollicitudo Rei Socialis*, n. 38.
102 The translation was taken from *Origins*, May 24, 1990, p. 1.
103 *Laborem Exercens*, n. 25.
104 Mt 25:31-46.
105 Ex 22:22f.
106 *Christifideles Laici*, n. 3.
107 *Laborem Exercens*, n. 7.
108 *Laborem Exercens*, n. 9.
109 *Laborem Exercens*, n. 14.
110 *Laborem Exercens*, n. 19.
111 *Sollicitudo Rei Socialis*, n. 45.
112 *Sollicitudo Rei Socialis*, n. 37.
113 *Sollicitudo Rei Socialis*, n. 27.
114 Mt 6:33.
115 The translation was taken from *L'Osservatore Romano*, December 3, 1990, pp. 9-10.
116 1 Jn 4:20.
117 Gen 1:28.
118 *Gaudium et Spes*, n. 67.
119 *Sollicitudo Rei Socialis*, nn. 38-40.
120 Mt 20:28; Mk 10:45.
121 *Gaudium et Spes*, n. 24.
122 The translation was taken from *L'Osservatore Romano*, December 10, 1990, p. 2.
123 *Sollicitudo Rei Socialis*, n. 15.
124 *Sollicitudo Rei Socialis*, n. 42.
125 *Sollicitudo Rei Socialis*, n. 42.

126 Lk 12:42-44.

127 The translation was taken from *The Pope Speaks*, September/October, 1991, pp. 261-3.

128 The translation was taken from *L'Osservatore Romano*, April 22, 1991, pp. 2, 5.

129 *Sollicitudo Rei Socialis*, n. 38.

130 *Gaudium et Spes*, n. 1.

CHAPTER 2: ADDRESSES TO MANAGERS, AND WORKERS

20. *Christian Faith Ennobles Human Work*[1]

Work and Society

[An address on December 4, 1980 in Rome, to miners and managers of S. A. Solvay and Co.]

I want to thank you first of all for having come to this meeting, which, taking place on the day of St. Barbara, the patroness of all those who work in mines, is an evident sign of your Christian faith, as well as of your devotion to Peter's Successor.

Therefore I cordially greet you and welcome you to this house, that of the common Pastor of the Church, all the more reason it must open to you, dear miners. You, in fact, represent a class of people whose work is among the heaviest of all, and furthermore you remind me of the work that I myself carried out for some years in my youth.

I know from experience that it is a hard job, even if improvements in work techniques have certainly been made in the course of the years;

I can therefore understand your problems and I assure you that I am close to you in affection.

Above all I wish to tell you that if the common saying that work ennobles man is true, it is also true that only Christian faith can ennoble work itself and even make it more human. Therefore the exhortation I address to you is to renew and strengthen your full adherence to Christ, man's Redeemer and our Lord. Only he enables us to harness all our energies for the construction of a society which will be new only if founded, finally, on respect, and above all on mutual love.

22. *Workers Possess Special Rights and Responsibilities in the Life of the Human Community*[2]

Christian Witness/Mission, Collaboration With God, Community of Persons, Dialogue and Cooperation, Human Development/ Progress, Human Rights/Dignity, Meaning of Work, Professional Training/Responsibility, Service, Solidarity, Unemployment, Work and Society.

[A homily on February 16, 1982 in Lagos, Nigeria, to Nigerian employers and workers.]

I would now like to direct my words to those members of the Church in Nigeria who are industrialists and workers, employers and employees. You are playing a vital role in the life of your nation, and people expect much of you. The Church too looks to you with great hope. She knows that you are able to give a powerful witness to the Gospel in the places where you work and among all those people associated with you in the service of humanity.

Human Work Shares in God's Creative Activity

People who work enjoy a God-given dignity. God could have created everything on earth in its final form, but he decided differently, for God wants us to be associated with him in the improvement of the things he has made. By our work we share in God's own creative activity. It was the same with Christ himself in his human nature. As I stated in my last encyclical, "The eloquence of the life of Christ is unequivocal: he belongs to the 'working world,' he has appreciation and respect for human work. It can indeed be said that he looks with love upon human work and the different forms that it takes, seeing in each one of these forms a particular facet of man's likeness with God, the Creator and Father."[3]

Work and Society

Work is also man's way of helping his neighbor. One person's work affects another person, and together workers help to build up the whole of society. Those who work can say: when we work conscientiously, we make a real contribution towards a better world. Our work is an act of solidarity with our brothers and sisters.

The Rights and Responsibilities of Workers

All who work, whether they are single or married, well-skilled or not, have important rights and responsibilities. For example, each one has the right to proper pay and to reasonable working hours, including time for holidays. And work should never hinder the exercise of one's religious freedom. Work is for man, not man for work. So, work must not be allowed to dehumanize the person who does the work.

Between employers and employees there can sometimes arise cases of misunderstanding. These are to be resolved, not by violence, harsh words and antagonisms, but by mutual respect, willingness to listen and patient dialogue. Workers have the right to form unions and to ask for proper working conditions. But they also have the obligation to render loyal service, and employers have the right to receive the services for which they pay. Workers should not too readily have recourse to strikes, which generally cause much suffering to many; strikes remain extraordinary measures for the defense of human rights.

Resources for the Benefit of All

As employers and employees, as industrialists and workers, you can and must serve your country by vigorous efforts at economic development. Your country is richly gifted by God with agricultural and mineral resources. Use them to the best advantage of all, especially the poor, the orphans, the sick, the handicapped, the old, and those who are overtaken in the struggle for economic betterment. Do nothing to sabotage the economy of your own country. Nothing can replace diligent, efficient and honest hard work on your part.

Unemployment

Some people are unemployed because they rush to the big cities and do not want to cultivate the land. Help is needed therefore to modernize agricultural methods and to install such facilities as water, electricity and telephones in the rural areas, so that the young can be persuaded to stay on the land.

Some people are unemployed because they were not adequately trained or because their expectations of the type of work they want are not fulfilled. Competent and dedicated economists, government planners and sociologists are needed to help solve these problems.

A Vital Task for Each

My words today are especially for you, industrialists and workers, employers and employees, all brothers and sisters in our Lord Jesus Christ. Each of you has a vital task to carry out in the mission of the Church, a task which you carry out in the toil and labor of your ordinary working lives. Side by side with your fellow workers, you share in the creative activity of God, you forge bonds of fraternity and friendship and, like the yeast of the Gospel, in quiet but effective ways you further the Kingdom of God.

Christian Mission

Through your work and through the holiness of life that comes from doing God's will, you are able to make a big contribution to the Church's mission of proclaiming the Good News to the whole world.

Where do you find the strength for this mission? What is the source of your inspiration? It is always Christ. Remember the words of the Gospel: "I am with you always."[4] Yes, Christ is with us, especially in the Eucharist. And this morning, in his Sacrifice, Christ offers us and all our work to his Father in heaven. In this way he gives an even deeper value to all work. He gives a whole new meaning to our lives.

In Jesus Christ our Savior and our Lord and in his Eucharist we find the source of our strength and the cause of our joy.

22. Managers Have a Responsibility to Respect the Moral Dimension of Enterprise[5]

Christian Witness/Mission, Collaboration with God, Common Good, Community of Persons, Dialogue and Cooperation, Dignity of Work, Dominion over the Earth, Economic Laws and Profits, Entrepreneurship, Gospel of Work, Human Rights/Dignity, Justice, Leisure, Meaning of Work, Solidarity, Unemployment, Work and Family, Work and Society, Work and the Worker.

[An address on November 6, 1982 in Barcelona, Spain, to Spanish workers and businessmen.]

The Church believes it has an unavoidable duty in the social field to help "fortify the human community according to the divine law,"[6] by recalling the dignity and rights of workers, by stigmatizing situations where such rights are violated, and by favoring exchanges leading to authentic progress for man and society.

Work corresponds to God's design and will. The first pages of Genesis present creation to us as the work of God, God's labor. So, God calls on man to work, so as to be like him. Hence, work is not something off on the side. Even less is it a curse from heaven. On the contrary, it is a primordial blessing from the Creator, an activity permitting the individual to realize himself and to offer a service to society. In addition, he will have a higher reward, for "your toil is not vain when it is done in the Lord."[7]

Gospel of Work

But it was Jesus who delivered the most thorough Gospel of Work, he who was the son of God made man and a man of manual work, subject to hard effort. He gave the most part of his earthly life to work as a craftsman and incorporated that same work into his task of salvation.

For my part, during these four years of my pontificate I have unceasingly proclaimed the centrality of man in my encyclicals and catechesis, insisting on his primacy over things and on the importance of the subjective dimension in work, based on the dignity of the human person.

In fact, inasmuch as he is a person, man is the center of creation, for he alone has been created in God's image and likeness. He has been called to "subdue" the earth[8] with the acuteness of his intelligence and the activity of his hands. He turns himself into an artificer in work – both manual and intellectual – and communicates his own dignity to his work.

Friends and brother workers, the Christian concept of work sees it as a call to collaborate with God's power and love, maintaining man's life and making it more in accord with his design. When understood in this way, work is not a biological necessity for the sake of subsistence, but a moral duty. It is an act of love and it turns into joy, the deep joy of giving oneself through work to one's own family and to others, the intimate joyousness of offering oneself to God and of serving one's brothers, even though such giving entails sacrifices. Thus Christian work has a paschal meaning.

The logical consequence is that we all have the duty to do our work well. If we wish to realize ourselves properly, we may not avoid our duty or perform our work in a mediocre way, without interest, just to get it over with.

A Christian Concept of Work

Your tenacious hard work and your feeling of responsibility make us understand, dear brothers and sisters, how far from the Christian concept of work – and from a correct vision of the social order – are certain attitudes of lack of interest, of waste of time and resources. These attitudes are spreading in our day, both in the public and in the private sector. Not to mention the phenomenon of absenteeism. This social ill not only affects production, but offends the hopes and sufferings of those who are desperately looking for work.

The Church wants, through fidelity to the good news of salvation, to be present for all, but especially for the poor and oppressed, to be present in the effort which drives believers and men of good will toward attaining a truly human society, and to do this by recalling teachings coming from the Lord's mouth.

Work is certainly a good of man and for man. In this respect, I emphasized in the encyclical *Laborem Exercens* that "work is for man and not man for work."[9] The marrow of Christian social doctrine on work is centered there: one does not achieve a correct concept of work except in strict dependence on the right concept of man.

Labor and hard work constitute a duty and a service to the family cell, to its life, unity, development and perfecting. Therefore, "the reason for the family" – I said to Polish workers three years ago – "is one of the fundamental factors determining the economy and policy of work."

When rightly understood, the naturalness of all work not only respects the demands of the common good but also directs and transforms all work activity into cooperation affecting the good of all, and so enriching the patrimony of the human family.

The Spiritual Problem of Unemployment

What I have already said leads me to touch briefly on a problem which is not exclusive to Spain, but which affects it to a large degree. I mean unemployment.

The lack of work goes against the "right to work," understood – in the universal context of the rest of the fundamental rights – as a primary necessity, and not a privilege, to satisfy the vital needs of human existence through labor activity.

It is an urgent problem and one which must push each Christian to assume his or her responsibility in the name of the Gospel, and its message of justice, solidarity and love.

Prolonged unemployment gives rise to insecurity, lack of initiative, frustration, irresponsibility and lack of trust in society and in oneself. Capacities for personal development are atrophied, enthusiasm and love for the good are lost, family crises and desperate personal situations break out, and so there is an easy fall – especially on the part of the young – into drugs, alcoholism and crime.

It would be false and deceptive to consider this distressing problem – which has become endemic throughout the world – as the product of passing circumstances or as a purely economic and socio-political problem. It is really an ethical problem, a spiritual problem, because it is a symptom of a moral disorder existing in society when the hierarchy of values is broken.

Responsibility of the State, Employers and Workers

Through its social magisterium the Church recalls that the ways to a just solution of this grave problem demand a revision of the economic order as a whole. Comprehensive planning of economic production, not simply planning by sectors, is needed. The correct and rational organization of work is necessary, not only on the national level, but also on the international level. The solidarity of all working men is needed for this.

The state must not resign itself to having to tolerate chronic high unemployment. The creation of new jobs must constitute for it a priority as much economic as political. But businessmen and workers together have to help in overcoming the lack of jobs. The former have to keep up the production rate of their factories, the latter should attend to their work with due efficiency and be disposed through solidarity to give up "double" jobs and recourse to systematic use of overtime, which reduces the possibility of providing work to others.

Need for Conversion

An economy that is at the service of man must be created by all possible means. To overcome clashes between private and collective interests, to overcome egoisms in the struggle for subsistence, a real change of attitude is demanded of all, a change in lifestyle, minds and wills, a conversion of man to the truth about man.

I have dwelt particularly on this matter because it is so topical. I know that you are preoccupied by many other problems concerning wages, health conditions at work, protection against accidents at work, the role of labor unions, management and profit sharing, and proper protection of workers coming from other places.

Labor Unites Humanity

These are complex problems and they are vital for you. But I would repeat once again: do not forget that the primary characteristic of labor is that of uniting humanity. "This is what its social power consists in: the power to construct a community."[10] Base yourselves on that and on the great Christian values which enliven you. Take your serenity and confidence with you to your places of work. Brighten your surroundings with charity and hope. In this way it will be easier for you to find the right solutions.

Christian Concept of Enterprise

Allow me now, dear men and women workers of Spain, to address my words to another class of workers in Spain: businessmen, industrialists, top administrators, qualified experts in socio-economic life and backers of industrial complexes.

I greet and pay honor to you, the creators of jobs, employment, services and job training, all of you in this dear Spain who provide work and support for a great number of men and women workers. The pope expresses his esteem and gratitude to you for the high function which you perform in service to man and society. To you, too, I proclaim the Gospel of Work.

And, as I invite you to reflect upon the Christian concept of enterprise, I would remind you above all that there is a deeper problem, above and beyond technical and economic aspects in which you are masters. I mean the moral dimension. Economics and technology really have no meaning unless they have reference to man, whom they must serve.

Work is actually for man, not man for work. Consequently, enterprise is for man and not man for enterprise.

An indispensable requirement for a society seeking to be a just society is that it overcome the unnatural and illogical opposition between capital and labor, which has often been artificially sharpened by programmed class struggle. This requirement is based on the primacy of man over things. Only man – entrepreneur and worker – is subject to work and is a person. Capital is nothing but "a conjunction of things."[11]

Give a Humane Face to Enterprise

You well know that the economic world has been suffering a great crisis for some time. The social question has turned from a class problem into a world problem. Development of energy sources and the effect of strong political interests in this field have created fresh problems. These have led to doubts about certain economic structures until recently considered indispensable and untouchable, making the running of them ever harder.

In the face of such difficulties, do not waver, do not doubt your mission. Do not fall into the temptation to give up business, to shut down, to devote yourselves egoistically to calmer and less demanding professional activities. Overcome such temptations to escape, and keep on bravely at your posts, trying to give a more humane face every day to your enterprise and keeping in mind the great contribution you make to the common good when you open up fresh work possibilities.

Major errors were committed by entrepreneurs during the development of the industrial revolution in the past. But that is no reason for failing, dear industrialists, to give public recognition and praise to your dynamism, your spirit of initiative, your iron wills, your creative capacities and your ability to take risks. These qualities have made you key figures in economic history and in confronting the future.

Social Function of Enterprise

Because of its intrinsic dynamism, enterprise is called to perform a social function under your direction, and this social function is profoundly ethical. It is that of contributing to the perfecting of man, of every man without any discrimination, by creating conditions making work possible and enabling it to be, at the same time, work in which personal capacities can be developed. In this way effective and reasonable production of goods and services can be attained, and the worker should thus be able to feel that he is really working at something of his own.

So, an enterprise is not just an organism, a production structure. It should also transform itself into a life community, a place where a man lives with and relates with his peers, where personal development is not only allowed but encouraged as well. Is not the main enemy of the Christian sense of enterprise perhaps a certain functionalism that makes efficiency the one and only and the immediate requirement for production and work?

Work and Efficiency

Work relations are first of all relations among human beings. They cannot be measured by the sole rule of efficiency. You yourselves, dear men of enterprise here present, if you wish your professional activity to be consistent with your faith, should not conform to the rule of "making things work," of making them be efficient, productive and effective; seek rather that the fruits of your enterprise shall redound to the good of all through overall promotion of man and the personal perfection of those who work at your side, collaborating with you.

I know that socio-economic reality is quite complex by its very nature, to the point that it seems difficult to keep it going at moments of acute crisis, above all when the crisis takes on planetary dimensions. Nonetheless, it is precisely in such situations that it is proper to let oneself be guided by a great sense of justice and total confidence in God.

Justice

When times are difficult for all – as times of economic crisis are – workers cannot be left to their fate, especially those who, like the poor and the immigrants, have nothing but their hands to support themselves. It is proper always to remember an important principle of Catholic social teaching: "The hierarchy of values and the deep meaning of work itself demand that capital be a function of work and not work a function of capital."[12]

Solidarity and Dialogue

And, as we end our meeting, I would say a last word to you, dear brothers and workers, and dear entrepreneurs of Spain: Live in solidarity!

The time in which we live urgently demands that, in human, national and international living together, each person and group get over its fixed positions and one-sided points of view that tend to make dialogue difficult and efforts at collaboration ineffective.

The Church is aware of the presence of tensions and even conflicts in the world of work. But it is not through antagonisms and violence that difficulties are resolved! Why reject patient and sincere dialogue? Why not have recourse to the good will of listening, of mutual respect, of efforts at honest and persevering effort together, and even acceptance of partial agreements which can after all always lead to fresh hopes?

Work has a power in itself that can give life to a community, to solidarity: the solidarity *of* work, which spontaneously develops among those sharing the same kind of work or profession, so as to embrace, through the interests of all individuals and groups, the common good of all society; solidarity *with* work, that is to say, with each man who works, which by overcoming all class egoisms and one-sided political interests makes its own the drama of the unemployed and those in hard working conditions; finally, solidarity *in* work, a solidarity without boundaries because it is based on the naturalness of human work, that is to say, on the priority of the human person over things.

Such solidarity, open, dynamic and universal by nature, will never be negative. It will not be a "solidarity against," but a positive and constructive one, a "solidarity for," for wages, for justice, for peace, for well-being and for truth in social life.

Most beloved brothers and sisters! May your sensitivity as believers, your faith as Christians, help you to live the "good news," the Gospel of Work. Be aware of your dignity as manual and intellectual workers. Collaborate in a spirit of solidarity in social problems facing you. Be the Christian leaven and presence in every part of Spain.

The Church trusts in you, follows you, supports you, loves you. Be ever worthy of your religious and family traditions.

Work and Rest

Permit me to remind you particularly not to neglect your families and children because of your work. And use the festive day for rest for renewing contact with God and having healthy recreation.

---

23. *The Gospel is Fundamental to the Meaning of Work*[13]

Christian Witness/Mission, Dominion over the Earth, Gospel of Work, Human Rights/Dignity, Meaning of Work, Solidarity, Technology, Work and Family.

[Given as a homily on March 18, 1984 in Rome, to managers and workers.]

The experience of human work – the whole experience, past and present, of human work – has its beginning in the words uttered by the Creator to the first man and woman: "Be fruitful and multiply and subdue the earth."[14] Even though the term "work" does not appear in these words, there is a clear reference in them to the reality of work.

The Creator's words establish work as the constant coefficient of human life in the prospect of earthly existence.

Subduing the Earth Through Work

Work binds man with the earth, the world, its various resources. Work serves for the exploitation of these resources and for the transformation of the world from the point of view of man's needs. This concept includes every sort of human work, whether physical or intellectual. It can be said that, beginning from the words contained in the Book of Genesis, humanity has begun its historical pilgrimage which links it with the earth and passes through the stages of the various civilizations and the successes achieved by man through work.

But at the same time, it is precisely to this man, bound through work to the earth and the visible world, that there are addressed, in the person of Abraham, the words: "Go from your country!" These are the words of the living God, which unveil before man's eyes the prospect of the Kingdom of Heaven as the "promised land," the symbol of man's definitive destiny, which is God himself. These words can be accepted only through faith. And it is thus that they were received by Abraham and the whole of his spiritual offspring.

The dimension of work in man's earthly vocation is linked with the dimension of the Kingdom of God by means of faith.

The Gospel of Work

Into both these dimensions enters Jesus of Nazareth: Jesus Christ, he in whom there culminates the promise made to Abraham. Christ proclaims the Gospel of the Kingdom of Heaven, and at the same time he devotes to work at the side of Joseph, the carpenter of Nazareth, the greater part of the years of his life.

Precisely tomorrow – 19 March – is the annual Solemnity of Saint Joseph. This occasion impels us to read carefully this Gospel of Work which Jesus proclaimed with the whole of his life, and especially with his hidden life at Nazareth, when he worked physically at the side of Joseph and Mary.

By this choice of his he made work an integral part of the work of the Redemption. Jesus Christ redeemed the world and humanity definitively through the Cross and the Resurrection. But this does not take away from the fact that the whole of his earthly life from the moment of his conception in the womb of the Virgin Mother – and in particular his work – forms part of the whole of the redeeming mission for which he came into the world. Christ redeemed the world also through work.

In this light, human work is presented to us as redeemed, that is to say, offered to us anew by God, the Creator and Father, in Jesus Christ. And at the same time the Gospel of Work proclaims that every person who works in union with Christ shares in the Redemption which he accomplished. Work thus takes on a new value for man: it becomes something sacred.

The Church down the centuries has constantly proclaimed the Gospel of Work. She has emphasized all its values: social, economic, cultural. In particular she has stressed the personal dignity of human work, and has taught her sons and daughters to share through work in the work of the Redemption of the world.

In this Jubilee Year of the Redemption, we are called to this in a particular way.

Work and Transfiguration

The Transfiguration on Mount Tabor, which the reading of the Gospel of Saint Matthew reminds us of in the liturgy of this Sunday of Lent, constitutes as it were a special day of that light which Jesus Christ casts upon man's life and immortality.

This is the summit towards which whole generations of the People of God are going on pilgrimage in faith. They are the generations of the people of work. And the three Apostles Peter, James and John, who were permitted to share in what happened on Mount Tabor, were also men of work.

Through the Gospel of the Transfiguration Christ casts a special light upon life and upon the immortality in which man is to take part in the Kingdom of heaven. This Gospel speaks of the spiritual raising up of man in Jesus Christ. And at the same time, consider how we are to link this dimension of faith – the dimension of the Kingdom of God, in which the Gospel unfolds before us the prospect of immortality – with the dimension of work, which from the beginning is man's earthly vocation. This vocation links us to the world and closes with the prospect of death.

Work and Redemption

How are we to link these two dimensions: work and the Redemption, temporality and immortality.

Let us listen to the words of the Apostle Paul in the Letter to Timothy: "take your share of suffering for the Gospel in the power of God, who saved us and called us with a holy calling . . . in virtue of his own purpose and the grace which he gave us in Christ Jesus."[15]

Take part in the toil of the Gospel!

Precisely this is the call of the Holy Year of the Redemption, which responds to our pilgrimage of faith. It responds in a particular way to your pilgrimage of the extraordinary Jubilee today.

"Take your share of suffering for the Gospel."

These two dimensions, the dimension of work and the dimension of faith, are not two separate things, any more than the dimension of the world and the dimension of the Kingdom of God.

They have been joined together in the eternal thought and will of the Creator. From the beginning, the path of faith passes through work, and the path of work through faith.

Jesus Christ – that beloved Son in whom the Father was well pleased – has confirmed this with all his Gospel of Work.

Faith and Work

So it is not true that the life of faith and hope in the Kingdom of God draws man away from work. The opposite is true: it is precisely this faith and hope that shed full light on human work, it is they that completely reveal its meaning and true value. It is the Gospel of Work which fully restores his work to man. It alone enables man to realize himself as man, while with the work of his hands he transforms nature. It alone gives work its dignity. And, at the same time, the Gospel leads up to the summit of a "transfiguration" through which work shares in man's immortality, becoming the path to his salvation.

Only when it is completely given back to man in Jesus Christ does work become a gift of God to the creature who must "subdue the earth."[16] And at the same time man's very work is to become a dimension of that land promised to man in God, towards which are travelling the generations of the People of God sprung from Abraham's faith.

24. The Parable of the Talents Tells Us of the Importance of Work[17]

Collaboration with God, Fair Wage, Gospel of Work, Human Rights/Dignity, Humanization/Dehumanization, Justice, Unemployment, Universal Destination of Goods.

[A homily on February 4, 1985 in Trujillo, Peru, to Peruvian workers and business people.]

Jesus Christ is the man of work. The Gospel text we have just heard speaks to us of human work, which for the Christian finds its greatest inspiration and model in the figure of Christ, the man of work. Before beginning his messianic activity, proclaiming the Gospel to the people, he worked for thirty years in the silent house of Nazareth. From his earliest youth Jesus learned to work at the side of Joseph in his carpenter's shop, and for this reason they called him "the carpenter's son."[18] This work of the Son of God constitutes the first and fundamental Gospel, the Gospel of Work.

Later, during his apostolic preaching, he will refer continually, especially in his parables, to the different types of human work.

Human Beings Are Saved through Their Work

Jesus preached above all the Kingdom of God, and at the same time man's definitive destiny, union with God. But this supernatural perspective made equally evident the profound significance of human work, for it does not belong only to the temporal economic order of human society, but it also enters into the economy of divine salvation. And even though it is not only work that serves for eternal salvation, man is saved also by means of his work. This is the teaching of the Gospel that Sacred Scripture transmits to us repeatedly, in the Old as well as in the New Testament.

Today's reading, taken from St. Matthew, contains this basic doctrine in the parable of the talents. Three persons receive talents from their master: the first, five; the second, two; the third, one. The talent at that time represented a certain amount of money, capital, we would say today. Today we would call it above all the capacity, the talents for work. The first and second servants doubled what they had received. The third, on the other hand, buried his talent and did not increase its value.

These three cases speak indirectly of work. Beginning with the gifts man receives from the Creator through his parents, each one can fulfill in his life, with greater or lesser success, the mission God has entrusted to him, always by means of work. This is the ordinary way of doubling the value of each one's talents. On the contrary, by refusing work, without work, not only is the "one talent" of which the parable speaks wasted, but any other talents received as well.

Jesus, through the parable of the talents, teaches us at least indirectly that work belongs to the economy of salvation. The divine judgment on the whole of human life and the kingdom of God as a reward will depend on work. On the other hand, "the wasting of one's talents" brings about rejection by God.

The Problem of Work is Fundamental to Christianity

The text of St. Paul from the Letter to the Thessalonians, which we heard in the first reading, can be considered an apostolic commentary on the parable of Christ and, in a certain sense, on the whole Gospel of Work, which Jesus of Nazareth taught us by his life and his words.

The Apostle warns all those who do not work, who live disordinately and in constant busyness, just as Jesus warned those who waste their talents. In addition, St. Paul gives to the recipients of the letter, the Thessalonians, an example of personal work, besides his untiring apostolic labor, "so as not to impose on any of you."[19] This behavior of the Apostle is an indication, and must be cause for remorse, for those who do not work. For this reason he adds that "anyone who would not work should not eat."[20] And he commands and exhorts everyone in the Lord Jesus Christ "to earn the food they eat by working quietly."[21]

In this way, the subject and problem of work appear as fundamental from the very beginning of the Christian life. They constitute a constant element of the social teaching of the Church throughout the ages, especially in the last century, when work became the center of what is called the "social question" and of all those problems related to a just social order.

Scandal to Christianity in Latin America

This problem presents itself with particularly grave and sometimes even tragic features in the regions of Latin America. The Church, in the person of her pastors, guided by the teachings of Vatican II, has been able to point it out and denounce it adequately, first at Medelín and more recently at Puebla: "In the light of faith the growing gap between rich and poor is a scandal and contradiction with being Christian. The luxury of the few becomes an insult to the poverty of the great masses. This is contrary to the plan of the Creator and to the honor due to him."[22] I myself recalled to your bishops "the tragedy of individual people in your rural areas and cities, daily threatened in their very subsistence, harassed by poverty, hunger, sickness, and unemployment; those unfortunate people who so often rather than living, are only surviving in subhuman situations. In these situations there is certainly no justice nor the minimum dignity that human rights demand."[23]

At the root of these evils of society are no doubt to be found situations and economic, social and political structures, at times of international magnitude, which the Church denounces as "social sins." But she knows at the same time that this is the result of the accumulation and concentration of many personal sins, which it would be necessary to avoid at their root: "sins of those who cause or support evil or who exploit it; of those who are in a position to avoid, eliminate, or at least limit certain social evils but who fail to do so out of laziness, fear or the conspiracy of silence, through secret complicity or indifference; of those who take refuge in the supposed impossibility of changing the world."[24] It is the sin of those who direct and are responsible for society, and also of those workers who do not fulfill their duties. In short, they are the sins of disharmony and egoism, of the search for power and wealth above service to others.

Church's Social Teaching

In the face of these situations, the Church continues to be inspired by the Gospel and her own social teaching to offer her constant and determined collaboration in the cause of justice.

For this reason she wants to be close to all those unjustly treated and to be the poorest of the poor, to improve their situation in every way, not only in the economic sphere, but also in the spiritual, cultural, and moral spheres.

The poor person is one who lacks material means, but no less poor is the one who is immersed in sin; who refuses to recognize his personal dimension which goes beyond the limits of death; who does not have the freedom to think and act according to his conscience; who is subjected by the leaders of society to restrictions by which one who practices his faith is deprived of the benefits granted to those who follow the norms dictated from on high; who is seen as a mere tool of production.

The Church wants a liberation from all these forms of slavery. Your bishops moved along the same line in the norms pointed out in their recent document on the theology of liberation.

The Rights of Workers

In the Christian conception of society there always appears as a basic principle the affirmation of the inviolable dignity of the person, and consequently of the dignity of every worker. To this personal dignity corresponds a series of fundamental rights. The first of these is the right to have a job; a job in order to live, to be able to fulfill oneself as a person, to provide bread for one's family; a job that enriches society; a job that must be carried out in conditions worthy of a person, that is, conditions which damage neither the physical health nor the moral integrity of the workers.

Therefore unemployment and also underemployment constitute an evil and often "a real social disaster."[25] It is humiliating for people and creates feelings of frustration, with dangerous psychological and moral consequences, especially for the young and for parents of families. The first concern of all responsible must be, therefore, to provide work for everyone. This is by no means an easy task, but it should mobilize the energies of the whole nation.

In addition the worker must be assisted, technically and culturally, to prepare himself to carry out a work that satisfies him and at the same time contributes to the well-being of society. The Church has in this area a tradition which she must preserve and perfect.

A just salary, which covers the normal needs of a family, continues to be the concrete measure of justice in the whole socio-economic system, and in each case, of its just functioning.[26] In the same way, all those social services (pensions, health and accident insurance, the right to rest, etc.) are to ensure the life and health of workers and their families.[27]

I am aware of the inherent difficulties which, in this time of such acute socio-economic crisis, impede the concrete and effective realization of these rights. However, I want to call it to the attention of all those responsible directly or indirectly for the socio-economic order, that they strive more than ever to make this ideal possible. The Church and Christians have the right and the obligation to contribute to this, as far as they are able, by diligently carrying out their respective duties; and they must do it united in associations and institutions that society creates for pursuing the common good of all the citizens.

The Social Function of Business

A word, finally, to the businessmen, without whom it would not be possible to render many of these rights effective. I would like to remind these, with the social teaching of the Church, that they must give their enterprises a social function. They must not conceive them only as instruments of production and profit, but also as a community of persons.[28] The gradual building of a more just society will depend on the union of workers and entrepreneurs, under the responsible direction of government leaders.

---

25. *The Problems of Work Must Be Seen in the Context of Human Dignity and Solidarity*[29]

Common Good, Dominion over the Earth, Environment, Human Development/Progress, Meaning of Work, Solidarity, Unemployment.

[An address on June 17, 1985 in Venice, Italy, to workers, contractors and executives of the Porto Marghera complex.]

It is with lively joy that I find myself in your midst, you who are representatives of the vast and important field of work, which here too at Porto Marghera embodies the greatness of man's work and also all the tensions of present day society. It likewise manifests the just aspirations towards a world in which man's labor is properly valued, by putting the human person at the center.

My greetings and my esteem go to you, workers, who every day experience physical fatigue; to you executives and technicians, who strive to alleviate this fatigue; to you contractors, who feel the duty to dedicate time and resources in the service of an economy for man.

Through you it is my desire to greet the whole working world of this region of Veneto, from which many of you come, leaving your villages to seek a source of livelihood here. I express sincere and warm solidarity with laborers, farmers, artisans, small businessmen, workers of the production and service sectors, and fishermen.

I come to you with the heart of a brother in order to share your thoughts and concerns, to underline your research and initiatives, to encourage everyone, the Christian community and men of good will, so that every effort might be made in all areas and at every level to face and to complete the processes of renewal and restructuring, together with the fundamental problem of employment for all.

Problems of Work

Serious questions arise from the situation of "crisis." They must not merely be read in an economic, political and technical key, but also, and above all, in an ethical one. Every crisis in fact obliges us to review and to verify our mentality and our life according to various aspects.

The world of work is today going through a time of great unrest: there is not enough work, and the number of unemployed, especially among the young, grows daily; living conditions, even though better overall, are not yet satisfactory; solidarity, threatened by personal and group selfishness, is achieved with difficulty; security of life, founded upon a concrete and just social peace, does not yet seem to have been attained; the economy resists bending its laws in the service of man; the error of economism which considers human work exclusively according to its economic result, is far from being corrected.

I know that here at Porto Marghera there has been a drop of nearly thirteen thousand in the number of jobs from the seventies to today; the problem of lay-offs is well known; many young people have great difficulty in finding a job, dignity, and a personal, family and social future.

This extraordinary reality of work and of problems, of hopes and expectations which is Porto Marghera, today faces a situation which can only be expressed in economic terms of "crisis."

There are the international fluctuations of the economy, of marketing and finance, and the conditions deriving from the rapid and widespread application of new technologies. To these, one can certainly add the national and local problems that it is your task to carefully analyze in order to deal with them by making the necessary interventions, according to your particular competencies, always honoring the commitments and responsibilities assumed.

And this must be done with urgency and courage in order to avoid the many negative effects of this critical situation, which in the end hurt those who are the weakest.

Need for an Ethical Spirit

While expressing my human and Christian solidarity with those who pay the greatest price in terms of personal and family suffering in the present situation – with the men and women who have lost their jobs, with the young people who at times despair of finding work – I wish at the same time to tell everyone that the reality of Porto Marghera is a patrimony of experience in the areas of labor, management, trade unions, professionalism and technological research that must be conserved, increased and made fruitful for the benefit of the region's development. But its revival will either embody an ethical spirit or it will not be authentic growth.

The climate of uncertainty and fear which is created by the crisis can lead to distrust, to turning in upon oneself, one's family or group, prompting fatalistic attitudes, the search for individual defense through having two jobs or working illegally: situations which, while at times understandable, in general easily cause inequality and injustice. Solidarity is harmed within consciences and within its institutional structures.

An increasingly economistic and consumer mentality is being spread, one which exalts the privileged and penalizes the weak; which strongly conditions the birth-rate, the education of children, relations with others, especially with the most disadvantaged and the elderly, weakening the motivations for gratuitous service and active participation. That which collapses is the religious and moral sense of life. The strong and motivated recovery of the deeper ethical reasons for communal life – in work, in solidarity and in generosity, truly carrying one another's burdens (Gal 6:2) – will give vigor to the inventiveness and courage necessary to look to the future with serious and realistic projects; to reweave the dialectic relationship – which is always constructive if pursued with fairness and justice – between contractors, executives and workers, all of them interested in the growth of Porto Marghera.

The Human Being Is both the Subject and Object of Work

In facing current challenges today's world – and the world of work as well – has need of reconciliation with "God's project." God has called man to be the "lord of created things." Man cannot be an object dominated by economic or political laws, nor can he be reduced to the level of an instrument. Man must subdue the earth, he must dominate it, because as the image of God he is a person, that is, a subjective being capable of acting in a planned and rational way, capable of deciding for himself and tending to realize himself. As a person, man is therefore the subject of work.[30]

There will not be true growth until there is an insistence on the fact that man is the primary foundation of the value of work and that the object of work, of any work done by man, is always man himself.

In present day circumstances the need for a new solidarity which is both generous and effective is emerging ever more forcefully: a solidarity which would help to single out new means of growth; a solidarity which would face up to the difficulties currently experienced in the world of work; a solidarity, therefore, before the problem of unemployment as well.

Everyone Is Responsible

As my predecessor Paul VI said: "Let everyone examine himself to see what he has done thus far and what he must still do. It is not enough to recall principles, affirm intentions, underline the strident injustices and offer prophetic denunciations: these words will not have real weight unless in each person they are accompanied by a more vivid awareness of his responsibility, and by effective action. It is too easy to shift the blame for injustices onto others, if one is not at the same time convinced that each man participates in them and that personal conversion is the first necessity."[31] Everyone is called to a serious commitment, in his own place and according to his responsibility.

To Management

You contractors have the duty to act in such a way that economic laws are increasingly at the service of man, and at the same time to find – in the current transformation of business and of work methods themselves – methods, technology and goals which restore man to his position as the primary foundation of work. How can the tension between capital and labor be resolved? I have already given a response in the encyclical on human work.[32] Still, new reflections can be made in this period in which new technologies enter more and more broadly into the productive cycle, and science daily provides new ways of actualizing the notions acquired.

To Workers

You workers have the obligation of founding your mutual solidarity upon new bases. The current crisis, new working conditions, new problems regarding the planning of one's own life, new areas of participation, the prospects of continual growth – these require new attitudes and a new mentality. Today you can be the protagonists of the new reality which is in the process of being formed. Insist and strive in such a way that this new reality assumes and realizes the great values of man's dignity, of the sanctity of the family, of community participation, of peace and justice. From this port, which in the past has seen ships from all over the world come and go, may your vision and your activity extend itself to the workers of the entire world. And in the same way that you strive to eliminate differences and discrimination concerning opportunities and rights among workers in your region and in your country, so also strive towards these goals for the workers of the whole world.

To Politicians

You who are involved in political affairs have the duty to discern new ways of dealing with the current crisis situation. Your perceptions, translated into wise and just laws, will make the transition to a more just and humane civilization possible. The recovery of the willingness to serve the common good is indispensable in order that each person might be able to question himself regarding the role which has been entrusted to him and to take his proper place in the life of society: with that ethical sense in choosing, that stringent and transparent morality in public activities, which alone can guarantee credibility and trust and promote a more active participation on the part of all citizens, culminating in that power which is love, capable of shaping human life in its various dimensions.

To Christian Communities

I address in a special way all the Christian communities from which you workers of Porto Marghera come; communities in which you should feel at home because they are open and hospitable; communities in which you yourselves must be present and participating, bringing the contribution of your ideas and experiences, values and hopes.

Pastors and laity can together render their service to the Gospel and to the world of work, with an ecclesial and missionary spirit and with a style of true communion and sharing. And with them, all the communities – not estranged, but sensitive and formed – will be ready to welcome what Pope John XXIII rightly considered the first among "the signs of the times, the economic and social ascent of the working classes," accompanied by the "need to be considered and treated not as beings devoid of intelligence and freedom, at the mercy of the will of others, but always as subjects or persons in all sectors of society."[33]

Jesus not only proclaimed but first of all accomplished with deeds the Gospel entrusted to him, the Word of eternal wisdom. Thus it was also the "Gospel of Work," because he who proclaimed it was himself a man of work.

26. Solidarity Is Needed to Solve the Problems of Work[34]

Common Good, Dominion over the Earth, Entrepreneurship, Meaning of Work, Solidarity, Technology, Unemployment, Work and Family.

[An address on May 10, 1986 in Ravenna, Italy, to workers and entrepreneurs at a petroleum chemical plant.]

I have come to Romagna, at the invitation of your bishops, in order to help the Christian communities prepare for the third millenium. The relationship between economic development and work is already showing itself to be the dominant problem of the coming decades; and it will take on increasing importance worldwide. It is sufficient to consider the fact that the vanquishing of starvation and the human liberation of entire continents is tied to this problem. All of this is going to require an immense common effort involving everyone: economists, researchers, public bodies, entrepreneurs and workers with their trade unions.

This also means that when, before the reality of unemployment, the Church reflects upon the relationship between technical-economic development and the moral principles that underlie it, she does not overstep her bounds or lose herself in abstractions: the acceleration of history is already demonstrating the social relevance of moral principles.

Technological Development and the Human Person

Returning to the question of Romagna, it is well known that the work crisis has been heavily aggravated by the introduction of automation in many areas of production; and everyone, among both workers and entrepreneurs, is aware of the difficulties and the problems that such changes bring with them. Still, our attitude in the face of technological progress cannot be one of rejection or fear. "Technology is undoubtedly man's ally. It facilitates his work, perfects, accelerates and augments it."[35] We might add, quoting your bishops' recent Pastoral Note, that the new technologies "can exalt people's creativity in the process of development, freeing man from its most alienating and repetitive aspects."

Even the most sophisticated technology and machines are thus the fruit and the instrument of human work, but the true subject of work is always and exclusively man. Instruments cannot be raised to the level of protagonists and placed above the working man without a reversal of the order of reality and a fatal inversion of the relationship necessary between the means and the end. The experience of recent years confirms the fact that technology, if its use is not guided and enlightened by a superior moral criterion, can change from being an ally to being almost an adversary of man, as when the mechanization of work "supplants" man, robs many workers of employment or, through the exaltation of machines, reduces man to their servant.[36]

We are called to dominate change and not to be dominated by it. But this can take place only to the extent that we are able to overcome that split between ethics and the economy that has kept the great conquests of the modern age from fully benefitting man.

Work for the Sake of the Worker

I would like to place the meaning of my visit to you, workers and entrepreneurs of Romagna, within the context of an effort to heal this split.

You know that, while in the past there was a tendency to present work as the only source and measure of man's value, now we are seeing the emergence of so-called "functional" perspectives according to which work is meaningful only as an occupation viewed in terms of material gain. For precisely this reason it is becoming more necessary than ever to recover the conviction that "work is a fundamental dimension of human existence on earth,"[37] on the condition, however, that it is not seen as the final end, but subordinated to that end which is man.[38]

Solidarity and the Principle of Subsidiarity

From this truth, dear workers and entrepreneurs, a pressing appeal rises up to you: the appeal for solidarity. In order to live and grow together, men have always needed to find paths to understanding, mutual assistance and collaboration.

Solidarity has its laws: it demands that no one be ambitious for a role of predominance, but that each instead be ready to recognize the functions of other forces and components and to welcome their contributions in a constructive way. This is valid within individual firms as well as in the entire productive process and, more broadly still, in the life of society.

Seen from the perspective of solidarity, the diverse but complementary roles of every sector involved in work and production acquire greater and more authentic significance. Entrepreneurs and executives will be recognized for their role in giving unity in decision making, coordination and dynamism to the firm's activity.

Those who are self-employed, and who thus continuously take upon themselves the responsibility, efforts and risks of work, give elasticity to the entire productive system, and must be suitably sustained according to the principle of subsidarity. This principle states that neither the State nor any society may take the place of the initiative of individuals and intermediate communities in those areas in which it is possible for them to act.[39]

For their part, employees not only have the right to a just wage, assuring them and their families of an adequate standard of living, but they are also called to participate co-responsibly in the initiatives and decisions that regard the life of the firm, and thus their own future. They must also be able to work under conditions that safeguard, together with their physical health, the dignity and the room for creativity proper to human work: in this way they will be able to see themselves as authentically "co-owners" of the great workbench.[40]

Solidarity within the Firm and Family

Dear workers and entrepreneurs, you know well that every right carries with it a precise duty: this principle of justice and equity regulates not only our mutual relations, but likewise the contribution that each of us is called to make to the common good. If we desire a more just society, a better quality of life, we must all be capable of looking beyond our own particular and immediate advantage, and be ready to carry loyally our portion of the collective burdens.

I would further like to invite you to broaden your vision beyond the realm of your direct work responsibilities, and this in two directions, one close at hand and the other more distant.

The first regards human relations within the firm. The world of work is not all to be found in the work contract; it also lies in the harmony of friendship. It becomes fully human only when, beyond the zone of the useful, fraternity appears, that communion of spirits which is the enlargement of the life of each individual through participation in the lives of others.

I recommend to your care the young who are making their first contact with this new world. Be attentive to the initial welcome you give them: they can receive from it a great and meaningful orientation.

Remember, too, your social commitments. I am referring especially to your family relations: in the past, the solidity of family ties has constituted a great reservoir of moral energies for the people of Romagna, with largely positive influences in terms of industriousness and rectitude of behavior. Today it is precisely the crisis of the family – evident from the scourges of divorce and abortion, from the low birth rate, and from people's reluctance to contract marriage – that could lead to a loss of meaning and values, with unforeseeable consequences on the level of commitment and fidelity to work as well.

Universal Solidarity

The other direction in which I exhort you to look embraces the immense mass of suffering and threatened humanity: from the immigrants who seek work and bread in your midst to the innumerable multitudes of starving people. This mass also includes all those who suffer the tragedy of war, terrorism, the deprivation of fundamental rights, beginning with the right to religious freedom.[41]

Ravenna is an ancient beacon of civilization which has projected its light from east to west, among ancient peoples and new peoples. May she now be capable of contributing to the realization of a universal solidarity that will be the builder of peace, and this through your work as well.

May the Lord bless these efforts and these proposals. May the world of work, which has often been the first to suffer from that separation of faith from life which has negatively conditioned the events of modern history and produced effects harmful to man, now benefit from a renewed encounter with Christ, the Redeemer of man.

27. Solidarity Directs Work to the Common Good[42]

Human Rights/Dignity, Solidarity, World Community.

[An address on December 6, 1986 in Rome, to representatives of the Workers' Movement of Catholic Action and the Christian Workers' Movement, plus participants in the Conference of Catholic Action Vice Presidents.]

This meeting gives me the opportunity to reflect with you on a theme that is common to your programs, the theme of solidarity. You plan to reflect on this question not only inasmuch as it is a social phenomenon that is felt with particular strength among workers, but also insofar as it is an ethical value that touches upon the consciences of Christians. You are in fact aware that solidarity is a proclamation very much present in the words of Christ: "This is my commandment, that you love one another as I have loved you."[43]

Network of Interdependencies

It is a fact that every person constantly receives help from persons far and near. He takes advantage of material, moral, cultural and religious goods created by entire generations. Everyone lives off the work, the efforts, the fervor and the sacrifices of many of his fellows. He benefits from their solidarity: it is thus right that he in turn offer his own solidarity to others. This is particularly true in our day, when all work is carried out within a very large network of interdependencies which condition from various angles its possibility and development. This fact reinforces the need – which is noted with ever greater clarity and awareness – to see work as a unique moment of participation and generous sharing: in a word, of constructive solidarity.

God desires a world founded on justice and fraternity. These virtues form the foundation for the order that must sustain interpersonal relations. But this order must be continually promoted and adapted as social structures and ways of life are gradually renewed and developed. We are seeking continual progress and a rapid transformation of man's living conditions, under the impulse of new economic conditions and possibilities, of new technical capacities and systems of production. In the context of this progress there have also developed further requirements of participation, and other forms of solidarity have been made possible.

Solidarity: Pursuit of the Good of All

It is necessary to see to it that the persons comprising the individual human organizations are able to cooperate ever more responsibly in providing the goods needed and desired by all. This presumes the involvement not only of people's technical skills, but also of their spiritual faculties, with the aim of reaching the understanding necessary for the pursuit of the common interest. This understanding is impossible unless each person makes an effort to open himself to the objective consideration of the good of others and not only of himself. Therein lies solidarity, which thus reveals itself as a fundamental expression of the social character immanent in human nature and a uniquely significant dimension of Christian love. It is in this dimension that every person can recognize himself as a brother to others.

Solidarity offers the exciting opportunity to communicate oneself to others in a peaceful and constructive way; it permits the establishment of coordinated and stable relations corresponding to the real needs of persons and communities; it also helps in overcoming those conditions of loneliness and isolation that often lead to the inability to communicate and to alienation. In solidarity, moreover, man tends to communicate to his brother his convictions regarding the deep meaning of life and work, from the perspective of the full realization of the transcendent destiny of every human being. It is obvious that this support found in the sharing of supreme values is today more urgent than ever, precisely because the growing automation of productive progress, while it tends to reduce the material intervention of man, also risks depreciating his spiritual significance, rendering the activity of the subject marginal and repetitive. It is therefore necessary to sustain and orient work by a strong spiritual motivation, which will be all the more easily transmitted and nourished in proportion to the liveliness and authenticity of the climate of solidarity which pervades the work environment.

Solidarity Pursued through Dialogue and Peace

An objective and complete discourse must at this point also refer to those disturbing phenomena of solidarity which are reduced to systematic opposition between classes, with consequent manifestations of struggle that often provoke an increase in conflict, social instability and ideological confusion among people.

It is certainly necessary to make every effort, through the solidarity of all workers, to eliminate all sources of injustice, disparity, and inequitable privileges. However, it is also necessary to affirm, with clarity and vigor, that the road to improvement does not pass by way of hatred, the systematic division of social groups, violence and domination. It is therefore essential that all movements of Christian inspiration be deeply united in the greatest solidarity so as to propose the authentic path to affirm forcefully – when faced with proposals of violence – the human value of dialogue and peace.

Global and National Commitments to Solidarity

Before the broadening and intensification of human relations in the various spheres of social life, other forms of solidarity can and must be considered, in order increasingly to adapt to the requirements of the person and the structures in which he is called to work.

It will first of all be necessary to make a deep commitment to promoting an active solidarity at a global level. Today, decisions made in one part of the world have repercussions through the rest of the world. Furthermore, social problems have become so widespread as to reach habitually the dimensions of all humanity. It is necessary, then, that the choices made by public authorities, as well as by union and management organization, be made in a spirit of solidarity, that is, with the consciousness that one cannot ignore the repercussions that such decisions will have on entire nations or on particular sectors of human society, involving rights, needs and aspirations common to all. The spirit of solidarity will lead people to consider the good of each community and to strive for a just share of all in the goods of this world, helping to avoid or reduce existing imbalances. Thus, solutions will be sought that respect the dignity of each particular community, including the poorest, because no people can pretend to reserve exclusively to itself the riches at its disposal.

At the national level, too, solidarity requires that in relations between corporations the criteria of conflict and domination be overcome. The development of technical civilization involves the establishment of new forms of work at the expense of others which are now obsolete. Still, this should not happen in such a way that it generates painful phenomena of recession in some sectors, with pockets of unemployment and poverty. Economic problems, even those technical in nature, must not be separated from their ethical and social aspects.

Solidarity at the national level therefore requires the efforts of all responsible powers, public and private, so as to avoid a situation in which the progress of some is paid for with the exorbitant sacrifices and humiliations of others. There must be a determined and courageous effort toward the arduous goal of creating continual employment opportunities through the proposal and support of jobs which, while being useful and productive, are at the same time within reach of those who, because of age or culture, find it difficult to keep pace with technological progress.

Solidarity among Organizations and Workers

Solidarity also requires opportune coordination between large and small firms. It is justifiable to fear at times that the great organizational capacity of the more powerful concerns might develop in a predominant and exclusive way, reinforcing privileges and powers to the detriment of smaller concerns and of participation in the common good of work. Everything possible must be done not only to keep development from permitting the persistence of unjust situations, but to prevent it from creating new ones.

Finally, there exists a new form of solidarity that calls out in a particular way to workers' movements such as those you represent.

It must be acknowledged that workers have shown themselves able to respond to the appeal of solidarity, working effectively in defense of man as the subject of work, in the face of pressing forms of exploitation present in the industrial structures created by capital.

Today, however, solidarity presents you with a broader field of action. It invites you not to favor certain categories of workers, but to consider the effects that the current technological revolution is having on all sectors of employment. As I recalled in the encyclical *Laborem Exercens*, "movements of solidarity in the sphere of work ... can be necessary also with reference to the condition of social groups that were not previously included in such movements but which, in changing social systems and conditions of living, are undergoing what is in effect 'proletarianization.' "[44] And so it is necessary that workers not close themselves off in a solidarity which is limited and circumscribed by the interests of the category or sector to which they belong, but that they consider the conditions under which others are living as well. True solidarity must be present wherever the subject of work – that is, man – finds himself in conditions of poverty, wretchedness, exploitation and injustice.

Christ and Solidarity

You lay men and women are the ones who must take upon yourselves the specific task of renewing in a significant way the relations internal to the working world, infusing them with a greater and more equitable solidarity.

The principle of solidarity, rooted at once in the personality and the social character of man, indicates a reciprocal bond and duty which finds singularly profound motivations in the Christian faith.

It is first of all the example of Christ that reveals the most sublime form of solidarity. He joined himself to all men, even the most miserable, unto death on the Cross, for the salvation of all. From His redemptive sacrifice sprang forth a "newly created" humanity[45] in which unity is so deep that "there is neither Jew nor Greek, there is neither slave nor free, there is neither male nor female; for you are all one in Christ Jesus."[46] In this mystery of unity we can discern the greatness, the dignity, the value, but also the urgency of a true solidarity uniting all men and women. Christians must become ever more credible heralds of this message in the world.

---

28. *The "Great Prospect" of a More Human Society Presupposes the Humanization of Work*[47]

Collaboration with God, Culture of Work, Humanization/ Dehumanization, Justice, Leisure, Work and Family

[An address on December 13, 1986 in Rome, to Italian executives, trade unionists and academics.]

In carrying out her task of evangelization, the Church has always been attentive to the context of those realities within which she lives, reflecting in her heart the joy and hope, the grief and anguish of humanity.[48]

Thus from the beginning she has taken an interest in the economic and social aspects of the human person, instituting even at the time of the Apostles seven "deacons" with the duty of presiding over and organizing the service of assistance within the Christian community.[49] In the period following the barbarian invasion and the fall of the Roman empire, the Church strove to respond to the social problems of the moment by creating hospices, charitable confraternities, Misericordiae, schools and centers of hospitality in the monasteries.

She was also present with her constant teaching, aimed at forming the consciences of the Christian people regarding the duty of charity, care of the poor, the use of goods and their social destination, the obligation to allocate superfluous goods to the needy, and the need to bear the misfortunes of life with fortitude and hope, while seeking to overcome them to the extent possible. The medieval era was to see great theologians developing the themes of justice, law, politics and international relations.

Later, with the rise of industrial society, the Church once again made herself heard, condemning economic amorality, whether in the form of capitalistic greed or of a socialism lacking respect for the dignity of the human person. At the same time, she strove to map out the great lines of a vision of the world and work that took its inspiration from the Gospel, for a just solution to the social question.

The Dynamic Character of the Social Encyclicals

Rerum Novarum of Pope Leo XIII was a document of such importance that it became the point of reference for subsequent papal social teaching, beginning with Pius XI on the fortieth anniversary of the encyclical, and then at ten-year intervals until Paul VI and his *Octogesima Adveniens. Laborem Exercens*, too was meant to enter into this river of tradition which swells as it flows along. It took work as its object of particular reflection. Five years have passed since that encyclical's publication: an arc of time dense with history and rapid changes, with new developments in technological, economic and political conditions. The developments have greatly influenced – and will continue to influence – the evolution of work, of this dimension of human existence from which man's life is built up every day, and about which there continually arise new questions and problems, new hopes, but also ever new fears and threats.[50]

It is not for the Church to analyze scientifically the consequences that these changes may have on human society.[51] However, in your capacity as lay persons animated by the faith, as Christian animators of the contemporary world, you are and must be capable of carrying out this analysis, of preparing the future.

Priority of the Worker

It is the Church's task to recall continually the dignity and rights of workers, calling attention to situations in which these are violated, and to contribute to orienting changes, so that the progress of man and society will be authentic.

There is no authentic progress when in the world of work the human dimension is in some way compromised. The encyclical which you are studying insists on the principle that the first foundation of the value of work is man himself, who is its subject.[52] Work is a means, never an end. Man is primary. The end of work is the worker, that is, the person who is working.

The perfection of man obtained through the development of his faculties has greater value than the external riches which he can produce with his work.[53] Whence the rejection of all solutions, old and new, in which work is considered merely an element of production and the worker is subordinated to his activity, transformed from subject into object, from end into means, from a person into a thing.

In your document you have expressed the hope that Christians might make themselves bearers of a culture of work, demonstrating an effective capacity for social initiative. This must be the point of departure for every project and program: the whole productive process must be adapted to the needs of the person and to the conditions of his life.[54] It is from this perspective that the growing tragedy of unemployment, especially among the young, must be reconsidered and resolved. Lack of work humiliates a person, making him appear useless in his own eyes, and it impoverishes society, which is deprived of effective and willing forces.

Work and the Family

The other sphere of values consisting in the family dimension of work must be re-examined from this angle. The family, which is a natural right and vocation of man, has an essential relation with work, for it is work that normally assures it of the necessary means of subsistence.[55] Moreover, when he works to ensure the means of subsistence for his family, a human being puts all his love into his daily labors. Love contributes to increasing the nobility of work. When, instead, work disintegrates the family, it ends by destroying its very purpose.

In this area, social legislation still leaves much to be desired. I am referring in particular to the situation of women, who, while seeing their work in the home go unrecognized and undefended from a juridical and economic point of view, are often subjected to a stressful pace in work outside the home, which keeps them away from their husbands and children, often leading them to renounce the grandeur of maternity.

Accelerated efforts must be made to find satisfactory solutions in this area, solutions which guarantee both effective equality among persons and their specific character.

Collaboration with Divine Providence

What I have said up to now finds its integration and also its highest motivation in the spiritual dimension of work.

The human being, with the satisfaction and the weight of his labors, is inexplicable without him who, after having created man, offers to him as a gift the universe with its complex forces (still largely unknown), so that he may cultivate, keep and dominate it.[56] In recognizing the reality of God as personal and transcendent, man – who does not create matter but finds it already existing – situates himself in a new and most original way with respect to the cosmos. With this attitude he frees himself from the enticing grip of natural forces, keeps from being dominated by them, indeed, elevates himself, consenting to be a collaborator with the divine design.

The spirituality of work consists in the awareness of this profound reality that man, through his work, can place himself in a relation with his ultimate destiny, becoming an ally of the living God. Furthermore, when the truth that work was done by the human hands of the very Son of God in the little workshop of Nazareth is embraced, the effort to transform the world becomes liberation from moral evil and insertion in a new long range project, extending beyond the confines of history. With faith in Christ, man participates in the project which is in the process of being realized: the salvation of the whole man.

Dear brothers and sisters, faced with the broad horizons of this vision proposed by the social doctrine of the Church, one conclusion appears certain: the realization of the prospect of a more human society, something to which we all aspire, is unthinkable without the simultaneous humanization of that fundamental component which is work. Yet we see that it is just as impossible to make the world of work more human if it is not treated and oriented in accordance with God's plan.

You, the laity, are called to this specific task, in the vast spectrum of your areas of work: you are called to strive as workers from within, as evangelical leaven in the midst of temporal realities.

29. *Business Should Recognize and Accept Its Integral Role in Society*[57]

Common Good, Community of Persons, Dominion over the Earth, Economic Laws and Profits, Entrepreneurship, Materialism and Consumerism, Solidarity.

[An address on April 17, 1988 in Verona, Italy, to managers and workers.]

Work, in all its forms, is an essential component of human life, or, as I wrote in the Encyclical *Laborem Exercens*, "a fundamental dimension of man's existence on earth."[58] This "fundamental dimension" is concretized today in the form of business, factories, laboratories and various offices. It is a pluralistic and very diversified reality, one in which, however, we see common elements which converge in a grand and fundamental design: the transformation of some material or pre-existing element resulting, through the cooperation of intelligence and manual labor, in goods and services for the use of the human community. There is also need of capital – that is, of various kinds of investments – of technology and of the labor of each individual worker in order to attain this goal.

Interdependence of Business and Society

The first characteristic of a modern firm and of its social function, in this context of great complexity, is without a doubt that of interdependence. Each of its components is equally necessary, and it is useless to speculate about the primacy of one or another of them.

However, there is a similar interdependence between society and the world of industry and services; society has need of what is provided by the activities of production, and these latter, in turn, have need both of the outlet offered by society in terms of its purchasing capacity and of the resources it provides in the form of potential workers, investments and technology. We are all well aware that that interdependence is no longer contained within the boundaries of a society or nation, but extends to continental and intercontinental dimensions.

Interdependence Implies Solidarity

If we are "all really responsible for all"[59] in every setting and dimension of human life, then this is all the more true in the dimension of productive activity and economic life.

Now this tightly woven and capillary interdependence can be endured because it is necessary or it can be accepted and assumed as a moral obligation. When it is interpreted in the second way – the only way truly worthy of the human, individual and social vocation – then interdependence is transformed from a more or less conscious reality into a value, the value of solidarity.

This in its turn means, dear representatives of the world of labor, that your activities, which are tied to the earthly dimensions of life, have radical moral implications; indeed, they must be governed by moral criteria. The first of these criteria is precisely that of solidarity.

In the encyclical *Solicitudo Rei Socialis*, I returned to this fundamental idea several times,[60] emphasizing that it is a question of a "moral category," of a "virtue," not of "a feeling of vague compassion." Solidarity is the "firm and persevering determination to commit oneself to the common good."[61] In the same context I added that this is the way, indeed the only way, to conquer, by a diametrically opposed attitude the causes hindering full development: the lust for profit and thirst for power at any cost."[62]

The Validity of Moral Criteria

The application of the criterion of solidarity to the activity of production, and in particular to the world of business enterprise, has very significant consequences for the solution of the problems to which your spokesman referred. The first consequence, as I have already noted in passing, is that of admitting the existence of moral criteria, and not just economic ones, at the base of production, and of feeling bound to observe them for reasons of conscience and not just of law. The other immediate consequence is that when the time comes to make practical decisions, those involved in that activity must deliberate and choose in the light of those criteria.

Among them, the criterion of the common good is certainly primary. In fact, the objective norm of solidarity is the good of "each man and of all men," considered in the light of their dignity as images, indeed as children, of God.

Profit Must Be Regulated by Moral Criteria

From this perspective it is clear that the sole criterion of profit is insufficient, especially when it is raised to the level of an absolute: "earning" more in order to "possess" more, not only tangible objects but also financial holdings, making it possible to enjoy new forms of property that are ever more extensive and ever more dominating. Not that aiming at profit is in itself unjust; a business cannot do without it. The reasonable attempt to make a profit is, for that matter, connected with the right of "economic initiative" which I defended in the encyclical just cited.[63] I merely intend to say that, in order to be just, profit must be regulated by moral criteria, in particular by those connected with the principle of solidarity.

A Business Is a Community

This principle also has a precise bearing on relations within the firm, requiring the respectful observance of the rights of all who collaborate in it. Indeed, a business firm is not merely an instrument at the service of the well-being of its management; rather, it is itself a common good of both management and labor, at the service of the common good of society.

Anyone who collaborates, at any level, possesses the rights that correspond to his role in the common enterprise, as well as the respective obligations. In particular, he enjoys those rights and duties which proceed from his dignity as a man or a woman called, indeed obliged, to live a life that is truly human in all its dimensions: affective, cultural, social, spiritual, religious. This, once again, is a consequence not merely of legal impositions, valid though they may be, but of the obligations of conscience, both human and Christian.

Management Must Be Open to the Poor and to Others

From this perspective the weakest and poorest of people certainly have a priority in our concern, as the recent encyclical,[64] along with the whole Christian tradition, affirms. The "poor" exist in business, too; above all, there are the true "poor," that is, the huge number of unemployed, or of those who have been laid off. The ironclad logic of profit would have us forget them or consider them superfluous, or, worse yet, add to their numbers. On the contrary, we must vigorously affirm that a man, a woman, a young person, is never superfluous, nor can he or she be left out in planning new projects.

I would like to add that entrepreneurs should not forget themselves when it comes to developing all the dimensions of a truly human life. The law of profit and the demands of ever more demanding managerial work can never take the place of every man and woman's duty to be open to family, neighbor, culture, society and, above all, to God. This multifaceted openness to the higher values of the human person will certainly help to give managerial tasks also their true meaning and proper measure.

Consumerism and the Common Good

The value of solidarity and of the common good must also govern relations between business and society both on the national and on the international levels.

There are instruments which should not be produced, or whose production and marketing should be rigorously controlled. The first example is arms,[65] but perhaps it is not the only one. Here also the law of profit cannot be supreme.

One could say, in this sense, that an important task of Christian entrepreneurs, and of anyone who has man's true good at heart, would be to establish in today's world a sort of scale of priorities among the goods to be produced. Not all goods, in fact, are equally useful or necessary. The criterion of solidarity and the common good should be applied here in a precise way in order to help us understand better that certain products have a more intimate impact on man's "being" while others serve only his "having and thus have less value from the human point of view, whatever their market value may be. Multiplying them, by means of an excessive and artificial substitution of ever new and immediately obsolete models is what we call 'consumerism.'[66] A business enterprise should not try to create superfluous needs in order then to seek to satisfy them with ever more sophisticated products which, in turn, create new needs.

Universal Dimension of Solidarity

Among the goods closest to man's "being," those which are necessary for sustenance, such as food, stand out. In this city, and in this fairground, I cannot fail to mention the very well-known traditions connected with farm production and the technology designed to increase and improve it. May further advances in the service of man's basic needs be made in this sector in Italy, but also in other parts of the world which are less favored and developed. The solidarity of which I was speaking in fact possesses this universal dimension, because the decisions made in one country always have effects, for good or evil, in the other countries as well.

Administrators of the Earth

Finally, respect for nature and for natural resources is part of the duty of solidarity and the obligation to promote the common good, as I observed in the encyclical *Solicitudo Rei Socialis*.[67] The use that our technologies make of these resources is also subject to moral norms. We are not absolute masters of these goods, but administrators who must be attentive to the consequences – in terms of the environment and the quality of life – which our decisions have on both the present generation and those of the future, to whom we must pass on a habitable world.

---

30. Christians Must Respond to God's Initiative and Collaborate in the Work of Redemption[68]

Christian Witness/Mission, Collaboration With God, Dominion over the Earth, Gospel of Work, Meaning of Work, Private Property/Co-ownership, Solidarity, Universal Destination of Goods, Work and Society.

[A homily on May 17, 1988 in Villarica, Paraguay, to farm workers, employers and politicians.]

From the beginning, man was called by God to "subdue the earth and have dominion over it."[69] Therefore, the work of the land is the first to be recommended, as we read in Genesis: "The Lord God took the man and put him in the garden of Eden to till it and keep it."[70] It was a simple and pleasant task, because the Creator entrusted to man's care "every plant yielding seed which is upon the face of the earth and every tree with seed in its fruit";[71] and in the garden of Eden God himself caused "to grow every tree that is pleasant to the sight and good for food, the tree of life also in the midst of the garden."[72]

Called to Share in the Work of the Creator

This story "is profoundly marked by the fundamental truth that man, created in the image of God, shares by his work in the activity of the Creator," and that he is a co-worker with his Creator.[73] This truth, which refers to any kind of human work no matter how insignificant it seems, is applied in a special way to the work of the field.

How can we not recall here the many expressions that have come from the lips of Christ! How often he compared the kingdom of heaven to phenomena or activities that we can observe in nature almost every day! How well he knew the work in the fields, as his examples show!

Jesus speaks of the farmer, of sowing and harvesting,[74] of the lilies of the field and of the birds,[75] of thistles and the wheat,[76] of wine and oil.[77] He compares himself to the true vine and his Father to the vinedresser.[78] Yet, how distant and irrelevant his teachings are to some! It could be said that the more they progress in subduing and dominating the land, the more they become forgetful of God, who created the earth and all that it contains.

The Effects of Original Sin

"The kingdom of heaven may be compared to a man who sowed good seed in his field. While everybody was asleep, his enemy came, sowed darnel all among the wheat, and made off."[79]

In this field where the seed was sown, which refers to life, God's gift to each one of us, one often finds the darnel, sowed here and there by the enemy. Actually, you know well the consequences of original sin. You have experienced the deep truth contained in those words of Genesis: "In toil you shall eat … all the days of your life; thorns and thistles it shall bring forth to you; and you shall eat the plants of the field. In the sweat of your face you shall eat bread."[80] How much work still has to be done so that the seed sown in the ground may bear fruit in abundance! Cleaning up the brambles and briars, removing heaps of dirt and rubbish, looking after the irrigation, watching for harmful insects and pests – all those activities demand your dedication long before the harvest. What hardships! How many worries and uncertainties with regard to the present and the future!

The Reality of Injustice

Although it is true that this fertile land that the Lord has given you does reward your efforts abundantly, how often it happens that those who work it cannot enjoy its fruits. The absence of peace and tranquility because of the uncertainty of the family's future or social security; the intransigence with regard to salaries and unjust labor contracts and even the difficulties that have to be overcome to get a property agreement: these are some of today's thorns and thistles that worsen the already difficult conditions of your work. Then, new problems are added to these: marketing of your products; the prices determined from the cities; the questions concerning commercial politics on the national and international levels; in short, the interests of so many who, without considering the demands of the common good or the ever-growing basic needs of the farmers, have as their only goal profit at whatever cost.

Limits on the Right to Property

Many concentrate all their efforts on the accumulation of more and more goods and consider the right to property as something absolute, forgetting that it is "subordinated to the right to common use, to the fact that goods are meant for everyone."[81] In this regard they forget the warning of the Apostle James: "Laborers mowed your fields, and you cheated them – listen to the wages that you kept back, calling out; realize that the cries of the reapers have reached the ears of the Lord of hosts,"[82] since they behave as if they will never have to give an account of their stewardship.[83]

Rural Problems Demand Solidarity

The solution of so many rural problems demands the solidary collaboration of all the sectors of society. Modern farming is also connected with the cities, where they can slow down or, on the contrary, bring to perfection the economic and juridical mechanisms without which work in the fields, no matter how abundant the results, will continue to benefit mainly only a few.

Out of a sentiment of solidarity and even more, out of a duty of justice, public authorities and all those whose business or professional activity is directly or indirectly related to the land, must recognize their obligation to seek a solution to the conflicts which face the farming sector of your land today. The progressive growth of industry, trade and services should not weigh unduly on the agricultural sector. Successively, the increase in productivity obtained in agriculture, cattle raising and forestry should bring in just recompense and an improvement in the quality of life for all the workers and their families. The small independent producers should be able, without any kind of opposition, to count on the possibility of having free access to systems of commercialization and transformation that will not prejudice them. Lastly, we hope that timely measures will be introduced so that more farmers will have access to owning the land they till; without doubt, this will be a guarantee of progress and social stability.

The values that form the Paraguayan character – generous friendship, readiness to share, solidarity with the needy, love for the family and a sense of the transcendent – are deeply rooted in the rural life and work. This should lead all the inhabitants of this country to feel personally the problems and needs of the people of the farming sector.

Work as Collaboration in Redemption

God continues to trust in man; hence, sin and its consequences do not make void the Creator's command: "Subdue the earth and have dominion over it."[84] Through his life, Christ announces and accomplishes an authentic "Gospel of Work." Besides being a direct, although not the only, way of participating in the creative task of God the Father, physical work is called to be a form of collaboration with God the Son in the redemption of mankind. Indeed, your hardships, beloved farmers, your sweat, your anxieties, are by no means useless. They are the cross which you must take up daily: Christ wants you to help him carry the cross; you are to be another Simon of Cyrene as it were, "who was coming in from the country,"[85] and took on his shoulders the cross Christ was carrying.

However, do not think that helping Christ carry the cross through work simply means the resigned acceptance of the difficulties you encounter. You know from experience that the cultivation of the land is a continuous challenge, since you have to take into consideration and cleverly cope with a whole range of natural elements as well as overcome many obstacles at the same time. Likewise, it is not totally wrong to think that the solution, at least in part, of many problems that afflict you, also depend on you. You must live in solidarity among yourselves, because solidarity is a Christian virtue that flows from charity, a distinctive sign of Christ's disciples[86] and, consequently, a sign of being united with his Cross.[87]

Respond to God's Initiative

At the same time the horizons of an effective solidarity among yourselves are immense, as limitless as the demands of love. Indeed, the conscious and submissive collaboration with God through your work implies not only putting all your effort into cultivating your plantations and farms, but also contributing all your imagination, intelligence and effort to productive common endeavor. God wants to help you, but he is waiting for your determined correspondence with his initiative. If you do not give it, you will not be fully living as his children and, without noticing it, you will be giving in to idleness and conformity. Very often, the desire for others to find the final solutions hides the escape from daily and intelligent effort.

Seek God in Your Daily Lives

Seek God in your work, in the circumstances of daily life. Seek him from the moment you wake up – very often before the first rays of the sun appear – until you take your well-deserved rest, perhaps exhausted from work. Seek God in work well done, in order to offer him something worthy: the best of your efforts.

In the celebration of the Mass the priest offers the bread, "which earth has given and human hands have made," and the wine, "fruit of the vine and work of human hands." Together with that bread and wine, you can offer your entire day and your lives: work and rest, sleep and waking periods, sorrows and joys. All this, united to the sacrifice of Christ on the Cross, receives its deepest value, a co-redemptive value.

"My plans are not your plans, your ways are not my ways,"[88] God says through the mouth of the Prophet Isaiah. When the Christian vision of work is lost, man's plans are no longer according to God's plans; man's ways are no longer God's ways.

Spiritual Growth

However, the Prophet continues: "Let the wicked forsake his way, and the unrighteous man his thoughts; let him return to the Lord, that he may have mercy on him, and to our God, for he will abundantly pardon."[89]

The Lord is always waiting for you. God, "rich in mercy," is always ready to help us. However, in order that this divine compassion truly be a source of peace for our spirits, it is necessary to return "to the Lord;" man must abandon "his own way" and enter through "the ways" of God. The soul of every person, like "good ground" needs continuous attention for it to bear fruit.[90] It is necessary to sow the Word of God in it; it is necessary to water it frequently with the sacraments that infuse grace – especially Penance and the Eucharist – it is necessary to pull out the undergrowth of misdirected passions. You should cultivate your soul – and the souls of your children – even with greater love than you put in the cultivation of the land; it is your proudest boast and that which will give you more fruit. You can never be "*caigue*" – weak or lazy – with the things of God.

Laity's Witness to the World

Every Christian is called to contribute by his life and work to the growth of the kingdom of God on earth. In today's Gospel the kingdom of God is also compared to a mustard seed. In this parable we can also see a similarity with the growth of the Church, which, from its modest beginnings, has spread out to so many peoples, nations and countries. In this country of yours, this process which began almost five centuries ago, possessed very special characteristics like the fertility of your fields and forests.

Today it is up to you to carry on that work until that small seed[91] produces "big branches so that the birds of the air can shelter in its shade and build nests in them."[92] This is the whole Church's mission; in it the activity of the laity occupies an eminent place. It is you, beloved laity, who are to give a Christian meaning to every temporal activity: the countryside and the city, industry and commerce, politics, culture and the entire social life. That is your mission: "to impregnate the temporal order with the spirit of the gospel and bring it to perfection."[93]

The words of the Prophet, "I made him a witness to the peoples,"[94] can be applied to the lay person who strongly feels in his heart the need for the apostolate. You, the laity, should fulfil this beautiful task, first of all, by the consistency of your life – witness to God's presence among men – so that, in seeing "your good works, they may glorify your Father who is in heaven."[95]

31. Work Is a Means of Sanctification[96]

Collaboration with God, Gospel of Work, Meaning of Work, Solidarity, Work and Prayer.

[A homily on June 12, 1988 in Reggio Calabria, Italy, to workers and entrepreneurs.]

It is precisely in the name of Christ, who came on earth to unite man in the love of the common Father and to make all brethren, that labor problems are rightly entrusted to the solicitude of the Church; while not having the duty to devise purely technical solutions, she cannot be remote from, and indifferent to, all that relates to justice, respect for the human person, peace in families and in society. Neither can she remain distant from those who suffer, or are without work, or live in conditions unworthy of a human being.

The "way for the Church is, in fact, man."[97] Christ himself wished to be united with him in a certain way.[98] The Church, the Pope, and also your bishops have at heart the lot of men and women in their particular situations, especially those of workers.

In one way or another, you all know the social encyclicals; your representative referred to the most recent of them. The teaching contained therein has, as it were, two goals. The first is respect for the dignity of every man and woman; their right to full economic, human, and spiritual development must be recognized, and they must never be reduced to mere means or instruments to achieve other ends. The second is the value of work, "a fundamental dimension of human existence,"[99] "a key to the social question,"[100] and a privileged means of development.[101] These two goals are summed up in the affirmation of justice, lived and applied at every level.

Economic Problems Are Solved through Solidarity

In the light of these principles, I would like to take a clear yet calm and confident look, with you and before the Lord, at the real situation in this region of the South.

It is generally admitted that the South is not as developed as the North; that wealth is not equally distributed between the two areas; that there is not the same possibility to find proper work for proper pay; and that this causes emigration both within and outside the country with the consequences which we know.

Dear brothers and sisters, they are real problems; they are certainly complex, but not insoluble, if one has trust in God and in man. Once again I would like to emphasize that people are of greater value than things, that profit is not the only valid criterion when there is a question of creating or developing an enterprise or selecting the type of goods one would wish to produce.

Besides, there is a duty of solidarity, not only between the less developed regions themselves, but also, and especially, between these and the regions which have already achieved the goals of higher development. It is a solidarity which should be realized at every level; it should involve also those responsible for economics and politics as well as the workers themselves and their organizations.

Revitalization of the Moral Climate

Here we are already in the moral sphere, which is precisely the sphere in which human activities are carried out, in the first place, the activities which aim at development, and therefore economic activities connected in some way with human work.

Therefore here in Calabria, a profound revitalization of the moral climate seems to be necessary, a true "ecological" environment; outside of this it is impossible to work. Neither is it possible for men and women to live if they wish to maintain a standard in keeping with their dignity. Every form of abuse, dishonesty, unjust oppression, organized crime, in so far as they are fundamentally opposed to human dignity, should be rejected and, with the Lord's help, overcome.

Human Work Is Collaboration in God's Plan

The true meaning of work and of the worker's identity we find already in the first pages of Sacred Scripture, as I stressed in my encyclical *Laborem Exercens.* There God himself shows that he wishes to be represented as a worker. By his word he gives being to the world in six days, and on the seventh he rests.[102] Having "formed man out of the clay of the ground he placed him "in the garden of Eden, to cultivate and care for it," and gave the human couple a command which is the departure point of all human work: "Fill the earth and subdue it. Have dominion over all living things."[103]

In fulfilling this command, every person reflects the example of the Creator of the universe, so that human work appears in Scripture as a collaboration in God's creative plan.

Work Is a Means of Sanctification

If original sin has weighed on human work and subjected it to the hardship of fatigue, the tragedy of social imbalances, the risk of being reduced to mere goods for exchange, this has not in any way lessened or destroyed its value. Indeed, Jesus, the Son of God, in becoming man, in the redemption also of work, has conferred on it, as it were, a new title of glory. He himself wished to be a worker, a carpenter, thus inscribing daily work in God's same salvific design.

After Jesus, the disciples. For example, the Apostle Paul, who first brought the gospel message to Reggio, made himself the spokesman for this Gospel of Work. Not only did he himself work to provide himself with the necessities of life, and not to be a burden on anyone,[104] but he condemned the idle person even writing, "if anyone will not work, let him not eat."[105]

Besides, we all know that "prayer and work" was the motto of those Benedictine monks who laid the foundation of a civilized Europe in a period of barbaric destruction.

Thus, work has become a means of sanctification when it acts as a means of one's own human fulfillment and fully respects the dignity of others.

Solidarity for Development

This is what the Church has always taught. This is what I wish to repeat today during this meeting with you, workers and entrepreneurs of Calabria.

I have already alluded to solidarity. I now wish to add that in my two social encyclicals, *Laborem Exercens* and *Sollicitudo Rei Socialis,* I wished to highlight a dimension of solidarity which I think is of special importance for you, workers of Calabria and the South of Italy, in resolving your longstanding problems: development in solidarity.

"The development of peoples begins and is most appropriately accomplished in the dedication of each people to its own development, in collaboration with others."[106] Therefore, solidarity for development! However this alone is not enough. "Development demands above all a spirit of initiative on the part of the countries which need it. Each of them must act in accordance with its own responsibilities, not expecting everything from the more favored countries, and acting in collaboration with others in the same situation. Each must discover and use to the best advantage its own area of freedom."[107] Every region concerned must "identify their own priorities and clearly recognize their own needs, according to the particular conditions of their people, their geographical setting and their cultural traditions."[108]

---

32. *The Structure and Design of Work Must Promote the Development of the Worker as a Person*[109]

Collaboration with God, Culture of Work, Dignity of Work, Economic Laws and Profits, Fair Wage, Humanization/Dehumanization, Materialism and Consumerism, Meaning of Work, Unemployment.

[An address on May 21, 1989 in Grosseto, Italy, to workers, contractors and representatives of the world of work.]

Every meeting with the world of work, as you know, is exceedingly welcome to me, because it allows me to express how much I share the concern which the Church has for workers. However, the type of work connected with mining activity has special significance for me, since it brings me back to the years of my youth when I personally experienced the problems connected with such an industry. The latter challenges every human being to discover and exploit the stores of good things which the Creator and provident God has generously bestowed on us, his children. Also from this point of view my greeting to each one of you is particularly affectionate.

Salvation and Solidarity

Beloved workers of the factories of Scarino and of the new Solmine! If you ask me what are the profound reasons which compel the Church to become involved in a direct and sharing way in your world, I will answer that they are primarily two, which are intimately connected and complementary.

The first reason is that the Church has received from Christ the mission of guiding man to salvation, orientating his involvement in the multiple sectors in which his earthly existence expresses itself and unfolds. Of this existence the vast and differentiated field of work forms an essential part. Work, therefore, forms part of the design that God has for man, a design which he has shown us in Revelation. There is a Gospel of Work which it is the Church's duty to preach, to ensure that man comes to an ever better understanding of his vocation and, by embracing it, contributes in a constructive way to common progress.[110]

The second reason why the Church concerns herself with the world of work consists in the profound solidarity which she preaches for man and for everything that influences or determines his full realization. If the first reason is set, so to speak, on the vertical line of the salvific word of God to be communicated to mankind, the second stands on the horizontal line of the sharing of human beings of their many problems and labors. In the matter of human problems the Church has many years of experience behind her. She is able, therefore, to make an original contribution of her own in the search for solutions which would respect human dignity and be effective in promoting its authentic affirmation.

The Dignity of the Worker

For these two reasons the Church invites the worker to take note of the noble design God has on him and for him. It is important always to reflect on who it is who works, why he works, what end his labor should serve.

The worker – I mean every one of you – is not a factory mechanism, is not a labor instrument: he belongs to an order of greatness superior to all material reality, endowed, by his nature, with intelligence and freedom; in a word, he is a person. Every human person, without any discrimination, is made in the image and likeness of God the Creator. His dignity, therefore, surpasses the value of all earthly things.

The Worker as Co-Creator

But there is more: the worker is called by God to insert himself into the creative plan and to become, in a certain sense, creator himself. From this flows an immediate and important consequence, one on which I dwelt in my encyclical on human labor: whatever be the level at which he operates or the category to which he belongs, the worker in the exercise of his own activity should be able to become more human, and not be degraded and humiliated as a result of his work itself.[111]

The Standard of Justice in the Workplace

All the injustices that have been committed or that are being committed in the work area should be measured according to this fundamental criterion: the criterion of the value and the true good of the person. If this is disregarded, there is the danger that the very protests raised against the injustices may become the source of other and perhaps even greater injustices.

Structure Work to Support Human Dignity

In my own country, which, as you know, is confronting grave difficulties, someone recently stated that what we urgently need today is a serious engagement in a "work on work."

What does "work on work" mean? It means, above all, to work on the organization of work, that is, to fashion it and to arrange it in such a way that it may serve to promote the integral development of the person. The concrete applications are, as everyone can see, many and urgent: it is necessary, for example, to see to it that everyone be assured a just participation in the fruits of his own labor; that to each individual be granted a just share of responsibility in the management of the firm or of the factory; that every industrial activity be carried out with respect for the natural environment and resources. It is necessary, in particular, that the work, to which man and woman devote the best of their years and their forces, serve them as the normal means to procure not only the minimum of subsistence, but the means to live a truly human life as well. If, for example, one were forced to do more work only to arrive at a level of life that is hardly human, would he not already be a victim of an unjust situation?

Anyone therefore who has a job in a factory, as well as in a mine or in an office, should be able to obtain access precisely through this activity to a worthy and dignified life-style as regards housing, food, health, insurance, as well as culture, free time, and spiritual and religious self-improvement. This is the criterion to distinguish between work that is "worthy of man" and the various forms – even modern forms – of exploitation.

In the light of these principles, those who have no work are in an objectively unjust situation, and society with its institutions is bound to help them find an adequate solution, rather than forcing them to resign themselves to unemployment, as through it were an inevitable phenomenon. In the unemployed it is society itself which is hurt, because it is being deprived of the valuable contribution of people who can and should be working.

The Moral and Religious Dimension Is Indispensible

"Work on work" means, in short, an effective commitment in the service of the worker. According to God's plan, work is the path on which man is to pursue the full realization of his own humanity. In work, therefore, not only the economic dimension should be considered; the cultural, spiritual and religious dimension should also be kept in mind and turned to account, so that the worker can express in his work not only his own physical or intellectual capacities, but also his own conscience, moral principles and faith.

In this regard I should reaffirm that man, when deprived of the moral and religious dimension, is emptied of his most genuine greatness. A society which would tend to confine development to within the borders of having, aiming exclusively at material well-being at the expense of a growth in being, would not resolve the basic problems of man, who, instead of "ruling" a patrimony of goods, however great it may be, would end up becoming a prisoner, with unsatisfying consequences.

Consumerism and Solidarity

As I wrote in the encyclical *Sollicitudo Rei Socialis*, "the evil does not consist in having as such, but rather in possessing in a way that fails to respect the quality and the ordered hierarchy of the goods one has. Quality and hierarchy arise from the subordination of goods and from their availability to the being of man and to his true vocation."[112]

It is clear how, in this kind of perspective, there is no room for egoism, whether individual or collective. From this outlook flows, by obvious consequence, the duty of solidarity not only with respect to those who work at the same work bench, but also towards every member of the human race.

The Necessity of Faith

Dear brothers and sisters! Faith in Christ the Redeemer, accepted and lived in its full authenticity, rebuilds in everyone the good of the freedom and of the most genuine dignity. Always remember that this faith is an indispensable factor in re-establishing internal equilibrium for individual, family, society, and nature.

Work and the Environment

I know that your firms, besides taking into account criteria of technological modernization, have concerned themselves with the ecological aspects. I hope and pray that these plants, thanks to the renewed and constant efforts of management, may become an industrial model, in which the relationship between man and environment, between worker and manager may be ever more human, in the sense of authentic development.

---

33. People Are More Important than Economic Figures[113]

Dignity of Work, Human Rights/Dignity, Justice, Solidarity, Unemployment.

[An address on October 28, 1989 in Taranto, Italy, to Italian steel workers, managers and government officers.]

I thank the representatives of the Italian Government, the management of this company, and the workers, for the kind words they addressed to me. I listened attentively to the reference they made to the difficulties of the current situation and your concerns for the future. I am here to tell you that I share intimately in your concerns.

Concern of the Church for Justice and Humanity

I have followed daily the developments of recent weeks and, although I do not want to discuss the merits of the labor questions which brought about the recent controversy, I want to express my satisfaction for the positive solution which, it seems, has finally been reached. Unfortunately, the problems involving the steel industry are especially complex and justify your fears, considering the effects that every job cutback has on your families and the prospects of the young people who hope to take their place in the cycle of production.

The Church cannot remain indifferent in the face of this situation which concerns so many of her children placing a heavy mortgage on their present and future. Economic, technological and political factors certainly figure in the social question; however, it has primarily directly human repercussions, which cannot be subject to the others in the search for an adequate solution. The Pope is here to recall this for all those who must make their contribution to the adoption of proper measures to confront the crisis.

This same intention impelled my predecessor, Pope Paul VI, to come to you, twenty years ago, when this steel mill was still growing. At Christmas of 1968, among these blast furnaces, he emphasized forcefully once again the necessity of combining technological progress and the search for justice, in the context of the message of "Jesus, the worker-prophet, humanity's teacher and friend, the Savior of the world."[114] Perhaps some of you were present then and can help us to recall that event which made Taranto the podium from which he issued, "like a trumpet blast resounding in the world," a renewed appeal to the unsuppressible ethical aspect of the social problem.

Develop the Whole Person

Dear friends, in the footprints of my great predecessor, I have come to meet you today, bearing the same message from Christ and the Church.

This plant in which we are gathered, and the workshops in which you labor and spend a great deal of your day, are an eloquent sign of man's ability to transform raw materials to adapt them to his own needs. This mill, which currently employs sixty thousand people, is beginning the celebration of the thirtieth anniversary of the laying of the foundation stone. It is a milestone which, while it marks undeniable success, also evokes timely considerations which cannot be put off; not only about operational techniques and market strategies (already underway with the creation of the ILVA Corporation) but also, and above all, about the concept of development by which they were inspired in the past.

Nevertheless, promoting the productive capacity of an industrial complex is not everything; neither is it the most important. The value and immensity of a production plant, even one as impressive as yours, must not be measured solely on the criteria of technological progress or productivity and economic and financial profit, but also, and above all, on the criteria of its service to mankind, and how it corresponds to what the true dignity of the worker, as God's image, claims and demands.

Now, then, from this point of view, what is the current situation of ILVA of Taranto? There is, first of all, the difficult problem of employment, which has been aggravated by the cutback in the productive capacity of the plant in the context of the more general crisis in steel production. There are the phenomena connected with early retirement and recourse to unemployment compensation, the latter a partial and temporary remedy for the lack of work or slow periods. I am certainly not unaware of the complex components of the crisis in the steel industry, which is a problem of international dimensions. However, I cannot fail to point out the serious consequences of this situation for the workers themselves and their families who receive their necessary sustenance from their work.

I want all those who experience such situations – men and women, and particularly the young people who cannot find work in line with their preparation – to know that I am near to each of the jobless and those who are laid off, and that I bring them the Church's understanding and solidarity.

Dignity of the Human Person and of Human Work

When we have to rethink a situation such as this one, dear friends, there are two basic moral criteria which must be taken into consideration.

The first is the dignity of the human person, created in God's image: "man, in fact, is the author, center, and end of all socio-economic life."[115]

The second is the dignity of work itself, which is part of the vocation of man, called to be fulfilled and perfected as a person.[116] Man has been given no other means by which to develop his talents and characteristics, than by earning his livelihood.

Now, all this means that work must be considered not only as a potential source of economic goods, but also as an occasion for spiritual enrichment in a process of growth towards the achievement of one's self fulfillment.

For workers this implies the moral obligation to work to the best of one's abilities, conscious not only of one's own rights, but of one's duties as well. For those who have the power to decide – management, economists, politicians – this means that the value of the worker and the dignity of work must prevail in decisions, even, and above all, in times of crisis. It is people, not numbers, that count.

Interdependence and Solidarity

It is true that decisions about the goals and dimensions of industrial complexes and their operations today must be made in the context of an economic planning that goes well beyond the limits of a single city, or even of an entire country. This is the effect of the ever-increasing interdependence of economic, commercial and financial relationships in the whole world, and especially in Europe.

However, such an interdependence has a very valuable moral result, that of solidarity, which I defined in the encyclical *Sollicitudo Rei Socialis* as "the firm and persevering determination to be engaged in the common good, for the well-being of each and every person."[117] This is, in reality, the way to remedy the effects of cutbacks. Whatever cannot be maintained because of the overall balance must, however, be adequately compensated in other ways, and, hopefully, in other industrial fields, in order to serve the good of all, especially the weakest, such as the jobless, those who are laid off, and those who are looking for their first job.

The new circumstances require everyone to make an effort for renewed analysis and creativity, so that the men and women of Taranto may be given new possibilities for work, possibly more suitable to the environmental situation in which they live: the so-called "service" economy, but also a renewed agriculture and all that can derive from the riches of the sea.

Constructive Dialogue

Dear friends, I conclude with a wish for peace and justice, rooted in good will and constructive dialogue, enlightened by the Church's social doctrine and the people of the south's tradition of balance and industriousness.

Furthermore, this meal will be for me and for you a living symbol of that other meal, the Eucharist, in which Christ, giving himself to us under the form of bread, makes all of us one in him. May he be ever in your midst, sustaining your work, nourishing your hopes for a better life, and strengthening your solidarity.

---

34. Business Needs a New Professionalism, Rich in Human and Cultural Values[118]

Dialogue and Cooperation, Economic Laws and Profits, Human Development/Progress, Materialism and Consumerism, Professional Training/Responsibility, Selfishness, Work and the Worker.

[An address on September 22, 1990 in Ferrara, Italy, to business leaders and members of labor unions.]

Your kind presence offers me the chance to express my pleasure and appreciation at what you have done and plan to do to help the entire community. At the same time, this meeting leads me to reflect with you on the importance and delicacy of commercial activity in our times when "competition" tends to prevail over "cooperation," to the detriment of the real common good.

Need for a New Professionalism

Business today needs a broad and updated professionalism; in other words, a professionalism which is above all "qualified." As the experts say, we must move away from a "job-centered professionalism" towards a "process-centered professionalism." That presupposes not only a serious competence in the area of one's own specific tasks, but a cultural sensitivity as well, which allows one to take stock quickly of technological progress and to gear up for it in a quick and effective way. In short, what is needed is professionalism with a wealth of operational qualities, but also rich in the human, social, cultural and ethical values which make work gratifying as well as productive.

Furthermore, professionalism in business must always be inspired by a "personalist" vision which has at heart the "human factor," above all and before all else. Estimates and analyses are certainly necessary, along with statistical checks and technical certification; the "philosophy of total quality" is also important for a continuing improvement of the product. But a business must be especially committed to respect the primacy of the human being over work and work itself over technology, profit and capital. "To humanize" companies means, therefore, to place the human person in a privileged position by eliminating special interests, which often enough harm the community; it means to draft solutions to problems in the light of basic ethical values which remain perennially valid. This presupposes the attempts by business leaders and employees to engage in a serene and constructive dialogue with the goal of foreseeing and resolving conflicts and disagreements which ultimately harm the well-being of all.

In this light Pope Paul VI in the apostolic Letter *Octogesima Adveniens*, wrote: "Economic activity which is necessary can be a source of fellowship and a sign of Providence if it is placed at the service of the human person; it is an opportunity for concrete exchanges among people, for recognition of rights, for the delivery of services, for affirming dignity through work."[119]

Openness to the Transcendent

Finally, business professionalism must not exclude an openness to the "transcendent." That is, it must take into account the destiny beyond this world of the human person, created in God's image and redeemed by Christ. As that expert in human life, St. Augustine, stated earlier, God made us for Himself and our hearts are restless and dissatisfied until they rest in Him! A professionalism bound only to earthly interests and to the achievement of the highest material well-being risks making the person a slave to selfishness within a tiresome competitive struggle; on the other hand, attention paid to the eternal dimension of human destiny fosters mutual esteem, prompts trust and understanding, inspires works of charity and fraternal aid, especially toward the weakest and those who have less.

Begin with the Least

In the document the *Church and the Country's Future Prospects* published in 1981, the Bishop's Conference rightly urged the Christian community to "begin again starting with the least, who are the dramatic symbol of the current crisis," and with them to "discover the values of the common good: tolerance, solidarity, social justice, shared responsibility."

It is an exhortation which has value for us too, as it does for every person of good will.

May the Lord help you not to give in to the temptation to be selfish, but to find inspiration in your work in a higher motivation based on the deepest aspirations of the human being. You will thus contribute in an effective manner to the human person's integral development.

Deepen your Christian faith and be always more convinced that only by loving and following the Gospel can the authentic progress of humanity be fostered.

35. Work Is the Apostolate of the Worker[120]

Christian Witness/Mission, Service.

[An address on November 26, 1990 in Rome, to staff of Italian restaurants and international hotels.]

I express my deep appreciation for the work you do; it has become so necessary especially in our day, marked as it is by great human mobility.

Work Is Service

In your hotels and restaurants, you welcome on a daily basis people who are travelling for a variety of reasons. In this way you come in contact with people of every race and social class and in a certain sense you come to know better the human mystery in its many expressions, with its concerns and troubles, its hopes and joys.

How many come to your establishments hoping to find a peaceful and respectful welcome characterized by understanding and friendship. That demands on your part patience and a willingness to serve, perceptiveness and prudence. May these be the traits which distinguish your profession. Try to meet the expectations of your guests by seeing each of them as your brother or sister. Kindness and politeness, professional seriousness and readiness to be of service, competence and generosity are gifts which make a positive impression and are not easily forgotten.

Apostolate in Concrete Acts

Make your work an authentic service to people and see it as your apostolate.

The Gospel reminds us that on the last day we will be judged by the love we show in concrete acts.[121]

---

36. Social Developments Require a New Attention to the Culture of Work[122]

Culture of Work, Dialogue and Cooperation, Human Development/ Progress, Human Rights/Dignity, Meaning of Work, Selfishness, Service, Solidarity, Spirituality.

[An address on September 8, 1991 in Venice, Italy, to representatives from politics, culture, industry, and work.]

You are rightly worried about promoting an ever more modern economic and social development, one which will not deaden the cultural and spiritual aspects of the human person, and which will respect nature and the environmental balance.

In truth, businesses here have continued to be involved locally and have not uprooted workers from their families and their parishes. This kind of management policy, which we could say is family-oriented, has guarded against alienation and has permitted the formation of "working communities" in which, more than elsewhere, there are present some of the typical virtues mentioned in the encyclical *Centesimus Annus*: "diligence, industriousness, prudence in undertaking reasonable risks, reliability and fidelity in interpersonal relationships, as well as courage in carrying out decisions which are difficult and painful but necessary, both for the overall working of a business and in meeting possible setbacks."[123]

All this is probably due as well to the ancient tradition of the Veneto, which is marked by love of sacrifice, by the industriousness of emigrants compelled to work in foreign lands to support their families, by the solidarity which links your residents around their parish churches. In the shadow of the church belltower people have learned to work together, sharing every difficulty and trial. I am thinking of labor cooperatives, for the most part parochial in character, whose regulations made precise moral demands on their members. I am thinking of the workers' first "white leagues," formed to defend their rights, which were forerunners of contemporary social-assistance organizations.

Danger of Regression

In recent decades, however, even the Veneto has changed profoundly. Scholars call attention to the spread of significant changes in your region, not only in people's actual behavior, but in their decision-making criteria as well: the lessening of religious practice, the existence of cultural models and life-styles typical of the secularized areas of the West and the lack of traditional forms of solidarity and altruism provide so much evidence of this process. And you ask yourselves with justified apprehension whether the lessening in the Christian inspiration of development will not in time be the cause of social and even economic regression for your land as well. The weakening of this centuries-old patrimony, which was able to join faith with daily life, cannot leave anyone indifferent who is concerned about the welfare of people in this area.

I know how attentive you are in seeking in general to resist the compelling temptation of putting profit above every other value, and I know that you are doing your best not to return to exhausting work schedules and undue extensions of the work period over the weekend and holidays, in order to keep abreast of competition.

Small and medium-sized businesses predominate in your territory, many of which originated in the transformation of the worker into an entrepreneur, as Pope Leo XIII hoped 100 years ago in *Rerum Novarum*. However, it is a question of a process which, on the one hand, exalts the primacy of the intellect and the will, and, on the other, can lead to an aggravation of motives and individualistic standards, giving priority to rapid development over all other aspirations. One can then run the risk of putting in second place respect for those values – e.g., rest, primacy of family and religious life, the sanctification of Sunday – to which business has until now rightly been sensitive and attentive.

Often the tensions and disturbances of society have repercussions on people's work, because through his work the individual establishes relationships and patterns of life.

In the 20th century we have witnessed a colossal attempt to organize work and human society apart from God and any relationship to the world of transcendent values. As a consequence, this has caused the human person to be uprooted from his local culture and has then led to the creation of artificial needs and models of life.

Spiritual Needs Should Be Acknowledged

Today an appeal is again being made to what in the past was denied, or at least neglected. Thus, "immaterial" needs demand to be taken into account, e.g., respect for a person's religious aspirations, appreciation for local cultures, promotion of tranquil and satisfying interpersonal relationships: in a word, a return to making room for the needs of the soul. The words of Christ are enlightening in regard to the spiritual anxiety of contemporary man: "Do not seek what you are to eat and what you are to drink, and do not worry anymore. All the nations of the world seek for these things, and your Father knows that you need them. Instead, seek his kingdom, and these other things will be given you besides."[124]

In the encyclical *Centesimus Annus* I called attention to how the spiritual void caused by atheism was one of the principal causes of the failure of the Marxist economic system.[125] Values motivate work, and by establishing a firm link between generations, they ensure the development of a people's civilization. However, if they are not brought back to the profound ethical roots of all human beings, they are spoiled and disappear.

The human person, searching for his own global orientation, needs decisive answers about the meaning of life. When the most interior of spiritual motivations are obscured, man is reduced to a productive machine, culture and ethnicity become "useless differences" and politics is "maximized," being changed into a type of "secular religion."[126]

Culture of Work

It is therefore necessary to rediscover a "culture of work" which is not simply dictated by productive demand, but by the global needs of the person and civil society.

To accomplish this, it is indispensable that businesses become authentic "working communities,"[127] in which initiative, entrepreneurship and collaboration find room and development. For this reason it is necessary to protect personal rights, a topic I covered extensively in *Centesimus Annus*.[128] It is necessary to increase various forms of participation and dialogue and to acknowledge the proper roles of every person, restoring them to a reasonable complementarity. This doubtlessly is easier to do in small and medium-sized businesses than in larger ones, for the latter often run the risk of becoming anonymous and alienating.

A "culture of work" also means service to, and not manipulation of, consumers. The working community of a business will actually do this if it can be involved harmoniously in civil society, which is the goal of service, and if it can respond to people's real needs, without creating illusory ones by manipulating certain improper forms of advertising.

A "culture of work," finally, means that management and workers are able to assume a common ethical perspective, which does not mean simply codifying some general rules of the game, but obeying the truth of the human person, who is the image of God. Thus, you are called to give vitality to the religious soul of the Veneto, which in the past guaranteed the quality of life and today deserves to be strengthened and developed.

Responsibility and Solidarity

Dear brothers and sisters, the challenge for Venice today is to make an exemplary contribution to this "culture of work." You will be able to do so if an attitude of responsibility and solidarity always prevails in every aspect of your political and economic planning.

For this reason, continue to be welcoming, open your structures to immigrants, and learn how to develop those social virtues without which you will fall inexorably into selfish individualism, alienation and exploitation. Christians of Venice, you have the opportunity of restoring to your brothers and sisters who are different in race, culture or religion and come among you in search of work, everything which you received from your ancestors who were once emigrants, and you can witness to the Gospel of openness and love. Jesus promises a reward to anyone who welcomes a stranger.[129] Through this integration you will build that civilization of Gospel love, which in some way already prefigures in this world the future kingdom of God.

37. Be Guided By Traditional Values[130]

Dialogue and Cooperation, Dignity of Work, Economic Laws and Profits, Human Development/Progress, Human Rights/ Dignity, Materialism, Meaning of Work, Saint Joseph, Solidarity, Technology, Unemployment, Work and Family

[An address on May 1, 1992 in Pordenone, Italy, to workers and managers of the Zanussi industrial complex.]

You are aware that technological progress, no matter how advanced and modern it is, must in no case cancel out those things which are properly human; it must rather make people ever more responsibly involved in the productive system and the management of society itself. Duly applied to industry in its various sectors, new technology will help make the human contribution less costly in terms of physical energy and will make a greater contribution to the spiritual.

Through the contribution of each person, the factory can thus take on *the characteristics of a family* in which management and labor live together in harmony, committed to generous cooperation aimed at making work less difficult and improving mutual relations. In this regard, may we always have before us the *model of the home in Nazareth* where serenity and simplicity existed along with the difficult, daily strain of work.

Working Conditions Worthy of the Human Person

It is precisely to that home that the Church invites us to look today on the feast of St. Joseph the Worker. On the day on which the world celebrates the feast of the worker, the faithful are offered the example of a worker, the carpenter, Joseph of Nazareth, to whose loving care the heavenly Father chose to entrust his only Son and the virgin Mother of the Redeemer. This is to remind us that "individual and collective activity, that monumental effort of man through the centuries to improve the circumstances of the world corresponds to God's plan."[131]

The celebration of the first of May reminds us of the long journey made by workers to guarantee for themselves and society just living conditions worthy of the human person, in a slow but steady progress towards the recognition of their own rights and responsibilities. Important accomplishments have been achieved in organizing work and in overcoming conflict among the sectors of society involved. But much remains to be done in order to overcome some corporate interests, some remaining ideological barriers and the obstacles which still prevent the realization of true communities of work marked by mutual respect and sharing.

Work can never be considered as a mere commodity nor can the working person be reduced to a simple cog in the production machine, no matter how progressive and efficient it may be. Even though it is obvious that work is the production of goods and services, and it is understandable that it naturally aims at making a legitimate profit, that must never be allowed to harm human rights. Neither the law of profit, the desire for power and domination, nor the search for purely material progress must be the decisive criteria for determining the direction of productive activity; rather, it must always be the person, his dignity and aspirations and attention to all his true demands, especially his spiritual needs.

Today, therefore, the feast of workers, we are celebrating first and foremost the feast of man in his many productive capacities and deepest desires. We are celebrating the feast of the working person who by his or her work enriches humanity and can broaden the areas for cooperation in solidarity between individuals and peoples.

You have before you, dear brothers and sisters, the noteworthy results obtained in your region through the great effort made by the whole family of work. Your experience has taught you how essential is cooperation among all the forces involved in order to build a society marked by true solidarity, acceptance and respect for every working person.

Unemployment

As I rejoice with you for such encouraging success, I urge you to exercise patient tenacity in facing the problems which cause you greater concern at this time. First of all there is the crisis of youth unemployment. You must act so that these young people gain access to the world of work. After many years of study or professional preparation, they rightly long to be able to make themselves useful to the community and want to provide a better future for themselves. The problem of lack of work, however, does not affect young people alone. Other groups of people are looking for work: we can think especially of the immigrants from developing countries who, in addition to work, need housing and assistance, and the disabled, who want to find a dignified way of finding their place in the field of production and service.

In our society, which is rapidly approaching the year 2000, new problems and unusual social challenges are facing us. There is urgent need of re-emphasizing certain traditional values without which the community of mankind would be notably impoverished and end up becoming closed up, even without desiring to, in a sterile, selfish concept of life. For example, how could we not realize that it is indispensable to reconsider some of the difficulties which the family faces today? How could we fail to emphasize among these the grave problem of the low birth rate which is causing, along with a serious decline in population, an aging population?

Work and the family are two things that are closely related: in both of them the person is called to work with God to fulfill his plan of love. We must never let ourselves be won over by a view of life dominated by purely earthly concerns which aims at pursuing merely material goods. Rather, believers must be open to the Gospel perspective that enlightens and gives meaning to every personal and social choice.

The Church is With You in Your Efforts

Dearly beloved, feel the presence of *the Church* at your side in your daily work. She is with you, experiences your concerns and encourages you in Christ's name never to give up hope. With trust in God's providence, create ever greater room for solidarity, particularly on behalf of the weak and the poor. May your financial investments and the plans which you are fulfilling in regard to the world of the East be a concrete sign of that solidarity. At this time, when the frontiers of Europe are opening up, it is necessary to do everything to promote a professional ethic that respects human rights and is capable of bringing about fraternal understanding and cooperation among peoples.

The Church follows with favor your efforts in this regard, which certainly are not easy; she shares in your plans, understands your problems, and appreciates your commitment. She wants to be at your service. She loves you, dear friends of the world of work. She wants to share your work, your effort, your insecurity, your ardent desire for joy and fraternity. An expert in humanity, she knows the heart of man and asks you to place at the center of your every project the supreme law of love, expressing it in concrete acts of distributive justice and generous sharing.

How could we forget that in your past people of thought and action have made their contribution, following the Church's social doctrine, to creating that deep union between the productive and social forces which characterizes your people? I urge you not to abandon the Christian roots which enabled your ancestors to give the world a sign of the hard work and enterprise of a proud and faithful people.

38. *People in Business Must Work Together to Build Hope*[132]

Community of Persons, Economic Laws and Profits, Entrepreneurship, Human Rights/Dignity, Justice, Meaning of Work, Solidarity, Universal Destination of Goods

[An address on May 23, 1992 in Nola, Italy, to business and labour representatives from the Diocese of Nola.]

What, then is work in the light of faith in Christ, the "truth" about man? The meaning and dignity of human work are to be sought primarily in the subject who performs it: the human person, created in the image of God, redeemed by Christ and called to subdue the earth as the coworker of the Creator. Thus work attains its true dignity as man's involvement in God's plan. From this principle, which is to be proclaimed with renewed energy today, some precise ethical demands flow, such as the illicitness of reducing labour to a commodity and the right of every person to a job and a just wage.

Idolatry of the Market

After the historical fall of communism, our days have seen the risk developing of yielding to a type of idolatry of the market[133] which, if it prevails at the national and international level, could have severe negative consequences for the poorest of people.

There is an urgent need to reaffirm the demands of justice which no rules of the market can infringe upon. The right to private property must be ordered to the principle of the universal destination of goods in a context of social freedom, becoming increasingly not only the guarantee of private autonomy but also an instrument of solidarity.[134]

In such a context, one can also understand the importance of business ventures which, if they are begun and developed in conformity with ethical demands, are not only the source of wealth and work, but are also factors of authentic social and cultural advancement.

Similarly the value of the activity of labour unions is also to be reaffirmed, on condition that they fulfill their task of representing workers and defending their rights of justice, without indulging in corporate shut-downs, without yielding to the temptation of corruption and abuse of power, without resorting to inappropriate methods which do not respect the common good.

A Community of Persons

Finally, in the organization of labour it is necessary to stress the demand that businesses become a "community" of persons[135] in which the employees are not only materially involved, but feel that in some way they personally participate in the production process and are actively involved in the service rendered to society.

Responsibility and solidarity: these are two indispensable conditions which together describe labour relations in the process of humanization: responsibility in fulfilling one's own contractual and occupational obligations: solidarity in building a development model which increasingly respects human dignity and the demands of the common good.

Thus at all levels and in all roles it is a question of the primacy of the human person, the primacy of ethics, the primacy of love.

Build Hope

Is this not, dear brothers and sisters, a great challenge for you, for each of you? Yes, together you are called to build hope. Build it first and foremost, you, dear young people. In the face of the difficulties of your environment and the uncertainty that weighs on your future, do not give in to discouragement; resist the allurements of consumption which present an easy life based on having. Be resilient people who do not shun hard work and sacrifice. You have enormous potential: your enthusiasm, your initiative, your commitment. Put the resources of your youth at the disposal of good.

You, businessmen, economic planners, those in charge of public services, have a strong, clear sense of your vocation. You are called to serve the good of all, using your own resources to seek, in addition to legitimate profit, the growth of your community of work in solidarity. Be careful to contribute to the joy and realization of all those who, even more than being your "employees", are your brothers and sisters.

I address you, the workers. Through your hard work, your attachment to the family and your work, the firmness of your ethical and spiritual principles, you can contribute in great measure to the authentic progress of this area. Be aware of this and carry out your mission with consistency.

To all those who hold public office and are responsible for the right ordering of society as a whole, I would renew the invitation to work in all circumstances for the true good of their brothers and sisters.

It is necessary to help raise politics to the level of its mission. In our day of rapid social change there is this urgent need which concerns "political" men and women first and foremost, but also demands the involvement of everyone, especially of all those who appeal to the Gospel ideals.

In the face of the immense work to be done and the gravity of the problems to be confronted, we may have misgivings and feel discouraged. Dearly beloved, do not be afraid of the difficulties which you may meet on your path. Alongside our uncertain steps there are always the footprints of the risen Lord who walks with us. Christ, only Christ, is the unshakable foundation of our hope!

Notes

1 The translation was taken from *L'Osservatore Romano*, January 19, 1981, pp. 17-18.

2 The translation was taken from *L'Osservatore Romano*, February 22, 1982, pp. 13, 14.

3 *Laborem Exercens*, n. 26.

4 Mt 28:20.

5 The translation was taken from *Origins*, November 18, 1982, vol. 12: no. 23, pp. 374-376.

6 *Gaudium et Spes*, n. 42.

7 1 Cor 15:58.

8 Gen. 1:28.

9 *Laborem Exercens*, n. 6.

10 *Laborem Exercens*, n. 20.

11 *Laborem Exercens*, n. 12.

12 *Laborem Exercens*, n. 23.

13 The translation was taken from *L'Osservatore Romano*, April 9, 1984, pp. 3-4.

14 Gen 1:28.

15 2 Tim 1:8-9.

16 Gen 1:28.

17 The translation was taken from *L'Osservatore Romano*, April 22, 1985, pp. 6-7.

18 Mt 13:55.
19 2 Thess 3.8.
20 2 Thess 3.10.
21 2 Thess 3.12.
22 *Puebla*, n. 28.
23 Address during the *ad limina* visit, October 4, 1984.
24 *Reconciliatio et Paenitentia*, n. 16.
25 *Laborem Exercens*, n. 18.
26 *Laborem Exercens*, n. 19.
27 *Laborem Exercens*, n. 19.
28 *Puebla*, n. 1.246.
29 The translation was taken from *L'Osservatore Romano*, August 12, 1985, p. 9-10.
30 *Laborem Exercens*, n. 6.
31 *Octogesima Adveniens*, n. 48.
32 *Laborem Exercens*, nn. 11-15.
33 *Pacem in Terris*, n. 267.
34 The translation was taken from *L'Osservatore Romano*, June 2, 1986, pp. 9, 15.
35 *Laborem Exercens*, n. 5.
36 *Laborem Exercens*, n. 5.
37 *Laborem Exercens*, n. 4
38 *Laborem Exercens*, n. 6.
39 Instruction on Christian Freedom and Liberation, n. 73.
40 *Laborem Exercens*, nn. 14-15.
41 Discourse to the Ecclesial Conference of Loreto, n. 8.
42 The translation was taken from *The Pope Speaks*, Summer 1987, pp. 121-125.
43 Jn 15:12.
44 *Redemptor Hominis*, n. 8.
45 *Redemptor Hominis*, n. 10.
46 Gal 3:28.
47 The translation was taken from *L'Osservatore Romano*, January 12, 1987, p. 3.
48 *Gaudium et Spes*, n. 1.
49 Acts 6:5.
50 *Laborem Exercens*, n. 1.
51 *Laborem Exercens*, n. 1.
52 *Laborem Exercens*, n. 6.

53 *Gaudium et Spes*, n. 35.
54 *Gaudium et Spes*, n. 67.
55 *Laborem Exercens*, n. 10.
56 Gen 2:15.
57 The translation was taken from *L'Osservatore Romano*, May 2, 1988, pp. 7-8.
58 *Laborem Exercens*, n. 4.
59 *Sollicitudo Rei Socialis*, n. 38.
60 *Sollicitudo Rei Socialis*, nn. 38,39, *passim*.
61 *Sollicitudo Rei Socialis*, n. 38.
62 *Sollicitudo Rei Socialis*, n. 37.
63 *Sollicitudo Rei Socialis*, n. 15.
64 *Sollicitudo Rei Socialis*, n. 42.
65 *Sollicitudo Rei Socialis*, n. 24.
66 *Sollicitudo Rei Socialis*, n. 28.
67 *Sollicitudo Rei Socialis*, n. 34.
68 The translation was taken from *L'Osservatore Romano*, June 27, 1988, pp. 12-13.
69 Gen 1:28.
70 Gen 2:15.
71 Gen 1:29.
72 Gen 2:9.
73 *Laborem Exercens*, n. 25.
74 Mk 4:26-29.
75 Mt 6:25-34.
76 Mt 13:24-30.
77 Lk 16:1-12.
78 Jn 15:1.
79 Mt 13:24-25.
80 Gen 3:17-20.
81 *Laborem Exercens*, n. 14.
82 Jas 5:4.
83 Lk 16:2.
84 Gen 1:28.
85 Mk 15:21.
86 Jn 13:35.
87 *Sollicitudo Rei Socialis*, n. 40.
88 Is 55:8.
89 Is 55.

90 Mt 13:8.
91 Mk 4:31.
92 Mk 4:32.
93 *Apostolicam Actuositatem*, n. 5.
94 Is 55:4.
95 Mt 5:16.
96 The translation was taken from *L'Osservatore Romano*, August 29, 1988, pp. 3-4.
97 *Redemptor Hominis*, n. 14.
98 *Gaudium et Spes*, n. 22.
99 *Laborem Exercens*, n. 40.
100 *Laborem Exercens*, nn. 3.
101 *Sollicitudo Rei Socialis*, n. 30.
102 Gen 1:31ff.
103 Gen 1:28.
104 Acts 20:34; 18:3; 1 Thes 2:9; 2 Thes 3:7f.
105 2 Thes 3:10.
106 *Sollicitudo Rei Socialis*, n. 44.
107 *Sollicitudo Rei Socialis*, n. 44.
108 *Sollicitudo Rei Socialis*, n. 44.
109 The translation was taken from *L'Osservatore Romano*, July 3, 1989, p. 7.
110 *Laborem Exercens*, n. 26.
111 *Laborem Exercens*, n. 9.
112 *Sollicitudo Rei Socialis*, n. 28.
113 The translation was taken from *L'Osservatore Romano*, November 27, 1989, p. 6.
114 *Insegnamenti*, p. 695.
115 *Gaudium et Spes*, n. 63.
116 *Laborem Exercens*, n. 4.
117 *Sollicitudo Rei Socialis, n. 38.*
118 The translation was taken from *L'Osservatore Romano*, October, 8, 1990, p. 4.
119 *Octegesima Adveniens*, n. 46.
120 The translation was taken from *L'Osservatore Romano*, December 3, 1990, p. 2.
121 Mt 25:36ff.
122 The translation was taken from *L'Osservatore Romano*, September 23, 1991, p. 3.
123 *Centesimus Annus*, n. 32.

124 Lk 12:29-31.
125 *Centesimus Annus*, nn. 24-25.
126 *Centesimus Annus*, n. 25.
127 *Centesimus Annus*, n. 32.
128 *Centesimus Annus*, nn. 6-9.
129 Mt 25:35.
130 This translation was taken from *L'Osservatore Romano*, May 6, 1992, p. 5.
131 *Gaudium et Spes*, n. 34
132 This translation was taken from *L'Osservatore Romano*, June 3, 1992, p. 6.
133 *cf. Centesimus Annus*, n. 40
134 *cf. Centesimus Annus*, n. 30
135 cf. *Centesimus Annus*, n. 35

Chapter 3: Addresses to Workers

39. *Work Is a Service and a Way of Putting Christianity into Practice*[1]

Christian Witness/Mission, Service.

[An address on June 16, 1980 in Rome, to members of the Italian Union of Hairdressers for the Cult of their Holy Patron Saint Martin de Porres.]

In the title of your Association, I read an addition that is also significant: "for the cult of their Holy Patron"; and I know that, in fact, you promote every year a worthy celebration in honor of St. Martin de Porres in the church of the Dominican Fathers in Milan.

Profession as Service

I wish, therefore, not only to thank you for your presence, but to express to you my satisfaction at the attachment you show in this way to the Christian faith, and, I would like to say, to faithfulness to the faith, at a time in which the dangers and temptations of belief have become, unfortunately, more serious. This importance that the religious element takes on within your Association deserves, in fact, praise and encouragement on the part of the Holy Church: in addition to guarding and protecting the legitimate interests of the profession, you have at heart the Christian formation of all its members, in order that the influence of faith may be felt, positive and exemplary, also in life. The very choice of a humble and great figure, such as that of St. Martin, who blossomed in the New World as a flower fragrant with virtue, reminds you and at the same time recommends you always to behave in consistent and shining faithfulness to Christian values. It reminds you, in particular, that your profession is essentially a service: just as your heavenly Patron, in the wide choice of his services (he was, according to the customs of his time, barber, nurse, doctor and chemist), always kept in mind "his neighbor" and loved him so much, according to the matchless lesson of the parable of the Good Samaritan,[2] so you, too, in the daily relations you have with brothers, must try to serve them with simplicity, kindly manners and, above all, with that fundamental attitude which respects the supreme causes of good and uprightness.

Personal Contribution to the Elevation of Morals

Each of you, in the variety of circumstances, and in the ways and forms in which you carry out concretely your typical professional work, must have the constant concern to follow this line of moral rectitude and thus offer a personal contribution to the elevation of morals. The Church expects a great deal from you too - from each of you individually and from all of you as members of your Union: a convincing demonstration of Christianity put into practice. I will say even more: she expects a clear testimony of love for Christ and, therefore, of love for brothers.

---

40. Action and Contemplation Support Each Other in Our Daily Lives[3]

Work and Prayer.

[A homily on July 7, 1980 at Castel Gandolfo, Italy, to the employees at the Papal summer residence.]

Since we are celebrating Holy Mass, we must glean from the Liturgy of the Word the teaching adapted to our life. We have just read in the Gospel according to Luke the episode of the hospitality given to Jesus by Martha and Mary. These two sisters, in the history of Christian spirituality, have been understood as symbolic figures, representing action and contemplation respectively: Martha is bustling around with household tasks, while Mary is sitting at Christ's feet to listen to his words. We can draw two lessons from this Gospel text.

Making Room for the World of the Spirit

First of all we should note the final sentence of Jesus: "Mary has chosen the good portion, which shall not be taken away from her." In this way he strongly emphasizes the fundamental and irreplaceable value that listening to the Word of God has for our existence: it must be our constant reference point, our light, and our strength. But it is necessary to listen to it.

It is necessary to know how to keep silent to make room for solitude, or rather for a meeting reserved for intimacy with the Lord. It is necessary to be able to contemplate.

Today man deeply feels the need of not limiting himself to mere material concerns, and of integrating his own technical culture with superior and purifying contributions coming from the world of the spirit. Unfortunately, our everyday life risks or even experiences cases, more or less widespread, of interior pollution. But the contact of faith with the word of the Lord purifies us, elevates us, and restores energy to us.

Therefore, we must always keep before our heart's eyes the mystery of love with which God came to meet us in his son Jesus Christ. The object of our contemplation is entirely here, and from here comes our salvation, redemption from every form of alienation and above all from that of sin. Essentially, we are invited to act like the other Mary, the mother of Jesus, who "kept all these things, pondering them in her heart."[4] It is on this condition that we shall not be men of one dimension, but right in the very greatness of God.

Complementarity of Action and Contemplation

But there is a second lesson to learn, and it is that we must never see a contradiction between action and contemplation. In fact we read in the Gospel that it was Martha (and not Mary) who received Jesus "into her house." Moreover, today's First Reading suggests to us the harmony between the two things: the episode of the hospitality given by

Abraham to the three mysterious persons sent by the Lord, who according to an ancient interpretation are actually an image of the Holy Trinity, teaches us that we can serve the Lord and be in contact with him even with our most trivial everyday tasks. And since this year is the Fifteenth Centenary of the birth of St. Benedict, let us recall his famous motto: "Pray and work," *Ora et labora!* These words contain a whole program, not of opposition but of synthesis, not of contradiction but of the fusion of two equally important elements.

The result is a very concrete lesson for us which can be expressed as a question: to what extent are we able to see in contemplation and prayer a moment of real impact for our daily tasks? And, vice versa, to what extent are we able to strengthen our work to its very core with a leavening communion with the Lord? These questions can serve as an examination of conscience and become a stimulus for a renewal of our daily life, which will be at the same time more contemplative and more active.

While we now continue the celebration of Holy Mass, we offer these resolutions of ours to the Lord, and above all we invoke his powerful grace, so that he may help us to put them into practice in the reality of our lives.

41. Human Work Unites Humanity and Participates in the Creative Activity of God[5]

Collaboration with God, Dignity of Work, Work and Prayer, Work and Society.

[An address on August 30, 1980 in Abruzzi, Italy, to workers and farmers assembled at the Gran Sasso tunnel.]

Beloved friends, the very name of the Gran Sasso once – but now no longer – described a chain that "divided" your noble region, according to the classical topographical and administrative division of *Abruzzo citerione* (Near Abruzzi) and *Abruszzo ulteriore* (Transappennine Abruzzi). Thanks to human work, which has been going on right here for a good many years and has "triumphed" over the most arduous difficulties of a geological and technical nature, the old "division" can now be considered overcome; and not only in the sense of soon being able to have road connections that are increasingly easy and quick, but from the ethnic and ethical point of view, in the very important and far more significant sense of a further growth in knowledge, in trade, in the mutual relations of collaboration between the populations of this and the neighbouring regions.

Work Overcomes Divisions

Friends and brothers who are listening to me! I have come to this place to honour and to celebrate work, and not according to the model of a vague and rhetorical exaltation, but in its actual value, that is, in its capacity and its "virtue" of being changed into a positive contribution to better understanding and to true fellowship among men. A source of material and moral life, work finds precisely here a convincing and eloquent proof of its nature and irreplaceable function which God the creator assigned to it "from the beginning"[6] and which the Apostle reaffirms forcefully.[7] Here it presents itself, moreover, not as an element of struggle and conflict, but of union and concord within society.

Nature as the Work of God

But in order that the subject may be clarified even better, I wish to refer now to the two forms of work, or rather to the two categories of workers whom I see represented here. I cannot confine myself to saying that I want to honour your human work; I must, rather, address you directly, dear miners, and dear farmers and shepherds, who have gathered to greet me and pay your respects to me.

How could I forget your persons in fact, if as the Second Vatican Council wrote with words so easy to understand – *hic labor ... a persona immediate procedit* (work proceeds from the human person)?[8] And how could I forget your professions, with the sacrifices and difficulties, uncertainties and dangers they entail? Certainly, there are evident differences in the type of work you carry out: you miners have worked and work, in the bowels of the earth, digging and penetrating it with a lasting and intense effort, which unfortunately is not exempt from risks to health itself; you farmers and shepherds, on the contrary, usually work in the open air, following the normal succession of the seasons. Yet, to both of you – here is an element in common – it is always nature that appears in its reality as God's creature. Working on the earth, outside or inside, you have always before you a work that can, and certainly does, offer you a whole series of reasons to reflect, to meditate, to worship. It has rightly been written that man is a religious being (*animal religiosum*); but it seems to me that those who, like you, live in daily contact with nature and discover it as an admirably ordered totality in its threefold mineral, vegetable and animal kingdom, feel not so much the opportunity but the facility, I would say, and as it were the invitation, to consider and contemplate in it the almighty and providential work of God, our Creator and our Father. You specifically, because of what you are and what you do, engaged either in the hard toil of digging in the mine or in the tasks of farming and sheep-raising by day and by night, always remember that you must be "ideally" religious spirits, open and attentive to recognize those vestiges that divine Wisdom has left, as numerous as they are evident, in the created world. "For all men who were ignorant of God were foolish by nature" – Holy Scripture warns us – and they were unable from the good things that are seen to know him who exists, nor did they recognize the craftsman while paying heed to his works; ... for from the greatness and beauty of created things comes a corresponding perception of their Creator."[9]

I wish, therefore, to appeal to your feelings as believers, or better, to your faith as Christians, in order that this faith, far from failing, may rather find in the very activity you carry out an opportunity and a cause for deepening and growth.

Human Work: Collaboration with the Creator

The last souvenir-thought of today's meeting springs from the things I have said up to now, and is a kind of comparison between them. Here, in the grandeur of the Appennine heights, everything speaks to us of the work of God; but here, too – I add in the presence of you workers – everything speaks to us of the work of man. Is there, therefore, a connection between these two works? Certainly there is: God creates in the originality of an operation from nothingness, which makes things exist that did not previously exist; man, on the contrary, transforms, intervenes in – by divine mandate – created things, rising in this way to the rank and to the honour of a collaborator with the Creator himself. Look at your work from this standpoint too: alongside the above-mentioned motive of contemplation, give it this further dimension, thinking that its dignity is a humble and modest, but actual and real, participation in the transcendent dignity of divine work.

---

42. Work Is a Service of Love[10]

Christian Witness/Mission, Collaboration with God.

[An address on December 6, 1980 in Rome, to the Third National Congress of the Workers' Christian Movement.]

You have assumed important tasks, often attended by serious difficulties, owing to the vast range of the problems involved, and above all to man's recurrent moral weakness in tackling them. In a society marked by deep ambiguities, straining, on the one hand, towards better conditions of civil society, but subjected, on the other hand, to a productive effort that risks being centered entirely on an ideal of mere material prosperity, excluding the perspectives and requirements of a human, spiritual and supernatural order, your movement wishes to affirm within the world of work the presence of Christ, the vitality of Christ. He is now, in fact, "at work in the hearts of men by the power of his Spirit; not only does he arouse in them a desire for the world to come but he quickens, purifies, and strengthens the generous aspirations of mankind to make life more humane and conquer the earth for this purpose." [11]

Christian Mission to the World

You wish to bear witness to this presence, at once redemptive, revolutionary and peaceful, and to live it in the first place in yourselves, by a precise effort of reflection on the reality that surrounds you, and on its requirements, for an evangelical understanding and interpretation thereof. This may be reached also in confrontation and in dialogue, carried out with lucid awareness of one's own faith, with other organized groups. Your task, therefore, assumes the form of Christian animation of the world of work and as evangelizing action within the forces that determine, at the present historical moment, the composition and increase of the workers movement.

Work in Its Spiritual Dimension

The Pope encourages you in this difficult but also exalting service of believers, aimed essentially at making people understand how human work, as the expression of man's creative capacities, beyond its evident productive aspect, is set in the perspective of the original Covenant between God and man himself, a Covenant renewed in Jesus Christ. Work, in this supreme light, while it is a means of improving the world and collaborating in God's work of creation, helps man to be more man, matures his personality, develops and elevates his capacities, thus opening him to service, generosity and commitment for others, in a word, to love.

The definitive meaning of work is contained in this availability with regard to brothers, that is, in practical exercise of the great commandment of love,[12] which is the fundamental law of human perfection and therefore also of the laborious transformation of the universe.[13] The Word of God, who became the Son of Man, and the anniversary of whose birth we are about to celebrate with joy, by giving his life for us won for us the grace of exercising that love which is the soul and principal incentive of human work.

---

43. Work Derives Its True Meaning from the Gospel[14]

Christian Witness/Mission, Common Good, Dignity of Work, Dominion over the Earth, Gospel of Work, Human Development/ Progress, Human Rights/Dignity, Humanization/Dehumanization, Justice, Leisure, Materialism and Consumerism, Meaning of Work, Saint Joseph, Work and Family, Work and Society, Work and the Worker.

[An address on March 19, 1981 in
Terni, Italy, to workers of Terni.]

Before meeting you here all together, I was able to visit at least some sections of this large factory, which is your place of work. I am at once pleased and honored to have been able to view close at hand the bench of your daily toil; to have met you personally, you who constantly spend the best of your days, in fact of your lives, at this work-bench; and to have been able in this way to realize from actual experience how heavy your occupation is, but also how productive it is and therefore how much it deserves to be appreciated, sustained and safeguarded.

Work Promotes Civilization

I realize that my visit was limited to only part of a far vaster industrial complex. And I know that it has an important place in Italy, with its specific productions of cold-rolled steel, rotors for turbines, machinery for the oil, chemical, cement, mechanical and structural work industries, and also of various parts for nuclear reactors, casts, pressure pipes, pressure vessels and rods. The work in question is certainly heavy but important, and it calls for special responsibility. At the same time, it is very interesting and highly useful. In fact, it meets certain necessities typical of advanced modern technology in all its components and specializations; and this is in turn geared to the greater good of mankind. In this way, therefore, your work is useful for all men, facilitates their lives, and raises the level of civilization.

Well, I have seen you at grips with this toil: I have noted what is the origin of many instruments which serve the welfare of man, but of which he does not always know the hard price. I have seen you, and my esteem and affection for you has grown. For this reason, I pay tribute to you, with full understanding!

Work Gives Meaning to Life

Your work-bench, dear workers of Terni and Umbria, is, moreover, similar to that of so many other men who, in different parts of the world, contribute day after day to the common good of the whole of society. And this simple fact concerning the universal and inseparable relationship between man and his work-bench leads us to see in these two poles, and above all in their mutual combination, an exalting creative possibility. Man, in fact, draws from his own intelligence and from matter, which is subjected to him, albeit by means of toil and the sweat of his brow, new and unsuspected products, small or gigantic, which are the documentation of his individual and social dignity. It is at his work-bench that man offers the measure of his own capacities and that, when all is said and done, he gives content and even meaning to his own life.

The Work of St. Joseph

While I was visiting your factory, so modern and mechanized, there took shape before my inner eye another work-bench, a very modest, artisan's one, directly connected with the family life of the home. It is the work-bench of Nazareth, at which St. Joseph worked every day. Today, as you know, is his feast day. But above all there grew up beside him, as the years passed, Jesus Christ himself, who helped him with the same work. And his fellow-townsmen spoke of him as the "carpenter's son," as we read in the Gospel according to Matthew.[15]

Well, dear brothers and sisters, I am very grateful to you for having invited me to Terni, to your work-bench, precisely on this day when the Church celebrates Joseph of Nazareth. Your bishop, several months ago already, had proposed to me to visit Terni sometime. And since I have known Mons. Quadri well since the time of the Council, I could not refuse his request. I am glad that 19 March was chosen for this visit and that it can take place at your place of work itself. I think it allows us to venerate and understand St. Joseph more fully. At the same time, it is possible for us to re-read together and in depth this Gospel of Work, which precisely today seems to be particularly expressive. It speaks, with all the depth of scriptural revelation, of the Word of God. And at the same time it enters human life with great simplicity: the life of Christ, Joseph and Mary; the life of all men and women engaged in work.

The Gospel of Work

The Gospel of Work was written particularly by the fact that the Son of God, of the same substance as the Father, on becoming a man, worked with his hands. In fact, his work, which was real physical work, occupied most of his life on this earth, and in this way entered the work of the redemption of man and of the world, which he accomplished with his earthly life itself.

So I was very happy to see at the entrance the statue of Jesus the Divine Worker: he is at home in your midst, because Jesus Christ knows by experience what work is. Work, moreover, has its beginning in God himself. If we open the Bible, we immediately find at the beginning of the Book of Genesis the description of the creation of the world. Well, though it is a question of a figurative description, rich in images, the work of creation is presented according to the pattern of a working week: God-Elohim carries out his work in the course of six days, and "rests" on the seventh. In this way, man is given the indication of connecting work with rest. In fact, there is a mutual conditioning between work and rest. This principle, which today occupies one of the principal places in the present-day codes of work, in the policy and above all the ethics of work, is already contained in Holy Scripture at the very beginning of the existence of the world.

Work: The Image and Likeness of God

The biblical narrative of creation – an activity which only God can carry out and which is presented in the likeness of human work – has a deep motivation of its own. It is not only a literary means of expression, but is impressed on the whole logic of the Word of God. In the same Book, in fact, we read that man, placed in the visible world as the culmination of the work of creation, was created in the image of God: "God created man in his own image, in the image of God he created him; male and female he created them."[16] For this reason, in the whole visible world it is only man who "works." Only his activity can be called "work" in the full sense of the word. On the contrary, the activity of the beings inferior to man, "animals," is not "work," even if it is sometimes called so. The fact is that in order to "work," physical ability and strength, which are characteristic of these beings as well, are not sufficient; and if man wishes to use this specific strength of animals in his work, he must "domesticate" them. The same thing holds true for the other forces hidden in nature. Man must "adapt" them, raise them, in a way, to his own level. But for "work," man is necessary. To be able to "work," one must be the "image and likeness" of God.[17]

Work, therefore, is not at all a servile occupation, reserved for slaves, as was believed in the ancient world and later, but it is characteristic of free men. In fact, it is an expression of creative freedom, in which man offers the measure of his own capacity of collaborating in creation itself.

The Dignity of Human Work

This short reflection already speaks to us of the dignity of work, in fact of the specific dignity of human work. It derives its own foundation from nothing else but the very humanity that carries it out. This truth is at the very center of the "Gospel of Work." And the Church has proclaimed it since the beginning of her existence, already from that simple house in Nazareth. She proclaims it daily. The 19th of March, furthermore, offers a special opportunity to speak about it and to live it together with all workers. Precisely in the present year it is possible to do so in a special way. This year, in fact, is the ninetieth anniversary of the Encyclical *Rerum Novarum*, the first social encyclical of the Church, published by my predecessor Pope Leo XIII in 1891. At the center of his message is the truth about the dignity of work, a truth which constituted the foundation of the whole morality of work. Every code of work should be built on it, if it wishes to have a really "humanitarian" and "social" character. That encyclical confirmed this teaching, without espousing any party ideology or theory which, albeit of opposite sign, is marked by materialism, that is, by the reduction of man to only one dimension, the economic one, which deprives him of the highest element of his dignity as a human person and son of God.

Well, today as yesterday, the Pope and the whole Church intend to be at the side of those who believe in man, because they believe in something or in someone that transcends him, in such a way as to reaffirm and promote all the values of the whole man, without stifling any.

Putting Belief into Action

And certainly this fundamental ethics is not honored when work becomes a means of exploiting man, a pretext for excessive profits, an opportunity for injustice on a small or large scale. The Council, too, expressed itself in this way: "The entire process of productive work must be accommodated to the needs of the human person and the nature of his life, with special attention to domestic life. ... Workers should have the opportunity to develop their talents and their personalities in the very exercise of their work."[18] Work must help man to be more of a man. But no one can grant himself the luxury of dreaming only, if he does not then try to put the highest ideals into practice. Woe to us if all these things remain only words, or just good intentions. Society must show, on the contrary, that it has acquired this truth, and show it concretely, with the same concreteness that qualifies everyday working activity.

The Church and the Gospel of Work

Dear brothers and sisters, speaking in Poland during my pilgrimage in 1979, I said that the Church is not afraid of the difficult problems connected with the world of work: "Christianity and the Church are not afraid of the world of work. The Pope is not afraid of the men of work. They have always been particularly close to him. He came from among them. He came from the stone quarries of Zakrzowek, from the Solvey boilers in Borek Falecki, then from Nova Huta. Through all these environments, through his own experiences of work – I venture to say – the Pope learned the Gospel anew. He realized and became convinced how deeply the modern problems of human work are engraved in the Gospel. How impossible it is to solve them thoroughly without the Gospel."[19]

But it is necessary to say more: that is, that the Church cannot be extraneous to, or far from, these difficult problems; she cannot break away from the "world of work," precisely because the "the Gospel of Work" is organically inscribed in her mission as a whole. And the Church cannot but proclaim the Gospel. Therefore she cannot but go forth to meet every man, and especially the man of work. In fact, as I wrote in *Redemptor Hominis*, "For the Church all ways lead to man."[20]

Although the attempt is being made in various quarters to create opposite opinions and sustain them at all costs, the Church has so many things to say to the man of work. Certainly not in technical, professional or similar questions, but in fundamental questions. And it is an important word. If it is lacking and if it is not put into practice, then the real "cornerstone" of the whole gigantic construction of modern technology, industry and the various sectors with which human work is connected is lacking.

Need for Internal Conversion

The frequent appeal of the Church to conversion, like the appeal of Jesus, is based on the certainty that nothing will improve, not even the structures of human society, if man does not improve from within; and, in practice, that means that it is impossible to obtain justice by creating new injustices, to establish peace by having recourse to violence, to create greater spaces of freedom by using physical or moral coercion.

It is not a good thing, therefore, to try to exclude the Church and the Gospel of Work. The cause of man suffers as a result. Moreover, it is precisely through work that man aspires to the development and to the maturing of everything that is human. I repeat to you what I said in France last year to the workers of Saint-Denis: "Christ will say one day: 'Blessed are those who hunger and thirst for righteousness, for they shall be satisfied.' "[21] However, this thirst for righteousness, this eagerness to struggle for truth and moral order in the world, are not and cannot be hate, or a source of hate in the world. They cannot be turned into a program of struggle against man, solely because he is, if one may so express it, "on the other side." This struggle cannot become a program of destruction of the adversary; it cannot create social and political mechanisms in which there are manifested ever greater forms of collective egoism, powerful and destructive egoism."

Apostolate of Work

In this way, therefore, I wish to express the conviction that this visit today will strengthen and consolidate your encounter with the Gospel of Work. I hope that it will bring the great bench of modern work, at which thousands of men work here in Terni, closer to that modest bench of the carpenter Joseph of Nazareth, to whom Jesus Christ, the son of God and the son of man, presented himself as a worker. And I hope that in this perspective you will be able to see in a fuller light the value and the meaning of your work and of your whole lives.

I am here today to give one and all confidence. In particular, I am here also to encourage that apostolate of work, which is already being carried out in an intelligent way by the bishop and his zealous collaborators. I liked what was written on the booklet published to prepare for this visit: the world of work is not to be considered "an area to be colonized, but a place from which there spring the strongest challenges for a Christian witness, which cannot remain helpless and passive before the historical tasks of realizing for man, for every working man, an environment of justice and peace, which do not bar him from human and Christian growth." Be men who are able to bear such witness, and who are Christians not only when it is convenient, but always and completely. I also saw with interest the results of an inquiry carried out by the inter-diocesan Commission for the apostolate of work, from which there emerge data which stimulate to ever greater commitment. I likewise express my appreciation for the institute of Theological and Social Studies, and for the various lay organizations.

I would like to exhort everyone to continue with strength and generosity in the valuable task of bringing the fresh and regenerating breath of the Gospel and of adherence to Christ more and more abundantly into the environments of work. And may the Lord generously reward the work of everyone.

Prayer for Workers

Brothers and sisters, I thank you again heartily for the welcome you have given me, and I will certainly keep in my heart the memory of you all, of your industriousness and hospitality. Rest assured that the Pope is with you, not out of opportunism, but with sincere and deep sentiments of human and Christian communion.

While I wish you all happiness, I am thinking not only of your work, but also of the difficulties it involves; I am thinking of your families, your children and your sick. I bless everyone and take everyone with me in my heart, invoking the most abundant heavenly graces upon each one.

I pray to God ardently for the happiness of all:

- that your just aspirations may be realized;
- that the moments and the reasons of crisis will be overcome;
- that work will never be an alienation for anyone;
- that, on the contrary, it may be honored by everyone as it deserves, so that justice and even more love may triumph in it;
- that the environment of work will really be fit for man, and that man may be able to appreciate it as an extension of his own family;
- that work may help man to be more of a man;
- and that, with the commitment of everyone, it may be possible to arrive at the construction of a new society and a new world, in the full realization of justice, freedom and peace.

44. The World of Work Should Be Molded Not Only by Justice but Also by Charity[22]

Christian Witness/Mission, Collaboration with God, Common Good, Dignity of Work, Economic Laws and Profits, Fair Wage, Gospel of Work, Human Rights/Dignity, Humanization/Dehumanization, Justice, Private Property/Co-ownership, Solidarity, Spirituality, Technology, Work and Family, Work and the Worker, Worker Participation.

[An address on March 19, 1982 in Solvay, Italy,
to the workers of the Solvay chemical factory.]

What I wish to reaffirm here is that I feel I am one with you because I feel I participate in your problems, having shared them personally. I consider it a grace of the Lord to have been a worker, because this gave me the opportunity to know firsthand the man of work, but also of every other type of work. I have been able to know the concrete reality of his life; an existence imbued with profound humanity, even if it is not immune to weaknesses, a simple life, hard, difficult, worthy of every respect.

Experience of Work

When I left the factory to pursue my vocation to the priesthood, I brought with me the irreplaceable experience of that world and the profound dignity of human friendship and vibrant solidarity with my fellow workmen, keeping these things in mind as something precious.

Proclaiming the Dignity of Work

Dear brothers and sisters! The Church, by virtue of her divine mandate, is near you; she is on your side, because she is on the side of man, of every man. The centrality and the dignity of the human person urge the pope and the bishops to proclaim their concern for the world of work. The Church has much to say to the man of work: not in technical matters but in fundamental questions and in the defense of workers' rights. She proclaims that the dignity of work is part of the dignity of man; and in protecting the dignity of work she can contribute positively to the defense of social justice. And if the achieved results, just reason for your pride, do not escape her, she then knows too well the "anxieties" and the dangers which they cost.

Labor and Technology

As workers in the industrial sector, you are part of the mechanism of modern labor which the inventive power of human genius has magnified. At the same time, however, you are exposed to the most exciting and the most dangerous consequences of this process, not only from the economic-social point of view but also the ethical-religious one.

The development of technology poses again in a new way today the problem of human work. Technology, in fact, which has been and is a coefficient of economic progress, can be changed from an ally to an adversary of man. In fact, it appears marked by an evident ambivalence: on the one hand, it has lengthened man's toil and has multiplied economic goods through massive production. However, on the other, with the mechanization of productive processes, it in fact tends to depersonalize the one who performs the work, taking away from him every satisfaction and every incentive to creativity and responsibility. In industrial activity we meet, in effect, two realities: man and matter, the hand and the machine, business structures and the life of the worker. Which will have pre-eminence? Will the machine become an extension of man's creative mind and hand or will man be subjected to the impelling mechanisms of organization, reducing him to acting as a robot? Will matter emerge ennobled by the workshop and man instead degraded? Isn't man worth more than the machine and its products?

It is known how the technical industrial era has fostered profound innovations, radical changes in society. The presence of the machine in the world of enterprise has changed not only the traditional configurations of work but has had a substantial effect on the worker's kind of life, on his psychology, his mentality, conscience, and on the very culture of the people, giving rise to a new type of society.

With the emphasis, then, on the scientific organization of work and the consequent assembly lines, there is greatly accentuated the situation of the alienation of man and his impossibility to participate responsibly in the work that he carries out.

Moreover, in recent decades, automation has made its entrance into the field of industry: automation, whose innovative character, based on electronics and computers, is not always completely in favor of man.

Growing Awareness of Human Dignity

In the modern age, the awareness that human beings, especially working men and women, are acquiring about their dignity is taking on universal dimensions. This phenomenon has been expressed on the historical level not only through the progressive proclamation and defense of human rights but also through the profound desire for a more living and concrete social justice.

It is not difficult to notice how from every part of our planet there arises today the aspiration to a greater justice, in connection with the new conditions of economy and the new possibilities of technology, of the production and distribution of goods. The perception and need of this justice are always made more insistent and sad in the human conscience, which if it recognizes on the one hand the results achieved, on the other hand it suffers more acutely the anxieties caused by discriminations and privations, which can harm the legitimate aspirations of workers.

Social Justice

In effect, social justice, in the Christian vision, constitutes the basis, the key virtue and the fundamental value of socio-political society. It directs and regulates the connections and relationships of citizens toward the common good in a viewpoint, therefore, that is not purely contractual and individual, but communitarian. As such, it represents a fundamental right of all men, conferred on them by the Creator and confirmed by the gospel message.

Overcoming the rigid limitations of commutative justice, social justice, therefore, seeks to subordinate things to man, individual goods to the common good, the right to property to the right of life, eliminating every condition of existence and of work that is unworthy of the human person.

Here we are, then, brothers and sisters, at the central point of the problem to which today's meeting of ours is dedicated.

A Human Economy

I will never tire of affirming that the economy and its structures are valid and acceptable only if they are human, that is, made by man and for man. And they cannot be such if they undermine the dignity of those – workers and directors – who carry on their activities; if they systematically erode in them the sense of responsibility; if they paralyze in them any form of personal initiative whatsoever; if, in short, they do not possess a human meaning and logic.

I now wish to refer to some elements that I consider essential for the social order to be truly inspired by justice in regard to human work.

In a society that wants to be just and human, profit and gain cannot prevail over man. It is absolutely necessary that man remain the subject of the economy and the various structures of production. I wrote in *Redemptor Hominis*: man "cannot relinquish himself or the place in the visible world that belongs to him; he cannot become the slave of things, the slave of economic systems, the slave of production, the slave of his own products."[23] God has created him to be the master and not the slave of work.

Right to Work

In this demand for justice, we must include the right to work and the other rights of workers.

Work, in fact, constitutes one of the great and fundamental inalienable rights of man, because it gives him life, serenity, meaning. Through work, people become more fully human and God's collaborator in perfecting nature. It is to be wished that this right truly represents a concrete reality for every citizen, a right promoted and protected by society.

To procure work or a position is not an easy task; yet it is necessary to affirm that this is a central aspect and a fundamental obligation of the political and economic order.

A Just Salary

I wrote in *Laborem Exercens* that the "concrete proof of the justice of the whole socio-economic system and its proper functioning is represented by a just salary." In effect, the most consistent way to realize justice in work relations between the worker and the employer, independent of the type of economic system in which human activity is carried out, is that of just remuneration.

Through the salary, in fact, the concrete access to goods destined for common use is generally opened. To adapt the salary in its multiple and complementary forms, so as to be able to affirm that the worker really and equitably shares in the wealth he jointly helps to create both in private enterprise and in the national economy, is a postulate and a requirement of a sound economy at the service of an effective social justice.

Worker as Co-Owner

The implementation of the proposals put forward in the Catholic field in order to ensure that the worker be considered a co-owner of the great workbench is a basic element of that proof to which I have already referred: not only that the man of work find full satisfaction in his aspiration to just remuneration, but also and above all that justice be safeguarded in all the structures of the economic process.[24]

Rights and Responsibilities of Labor Unions

Again I wish to draw your attention to another essential aspect of social justice, and that is the freedom of association, through which there must be recognized for workers the effective possibility to participate freely and actively in making and controlling the decisions which concern them, at all levels. The experience of history – as I have already stated on other occasions – shows that these associations or unions are an indispensable element of social life, especially in the modern industrialized society. Having arisen to defend the just rights of workers with regard to the owners of the means of production, the trade unions, particularly those in the industrial sector, have increased on the basis of the struggle. Nevertheless, in their attitudes of social opposition, they must give essential prominence to the positive values that inspire them, to the desire for the just good in the context of the common good, to the thirst for social justice, but never to the struggle "against" others, because the first characteristic of work is that of being "for," of uniting many men. Here it is of great social strength. It is precisely through union and solidarity that the trade unions have been able to protect the interests of workers by obtaining a just salary, dignified work conditions, security for the worker and his family.

The public powers, called to serve the common good, must, therefore, consider it their duty to protect these associations in the civil sphere through wise laws. On their part, the trade unions must always adequately realize the limitations that the general concrete economic situation can sometimes demand in the framework of the common good of the whole nation.

Justice Needs Charity

All of you, dear brothers and sisters, rightly desire that in your workyards, in your factories, justice reign as the fundamental dimension of your work activities. Isn't this so? This does you honor, but it certainly is not enough! From the world of your work must also spring the solution for realizing social justice: newer movements of solidarity among men of work and with men of work are necessary to create a union of hearts, a constructive union, sincere, inspired by moral formation and a spirit of responsibility.

"The experience of the past and of our own time demonstrates that justice alone is not enough, that it can even lead to the negation and destruction of itself, if that deeper power, which is love, is not allowed to shape human life in its various dimensions. ... This statement does not detract from the value of justice and does not minimize the significance of the order that is based upon it; it only indicates, under another aspect, the need to draw from the power of the spirit which condition the very order of justice, powers which are still more profound."[25]

You know, in fact, that Christian love animates justice, inspires it, discovers it, perfects it, makes it feasible, respects it, elevates it, surpasses it, but it does not exclude it, does not absorb it, does not replace it, but rather presupposes it and demands it, because true love, true charity, does not exist without justice. Is not justice perhaps the minimum measure of charity?

I listened attentively to the worker who spoke at the beginning of this meeting. She emphasized very well the need to search in love for the inspiration for a fuller social commitment. I think this perception is important. If, in fact, social justice gives a human countenance to enterprise, charity pours into it the vital energy of true solidarity.

The Gospel of Work

Dearest brothers and sisters, I nourish confidence that this meeting today will strengthen in each one of you sincere attachment to the Gospel of Work proclaimed by the one who, being the Son of God made man, wanted to belong to the world of manual labor at the bench of Joseph the carpenter, the spouse of Mary Most Holy.

Jesus looks with love on our work, in its various forms, seeing in each one of them a reflection of man's likeness to God the Creator. Work is willed and blessed by God: it no longer carries with itself the weight of condemnation, but the nobility of a mission, that of making man a protagonist with God in the building of human society and of the dynamism that reflects the mystery of the Almighty.

Giving Work a Soul

The Church looks on your work. Together with all men of good will, it seeks to validate the achieved "results" and to find the answer to the "anxieties" that are churning in your mind. Christian faith has the mysterious power to give work a soul, to confer on it serenity, peace, strength, rationality, thus making work an occasion of human growth that is not only personal, familial and communitarian, but also religious.

Work as an Expression of Love

And now allow me to address all of you who are taking part in this meeting – each and every one in particular. In doing this, I am at the same time thinking of your families, your babies, your children, your spouses, your mothers, your sick, and all of those who are dear to you. I know what place they have in your hearts; I know what value they represent for you. Through them you find in the toil and work of every day the full expression and the spontaneous measure of your love.

Love your families! I repeat to you: love them! Be for them joyous guides, sure light, vigilant guardians against the seeds of moral and social disintegration, which unfortunately lead inexorably to the breakup of so many families.

Family, Society and Church

Open your families to social values, to the requirements of the spirit! Family life must be an experience of communion and participation. Far from withdrawing into itself, the family is called to open itself to the social environment to become – moved by the sense of justice, by concern for others, and by the duty of its responsibility toward the whole of society – an instrument for humanizing and personalizing, a service to neighbors through various expressions of fraternal help, a defense and conscious guardian of its own rights and duties.

Open your families to Christ and to His Church! It is not by chance that the Christian family has been called the "domestic Church." Among its fundamental tasks there is the ecclesial one of being a witness for Christ to the world: "that is, it is placed at the service of the building up of the Kingdom of God in history by participating in the life and mission of the Church."[26] It is called to become more and more each day a believing and evangelizing community, overcoming the temptation to live its faith timidly in the intimacy of their homes.

Keep alive and consistent your sensitivity for the respect for social justice in the world of work, nourishing and sustaining it with the love that is "the bond of perfection."[27]

In your factories, in your places of work, may the serenity of the modest shop of Nazareth always reign, the serenity that comes from the knowledge that you have daily fulfilled your duty, the serenity that makes human work a growth factor and gives it the dimension of a fruitful vocation. The Church is greatly sensitive to the value of the factory environment, the place where the life of the worker – your life! – is lived, but also where you must bring the faith to have a positive influence, to make it become active.

God with Us

The Lord is here with us: not only now, He is always with you at your workbench to give to everyone the regenerating strength of his Gospel, of His grace and His love. Never ignore Him! Never put Him aside!

As a goal of your activity, always have that building a world that is more human, more fraternal, more Christian; the will to create more perfect forms of union, of solidarity, of sociality according to the requirements of the times; the ideal of growing in humanity, maturing more each day in justice and love.

45. A Common Effort Is Necessary to Confront Contemporary Socio-Economic Problems[28]

Common Good, Community of Persons, Dominion over the Earth, Economic Laws and Profits, Fair Wage, Gospel of Work, Human Rights/Dignity, Humanization/Dehumanization, Justice, Leisure, Materialism and Consumerism, Meaning of Work, Private Property/Co-ownership, Service, Spirituality, Technology, Unemployment, Work and Family, Work and Society, Work and Women/Mothers, Work and the Worker.

[An address on May 15, 1982 in Porto, Portugal, to a group of workers.]

I would like at this moment to shake hands with all of you, to feel your hands, calloused as they are, as proof of your professional activity. When you shake hands with someone as a sign of friendship, you allow him to feel the weight and value of your work. Noble is the hand that works, the hand that transforms the world, the hand that builds a new reality for a more human society. Generous is the hand that works for the benefit of mankind.

Value of Work

I have come to Porto to honor and celebrate work. I know very well that the people of this city and this region and all of Portugal have always felt proud of their earnestness in work and their devotion to work. I have been told that Porto is known locally as the "City of Work." So what else could I do here but proclaim to you the Good News, the "Gospel of Work"?

In my recent encyclical on human work, for the 90th anniversary of *Rerum Novarum*, the great document of Pope Leo XII on the social question, I wanted to pay special tribute to man seen in the full context of this reality which is work, in the light of the mystery of Christ, to reveal its richness and at the same time all that is arduous in human existence.

The Church, which believes in and thinks of man, considers it part of her mission "always to call attention to the dignity and rights of those who work, to condemn situations in which that dignity and those rights are violated, and to help to guide the above-mentioned changes so as to ensure authentic progress by man and society."[29]

The Worker Is the Goal of Work

In fact, according to the original designs of God, man is called to become lord of the earth, "to master it"[30] by the superiority of his intelligence and the activity of his arms. He is the center of creation. The primary basis of the value of work – and therefore of its dignity – is man himself. The dignity of the person who works must be the basis and the criterion to keep in mind when evaluating any kind of manual or intellectual work. In reality the protagonist and the goal of work, its true creator and craftsman, even in the most humble and monotonous activities, is always man as a person. It is man who was created "in the image of God."

Threat from Materialism and Technology

The growing materialistic civilization which is invading our world tends to relegate to second place the subjective dimension of work, based on the dignity of man. In this situation there is a danger that workers might become robots, faceless beings, a shapeless depersonalized mass, at the mercy of powerful forces that do not always respect the interests of the worker: the interests of man, the family, and the community.

The problem is not a new one, as you well know. The invention of the machine has certainly given a new dimension to human work. If the use of the instrument lengthened and strengthened the human arm, the machine tended to replace it. When he invented the machine, man hoped to remove the burden of muscular effort, to lighten his load.

Even if machines have improved the living conditions of the workers, after the first impact of novelty it became clear that mechanical precision and speed, greater every day, had begun a new condition of human life. It is the machine that imposes its rhythm upon man; there is no longer time for anything, nor for anyone, with all the problems that arise from this.

However, it should not be like that. Even when it is meant to improve this standard of living, to subject man "created in the image of God" to a productive effort directed almost entirely towards material well-being and profit, shutting him off from the prospects of the human and spiritual order, opposes his dignity.

Creating a More Human Conscience

If work is for man and not man for work, the gradual solution of the problems of the working world must be sought in the effort to create a conscience that is more just, more Christian and more human.

Only with this conscience as a basis can we tackle the problems of the working world, beginning with the difficult and delicate problem of the relationship between capital and labor, between the owner and the work force, between the employer and the employee.

Need for Balance between Labor and Capital

We must not underestimate either side of the problem: without capital there is no work. Therefore the holders or providers of capital are performing a great service to the common good which deserves everyone's consideration and respect, because they create new possibilities of work and employment. On the other hand, human labor cannot be considered merely a function of capital. It completely transcends it. Man was not made for the machine but the machine for man.

The argument that the machines must never stop cannot be used to try to make man a slave to their rhythm, depriving him of the rest he deserves and of a really human way of life.

If, on the one hand, recent profound changes reveal a real will to create an ever more perfect climate of economic well-being and social justice, they cannot however hide the inevitable tensions, uncertainties and weaknesses which sometimes accompany the search for solutions and adjustments following great changes in the socio-political order.

Cooperation in the Common Good

In these circumstances, each citizen has a duty to co-operate sincerely to build, with his serious and faithful work, an ever better national community, where social justice – the new name for the common good – is promoted, where personal dignity is at every moment respected. In the light of this common good must be judged the timeliness and justice of certain forms of demands, which while they seem to defend the legitimate interests of the workers, sometimes cause great damage to the whole community.

It is certain, dear workers, that you will never be able to obtain the best solution to your problems if each of you remains isolated. So that you can take part in the solution of social problems, you also have the right to form associations and unions, with the goal of defending the vital interests of the men employed in the different professions. Up to a certain point, these interests are common to all; but each work, each profession, has its own special characteristics, which should be reflected in these organizations. I refer as you know, to the unions.

Peaceful Struggle for the Rights of All

Catholic social teaching does not hold that unions are no more than a reflection of a "class" structure of society and that they are a mouthpiece for a class struggle, which inevitably governs social life. They are indeed a mouthpiece for the struggle for social justice, for the just rights of working people in accordance with their individual professions. However, this struggle, as I have already said in the aforementioned encyclical *Laborem Exercens*, "should be seen as a normal endeavor for the just good: in the present case, for the good which corresponds to the needs and merits of working people associated by profession, but it is not a struggle 'against others.'[31]

And so it is up to you to seek the solution to your problems, never, however, with hatred or violence.

Christianity teaches us to love all men, even when we are defending our interests and we are involved in fighting a claim. We cannot think only of ourselves or of our own social group. Everything must be subordinate to the common good. It is not just or Christian for one class, because it has greater opportunities to exert pressure, due to the position it occupies in the social context, or because of the fighting strength that it has managed to achieve, to prevail over others, neglecting the legitimate rights of others.

Common Effort to Reduce Unemployment

Following this line of thought, there is, at the opposite pole, the situation of those who do not have the opportunity, and so are prevented from having a "voice": the unemployed. "It is known that in our country," your bishops wrote in a recent pastoral letter, "there is a serious employment crisis, which is giving rise to intolerable situations, at the personal, family and social levels." I would like to make my own the words that they then added: "We must try everything to resolve or diminish this crucial problem as soon as possible. ... It is an authentic, patriotic and moral imperative that all the forces concerned, putting aside all differences, recriminations and conflicts, should make one concerted effort for the rapid reduction of unemployment, and that the national community undertake this together. With this aim in mind, no one should consider himself free from the obligation to make the necessary sacrifices."

Desire to Work

In these days there is a general aspiration to work. To work is to integrate oneself actively in the process of human development, and with this, to feel useful in relation to others. This desire to participate in the great achievement of the community in which he belongs is a desire innate in the human individual. Everyone feels his own share of responsibility. In fact, every man who comes into this world must make his own real contribution to human progress in the sense of bringing this world closer to the true aspirations of mankind. For this reason the consideration of the subjective and social value of work demands that in the whole political community there is recognized not only the importance of work itself, but also of the right to work, and that everything be done to eliminate unemployment and under-employment.

Economic Surplus Tested by the Provision of a Fair Wage

Related in a certain way to this problem of unemployment is the problem of fair wage. Without ever forgetting that private ownership is always under a public mortgage, and so must always serve the common good, this is a suitable point to recall the criteria for establishing a just salary. This remains in every case the concrete test of any socio-economic system.

Work, Motherhood, and the Family

But I must now bring our talk to an end, dear brothers and sisters. And I do not want to do so without a special reference to your families. When I see you, men of work, I also think of those dear to you: your spouses, your mothers, your children and your sick. I think of all those who make up your homes. You, who exhaust yourselves at work to maintain your home and support your children, continue to be faithful to the traditional wholesome values of the Portuguese family.

Continue to love your families because you also need your family. Do not let your work break up your family life. Do not let a certain life-style separate parents from children. Do not let your homes be simply a place for resting and eating. Be yourselves the educators of your children.

The mother occupies an important place in the home. The well-being of the family depends a great deal on her. May you not be forced, through lack of means or low wages, to sacrifice the time that would normally be dedicated at home to the education of the children. May your home never be the victim of inhuman situations. And if you must take a job outside the home, may you not sacrifice things more important or be drawn away from your home, your husband or your children!

An Ideal of Being

In conclusion I remind you once again of the great dignity of your work; I hope that you are never displeased with it. May you never succumb to easy demagogy, nor let yourselves be deluded by an ideology that is not open to the spiritual. You would be dreaming of a world less human if you were to commit yourselves only to having more everyday. As men, as persons and as workers, I encourage you always to the ideal of *being* more.

Poor in Spirit

I recall here, as on other occasions, the Gospel beatitude: "Blessed are the poor in spirit, for they will inherit the Kingdom of Heaven." Those who have goods must open their hearts to the poor through an inner conversion, without which a just and stable social order will never be achieved. Those without goods must learn to live in poverty of spirit, so that material poverty will not deprive them of their human dignity, which is always more important than all possessions. In its most exalted and beautiful form, the "Gospel of Work" was written and proclaimed by Christ. He, being God, made himself like us in all things, except sin, and dedicated most of the years of his life on earth to manual labor, thus assuming labor and rest in the work of the Redemption which he came to bring about.

Dignity of Work

But in the mind of God, work "right from the beginning" was incorporated in the marvelous prospect, "Let us make man in our image and likeness"[32] as we read at the beginning of Genesis. Do we not find here the first expression of the "Gospel of Work?" The reason for the dignity of labor lies in this divine "likeness." So man, when he works, imitates God, his Creator, because only he bears within himself the likeness of God. To work, it is necessary to be man, to be a person; to work, it is necessary to be the "image" of God.

So it is that the dignity of work rests not only on its natural aspect but also on its spiritual dimension. It is certainly the prerogative of the person. It is a factor in human achievement and a service to the human community.

46. True Human Progress Depends on Respect for the Dignity of All Work[33]

Common Good, Community of Persons, Dialogue and Cooperation, Dignity of Work, Dominion over the Earth, Gospel of Work, Human Development/Progress, Human Rights/Dignity, Justice, Meaning of Work, Selfishness, Solidarity, Spirituality, Unemployment, Work and Society, Work and the Worker, World Community.

[An address on June 15, 1982 in Geneva, Switzerland,
to the International Labor Organization.]

In addressing you, Ladies and Gentlemen, I wish first of all, through you, to pay tribute to human work, whatever its nature and wherever in the world it may be performed – a tribute to all work, and to each and every man or woman engaged in it, irrespective of its specific content and including "physical" as well as "intellectual" work; irrespective too, of its particular purpose, whether it be "creative" or "reproductive"; and irrespective of whether it consist of theoretical research providing a basis for the work of others, or an activity aimed at organizing the conditions and structure of such work or, again, the management or the actual performance, by workers, of the tasks involved in carrying out programs. Work in any of its forms deserves particular respect because it represents the output of a human being and because behind it there is always a live subject: the human person. That is the source of its value and its dignity.

Work: A Basic Dimension of Human Existence

The message which you expect from me, Ladies and Gentlemen, is bound to be no different from that which I delivered to other gatherings of representatives of the peoples of all nations: the General Assembly of the United Nations, the United Nations Food and Agricultural Organization and the United Nations Educational, Scientific and Cultural Organization. My thinking aims at reflecting, in a coherent way, one fundamental idea and one basic preoccupation: the cause of man, his dignity and the inalienable rights flowing therefrom. Already in my first Encyclical *Redemptor Hominis*, I stressed the fact that "man is the first road which the Church must travel in fulfilling its missions; it is the first road and the fundamental road of the Church, mapped out by Christ himself." That is also the reason why, in celebrating the 90th anniversary of *Rerum Novarum*, I felt I should devote a major document of my papacy to human labor, to man at work – *homo laborem exercens*. For not only does work bear the imprint of man, but it reveals to man the true meaning of his existence – work considered as a human activity regardless of its concrete content and circumstances. Work is endowed with this basic dimension of human existence through which man's life is built up every day. From work "it delivers its specific dignity but at the same time contains the unceasing measure of human toil and suffering and also of the harm and injustice which penetrate deeply into social life within individual nations and on the international level."[34]

Solidarity and Common Effort

The problems of work – problems that have repercussions in so many spheres of life and at all levels, whether individual, family, national or international – share one characteristic, which is at one and the same time a condition and a program, and which I would like to stress before you today: *solidarity*. I feel impelled to place these considerations before you partly because solidarity is inherent in one way or another in the very nature of human work, and also because of the objectives of your Organization and above all the spirit which imbues it. The spirit in which the International Labor Organization has carried out its missions since its foundation is a spirit of *universalism*, which rests on the fundamental equality of nations and the equality of men, and which is perceived both as the starting point and the point of arrival of any social policy. It is also a spirit of *humanism*, which seeks to develop all of man's potentialities, both material and spiritual. Lastly, it is a *community spirit*, which is successfully reflected in your tripartite structure. At this juncture, I can only repeat the words pronounced here by Paul VI during his visit in 1969: "Your original and organic instrument is to bring together the three forces at work in the human dynamics of modern labor: men of government, employers and workers. And your method, that has become a model, is to harmonize these three forces, so that they do not oppose each other, but combine 'in a courageous and fecund collaboration' by means of constant dialogue for the study and solution of ever renewed and recurring problems." [35] The fact that the solution to the problems of work has been seen to lie in a commitment by all the parties involved, and in peaceful bargaining aimed at the well-being of man at his work and peace between societies, shows that you are conscious of the need for solidarity, which unites you in a common effort transcending the real differences that exist and the divisions that may always occur.

Universal Significance of Work

This fundamental intuition which the founders of the International Labor Organization so strongly emphasized in the structure of the Organization itself and whose corollary is that the objectives it pursues can only be achieved through community and solidarity, reflects the reality of human work. For, in its fundamental characteristics, the reality of work is the same all over the world, in every country and in every continent; among men and women of every race and nation, who speak different languages and represent diverse cultures; among men and women who profess different religions or express their relationships with religion and with God in a variety of ways. The reality of work is the same behind a multiplicity of forms: manual work and brain work; work in farming and work in industry; work in the service sector and work in research; the work of the craftsman, the technician, the educator, the artist or the housewife; the work of the factory operative and the work of the supervisors and managers. Without concealing the specific differences which remain and which often quite sharply differentiate the men and women performing these very varied jobs, work – the reality of work – unites all in an activity which has the same significance and the same source. For all, work is a necessity, a duty, a task. For each and every one, it is a way of assuring a livelihood, family life and certain fundamental values. In the diversity and universality of its forms, human work unites men because every man seeks in work "to realize his humanity, to fulfil the calling to be a person that is his by reason of his very humanity."[36] Yes, "work bears a *particular* mark of man and of humanity, the mark of a person operating within a community of persons."[37] Work bears the stamp of unity and solidarity.

Dominion Over the Earth

Moreover, it is difficult in dealing before this Assembly with such a vast, such a varied and at the same time such a universal subject as the work of the entire human family, not to hear in the depths of one's heart the words of the Book of Genesis, in which work is given to man as a task so that he may subdue the earth and dominate it.[38]

Work Belongs to the Realm of the Spirit

The fundamental reason why I single out the theme of solidarity lies therefore in the very nature of human work. The problem of work has a very profound link with that of the meaning of human life. Because of this link, work becomes and indeed is a problem of man's spiritual nature. This observation in no way detracts from the other aspects of work, which one might say are more easily measurable and which are related to the various patterns and operations of an "external" character, arising out of the organization: this same observation indeed enables us to set human work, in whatever way it is performed by man, within man himself, in other words, in his innermost being, in the essence of his nature, in what makes him a man and therefore destined to work. The conviction that there is an essential link between the work of every man and the overall meaning of human existence is the whole foundation of the Christian doctrine of work – one might say the foundation of the "Gospel of Work" – and it permeates the teaching and activities of the Church, in one way or another, at each stage of its mission throughout history. "Never again will work be against the worker; but always work will be ... in the service of man" – it is worth repeating today the words spoken in this same place in 1969 by

Pope Paul VI.[39] If work must always serve the welfare of man, if the program of progress can only be carried out through work, then there is a fundamental right to judge progress in accordance with the following criterion: does the work really serve man? Is it comparable with his dignity? Through it, does human life achieve fulfillment in all its richness and diversity?

True Human Progress

We have the right to conceive of human work in this way; and we also have a duty to do so. We have the right and the duty to consider man not according to whether or not he is useful in his work, but consider work in its relation to man, to each man, to consider work according to whether or not it is useful to man. We have the right and the duty to take account, in our approach to work, of the various needs of man, in the spheres of both the spirit and the body, and to take this approach to human work in each society and in each system, in areas where well-being prevails, and even more so, in areas where destitution is widespread. We have the right and the duty to take this approach to work in its relation to man – and not the reverse – as a fundamental criterion for assessing progress itself. For progress always requires an evaluation and a value judgement: one must ask whether a given progress is sufficiently "human" and at the same time sufficiently "universal"; whether it helps to level out unjust inequalities and to promote a peaceful future for the world; whether in the work itself fundamental rights are ensured for each nation. In a word, one must constantly ask oneself whether the work helps to fulfill the meaning of human life. While seeking a reply to these questions when analyzing socio-economic process as a whole, one must not overlook the aspects and the content which form man's inner self: the development of his knowledge and his awareness. The link between work and the very meaning of human existence bears constant witness to the fact that man has not been alienated from work, that he has not been enslaved. Quite the contrary, it confirms that work has become the ally of his humanity, which helps him to live in truth and freedom in a freedom built on truth which enables him to lead, in all its fullness, a life more worthy of man.

Increased Solidarity

Confronted with the blatant injustices arising out of the systems of the last century, workmen, especially in industry, reacted and thereby discovered not only their common poverty, but the strength that comes from concerted action. As victims of the same injustices, they combined in a joint effort. In my encyclical on human work, I called this reaction a "just social reaction"; this situation "caused the impetuous emergence of a great burst of solidarity between workers, first and foremost industrial workers. The call to solidarity and common action addressed to the workers – especially to those engaged in narrowly specialized, monotonous and depersonalized work in industrial plants, where the machine tends to dominate man – was important and eloquent from the point of view of social ethics. It was the reaction against the degradation of man as the subject of work. ... This reaction united the working world in a community marked by great solidarity."[40] Despite subsequent improvements, despite the greater and more effective respect for workers' fundamental rights in many countries, various systems based on ideology and on power have allowed flagrant injustices to persist or have created new ones. Moreover, there is an enhanced awareness of social injustices which, because of their geographical extent or contempt for the inalienable dignity of the human person, are nothing less than challenges to mankind. The need today is to forge a new solidarity based on the true significance of human work. For it is only through a just concept of work that it will be possible to define the objectives of this solidarity and the various forms it should take.

Justice for All

The world of work, Ladies and Gentlemen, is the world of all the men and all the women who, through their efforts, are trying to respond to the call to dominate the earth for the benefit of all. The solidarity of the world of work will therefore be a solidarity that broadens horizons to include not only the interests of individuals and particular groups but the common good of society as a whole, whether nationally, internationally or worldwide. It will be a solidarity for work, manifesting itself in the struggle for justice and for the truth of social life. For what justification would there be for a solidarity that spent itself in uncompromising opposition to others, in a struggle against others? Of course, the struggle for justice must not ignore the legitimate interests of workers associated in the same occupation or suffering from certain forms of injustice. It cannot ignore the tensions between groups which are often liable to break into open conflict. True solidarity seeks to struggle for a just social order in which all tension can be absorbed and in which conflicts – whether between groups or nations – can be settled more easily. In order to build a world of justice and peace, solidarity must remove the foundations of hatred, selfishness and injustice, which have too often been erected into ideological principles or as a vital law of life in society. Within the same community of work, solidarity sets out to discover the unity inherent in the nature of the work rather than the forces making for division and opposition. It refuses to conceive of society in terms of a struggle "against" and of social relationships in terms of uncompromising opposition between classes. Solidarity, which derives its origin and its strength from the nature of human work, and therefore from the primacy of the human person over things, will create the machinery of dialogue and cooperation that is needed to resolve opposition without seeking to destroy the opponent. No, it is not utopian to assert that the world of work can also be make a world of justice.

International Solidarity

The need for man to safeguard the reality of his work and to free it from any ideology in order to bring out once more the true meaning of human effort, becomes particularly apparent when one considers the world of work and the solidarity that it calls for in the international context. The problem of man at work today must be set against a worldwide background which can no longer be ignored. All the major problems of man in society are now world problems! They must be approached on a worldwide scale, in a realistic spirit of course, but in an innovative, critical spirit as well. Whether we are dealing with the problems of natural resources, development or employment, a satisfactory solution can be found only if the international aspect is borne in mind. As long as fifteen years ago, in 1967, Paul VI noted in his encyclical *Populorum Progressio*: "Today, the major fact that everyone must grasp is that the social question has become worldwide in character."[41] Since then, many events have borne out the truth of this observation. The world economic crisis, with its repercussions throughout the globe, compels us to recognize that the horizon of the problems is increasingly a world horizon. The hundreds of millions of starving undernourished human beings, who also have the right to rise up out of their poverty, should make us realize that the fundamental reality today is mankind as a whole. There is a common good which can no longer be confined to a more or less satisfactory compromise between sectional demands or between purely economic requirements.

New ethical choices are necessary: a new world conscience must be created; each of us, without denying his origins and the membership of his family, his people and his nation, or the obligations arising therefrom, must regard himself as a member of this great family, the world community.

In other words, Ladies and Gentlemen, we must also seek a fresh significance in human work seen in a world context, and therefore set ourselves fresh tasks. This also means that the worldwide common good requires a new solidarity without frontiers. In saying that, I do not wish to belittle the importance of the efforts that each nation must make, within the limits of its own sovereignty, its own cultural traditions and in accordance with its own needs, to achieve the type of social and economic development which respects the distinctive character of each of its members and of the entire people. Nor must it too readily be supposed that consciousness of solidarity is already sufficiently developed because of the simple fact that we are all aboard this space-ship, Earth. On the one hand, we must ensure that nations complement each other in their efforts to develop their own spiritual and material resources; and on the other hand, we must proclaim the demands made by universal solidarity and the structural consequences it implies. We must maintain this creative tension and in so doing demonstrate how these two realities complement each other; for like the human person, the nation is distinctively individual and outward looking at one and the same time.

Unemployment

Solidarity in the world of work, among men at work, has several facets. It means the solidarity of the workers; above all, in its deepest sense, it means solidarity with work, seen as a fundamental dimension of human existence, on which the meaning of that existence in fact depends. Taken in this sense, solidarity casts a special light on the problem of employment, which has become one of the major problems of our present society and one with harsh consequences for the workers which are too often overlooked, especially when they receive no assistance from society; with harsh consequences for the developing countries as a whole, and for a long time past; with harsh consequences for rural workers whose lot is so often precarious whether they remain in the countryside where there is less and less work for them or whether they try to compete for the few jobs available in the towns; with harsh consequences for professional workers and indeed for all those who, in various categories and segments of the world of work, run the risk of a new form of proletarization whenever their specific contribution is not appreciated at its true value because of changes in social systems or living conditions.

As we know, the causes of involuntary unemployment may be, and indeed are, many and varied. One of these causes may lie in the improvement in the instruments of production which progressively curtails the direct share of man in the production process. This involves us in a new antimony which may well set human labor against capital, defined as the means of production as a whole, comprising natural resources together with the means by which man appropriates this wealth which has been freely bestowed upon him and converts it to meet his needs. Thus we face a new problem which is only beginning to reveal its scope and its consequences. To identify it, even in vague and imprecise outline, means being prepared to seek a solution from the outset, without waiting for it to force itself upon our attention by the harm it causes. The solution must lie in solidarity with work, in other words, in accepting the principle of the primacy of human work over the means of production, and the primacy of the individual at work over production requirements. ... We have the first and ultimate criterion in the planning of employment: solidarity with work must be the overriding theme in any search for a solution, and it opens a new field to man's ingenuity and generosity.

For this reason I ventured to say in *Laborem Exercens* that unemployment "in all cases is an evil and ... when it reaches a certain level, can become a real social disaster. It is particularly painful when it especially affects young people." Yes, here again, solidarity is the key to the employment problem. I say so emphatically: whether at the national or international level, a positive solution to the problem of employment, and more particularly employment for young people, presupposes solidarity of the highest degree within and among all peoples. All must be prepared to accept the necessary sacrifices; all must cooperate in the establishment of the programs and agreements through which economic and social policy will become a tangible expression of solidarity; all must help in erecting the appropriate economic technical, political and financial structures which the establishment of a new social order of solidarity indisputably requires. I refuse to believe that mankind today, with its prodigious scientific and technical prowess, is incapable of the kind of creative effort, inspired by the very nature of human work and solidarity among all living beings, which will yield fair and effective answers to the essentially human problem of employment.

Free Association

A society of solidarity is built up day by day, first by creating and then by preserving the conditions on which the free participation of all in the common effort effectively depends. Any policy to achieve the common good must be the fruit of organic and spontaneous cohesion of the forces of society. This is another form of solidarity – solidarity as an imperative of social order, the kind that manifests itself typically through the existence and the work of associations of social partners. The right to associate freely is a fundamental one for all those who are connected with the world of work and who constitute the work community. It means that no working man need be either alone or isolated; it expresses the solidarity of all in the defence of the rights which are rightfully theirs and flow from the requirements of their work; it affords a normal channel for participating actively in the performance of work and everything related to it, while being guided at the same time by a concern for the common good. This right presupposes that the social partners are truly free to form or join an association of their own choosing and to run it. Although the right to freedom of association seems beyond a doubt to be one of the basic rights most generally recognized, as attested by International Labor Convention N. 87 (1948), yet it is severely threatened, often flouted either in its principle or – more often – in practice, with the result that freedom of association is disfigured. It seems essential to point out that cohesion among the forces of society, always desirable in itself, must be the outcome of free decisions by those concerned, taken in full independence from the political authorities and arrived at in full freedom as regards the determination of the internal organization of trade unions, their operating methods and their activities. The working man must assume the responsibility for defending the truth, the true dignity of his work. He must not be prevented from exercising that responsibility, though also bearing in mind the good of the community.

47. The Christian Worker Bears a Responsibility to the World of Work[42]

Christian Witness/Mission, Collaboration with God, Dignity of Work, Dominion over the Earth, Economic Laws and Profits, Fair Wage, Gospel of Work, Human Rights/Dignity, Meaning of Work, Solidarity, Work and Society, Work and the Worker.

[An address on December 19, 1982 in Rome, to representatives of the Christian Workers Movement.]

The task of a movement such as yours is above all that of being a witness to Christ in the world of work. It is a matter of an ecclesial task in which the entire Christian community must feel committed, but in a special way those workers who are enlivened by Christian faith! and as Pastor, I feel the duty to renew a pressing appeal to the entire world of workers: open the doors to Christ and to his saving power, throw open the doors of your hearts and minds to Christ's message, which is the proclamation of salvation, freedom and true human development.

Christian Witness in the World of Work

Dear brothers and sisters, your movement takes on the form of an ecclesial movement precisely when it places among its primary aims that of carrying this message into the world of work. In particular, Christian workers must carry into the world of work that social message, rich in values and proposals, which springs from the same evangelical teaching and which the Church has always, but especially during this past century from *Rerum Novarum* to *Laborem Exercens,* offered as an instrument of authentic social development. The contribution of this doctrine operates above all on the level of principles of the moral order, but without them the so-called social question will never be able to find an adequate solution.

Gospel of Work

The task of every Christian worker, just as that of every workers' association, is to be the bearer, proclaimer and witness of what I called the "Gospel of Work" in the cited encyclical, *Laborem Exercens.*[43]

In the light of this Gospel the worker in workshops, the worker in the fields, the employee and the professional, or in any case every man who carries out an activity, discovers that "the primary basis for determining the value of work is not first of all the type of work performed, but the fact that the one who performs it is a person."[44] It is upon this principle that the true meaning and value of work and the dignity of the worker are based.

The work of man – whatever kind of work, manual or intellectual – is an act of the human person; every type of work has its human value and every worker has his dignity as a human person.

Primacy of Work over Capital

In the light of these basic principles, it can be understood why work's primacy over capital and every produced good must be recognized: capital, insofar as it is the overall means of production, is only an instrument, while work is a primary cause, which leads back to man and to his dignity. Through work man fulfills himself, discovers his true identity, and at the same time makes society grow, not only because of the material goods he is able to produce and place at everyone's disposal, but above all because of the moral values which enrich the community and foster the achievement of the true common good.

Every Christian, and especially the Christian worker, must carry this concept of work into society, since it is the key to dealing with the solutions to all the problems inherent in this area; the remuneration for work (which demands a just family salary); working conditions (which must correspond to the dignity of the worker himself); types of social security (necessary to ensure the worker during illness, incapacity, old age, unemployment, etc.).

Work: A Participation in God's Creation

But in addition to the human and social dimension of work, the Christian worker is the bearer of a spiritual and theological dimension of work itself, which brings us closer to God, Creator and Redeemer, and makes us rediscover Christ our Savior, who during his earthly life was also "a man of work."[45] In fact, human work, seen in its spiritual and theological dimension, is a participation in God's creative work; it is the continuation of creation. "Individual and collective effort," we read in *Gaudium et Spes*, "that monumental effort with which men throughout the course of the centuries have labored to better the circumstances of their lives, considered in itself, accords with God's will. For man, created in God's image, received a mandate to subject to himself the earth and all that it contains, and to govern the world with justice and holiness; a mandate to relate himself and the totality of things to him who was to be acknowledged as the Lord and Creator of all. Thus, by the subjection of all things to man, the name of God would be wonderful in all the earth."[46]

Solidarity of Work

Christian workers, therefore, have a rich and profound concept of human work, which not only exalts the dignity of the worker, of work and of the world of work, but as a natural consequence urges toward solidarity the men of work and commits them to work tenaciously for the defense of workers' rights as an integral part of human rights.

Your movement is itself an expression of this solidarity among men of work, operating in Italian society in the light of the social teaching of the Church.

The solidarity of your movement aims especially at the formation of Christian workers: human, religious and social formation. The Church is in a position to supply every element for this formation, in such a way that Christian workers may become able to insert themselves into the world of work with the proper concept of life and of society, and thus be Christian leaven in the world in which they operate.

Bearers of a Heritage

I therefore exhort you to continue this essential work of formation, to be always faithful to the teaching of the Church as it springs from the Gospel: I exhort you to be always consistent with your concept of life, convinced that, as Christians, you are the depositories of a heritage of values which can truly make not only the world of work grow, but all of society as well. The Church, in its evangelizing mission, needs your Christian witness. Commit yourselves therefore, as a movement and as Christians, to be witnesses always of your faith: you yourselves are to be the Church in the world of work.

48. *Christians Have a Responsibility to Bring Peace to the World of Work*[47]

Christian Witness/Mission, Dialogue and Cooperation, Economic Laws and Profits, Justice.

[An address on January 4, 1983 in Rome, to the National Youth Congress of the Italian Christian Workers' Association (ACLI).]

The world of work today more than ever needs Christian witness; and you young people, if faithful to Christ and the Church, are, with the dynamism and enthusiasm that characterize you, the most suited to attest to the values proper to Christianity.

The World of Work Needs Christian Witness

In the working environment, you young Christians are the bearers of a message which, because of its incomparable grandeur, paradoxically sometimes risks not even being noticed. It is up to you to translate it on a daily basis, almost breaking it up, to make it perceptible and liveable, within reach, and above all appealing. What is at stake is the fulfillment of man's potential, which only the Gospel makes fully possible.

I know the motto of the ACLI: "As Christians in the workers' world." Be faithful to the challenging commitment that it demands. We must finally consider obsolete the unfortunate conflict which some ideologies of the past century attempted to establish between the workers' identity and the ecclesial identity, between work and faith. This unfortunate opposition often caused man's further humiliation, attempting to extinguish in him a light which in reality is inextinguishable. By its very nature, Christianity never tends to extinguish anything which constitutes the true nobility of man,[48] but instead tends to kindle or even to light in him new fires of high ideals and generous dedication to his brother, in whom faith helps us to see almost a sacramental sign of God himself.[49]

Therefore, you have new reasons for pursuing a fruitful solidarity among men of work and the achievement of authentic social justice, prescinding from theories which reduce man to a single dimension, the economic and materialistic one.[50]

You will be able to give the witness that society needs today, to the extent that you make the Christian identity which gave birth to your movement, and which at times diminished during the history of your movement, always stronger and more creative.

Role of the Church and the Liturgy

Commit yourselves generously to this effort while you continue your active presence in the social fabric of your country. Always remember that your presence would be sterile if it should take place while neglecting to measure yourselves constantly by the word of God authentically interpreted by the ecclesiastical Magisterium, and to immerse yourselves ever more in the faith life of your ecclesial communities. It is rather from there that you must start: nourish yourself on this reality, and direct your every effort to this.

As the Italian bishops expressed so well in the document on "The Italian Church and the Prospects of the Country" of 23 October 1981, "There is no future for a Christianity made up of purely social tradition. It would be a grave error to pursue the press of daily problems while diminishing the basic commitment which finds its organic aim in daily confrontation with the word of God, in the Eucharistic celebration and in the duty of witnessing to the Gospel. We shall always be able to derive new ways for serving the country from an intense ecclesial life."[51]

Call for Peace and Dialogue

The theme of your congress reads: "Peace is the Destiny of Mankind." What profound concepts are contained in this motto! It is radically Christian, and recalls those ancient and solemn Biblical texts in which the Prophet foretold to the People of God glowing prospects of harmony, accord and, precisely, of peace: when "they shall beat their swords into ploughshares"[52] when "the wolf shall dwell with the lamb,"[53] when "the warrior's bow shall be banished."[54] Is all this perhaps a utopia? Vain hope? An illusion? No! On the contrary, the Christian knows that this is the destiny of mankind! He knows that, even if it is not a matter of an imminent goal, it is a certain one and merits all the most generous dedication in order to bring it ever closer. And every effort toward this end is not useless, but fruitful. The Prophet's words, indeed, are not only our comfort, but also our incentive. "For the vision still has its time, presses on to fulfillment, and will not disappoint; if it delays, wait for it, it will surely come, it will not be late."[55] One thing is certain: the Lord has "plans for peace and not for woe, plans to give you a future full of hope."[56]

But this is a destiny to which man must contribute, precisely because it concerns him. And a destiny of peace is certainly not prepared by resorting to conflicts, violence, suppression, both in international life and in relationships between social groups and forces. As I stated in my message for the World Day of Peace on 1 January of last year, not disputes but "dialogue is necessary for true peace."[57] Only dialogue allows us to know one another. In fact, it is already of the same nature as the goal we want to achieve, since in order to achieve peace, peaceful means are necessary which conform to the principle according to which only similar things generate things similar to themselves.

You, dear young Christian workers, are called to make these values alive and active in the world of your employment.

I exhort you to strengthen ever more your Christian identity and to live it with consistency and in full fidelity to the directions of the pastors of the Church.

---

49. Work Is an Essential Aspect of Human Dignity[58]

Christian Witness/Mission, Dignity of Work, Justice, St. Joseph, Work and the Worker.

[An address on March 19, 1983 in San Salvo, Italy, to workers of the Italian glass industry.]

A short time ago I was able to make a tour through your factory and I was able to realize personally not only how big and modern it is, but also to realize the nature of your work. And when one knows firsthand what a man does, especially if this is his everyday life, then not only does he appreciate him, but he loves him even more. It is as if a sharing, and therefore a communion, were created, which normally is impossible at a distance. Well then, this very current has been established between you and me. You thus have the assurance of my esteem and furthermore of my complete affection.

Appreciation of Daily Work

Today, as you know, is the feast day of St. Joseph, that is, the feast day of a man who was not only the putative father of Jesus, but who practised manual labour, certainly not as a hobby, but to procure the necessary sustenance for himself and for his singular family. This is why I have come among you today here in San Salvo: to venerate the greatest worker Saint and in a special way to honour work in itself, which constitutes your daily occupation.

Work is an essential part of man's life on this earth, already starting from the moment of his creation. Our Lord Jesus Christ himself accepted it and practiced it for many years: it could not have been otherwise, for from the moment that he assumed the most common human condition and lived as a man among men, one could say he hired as a worker among workers.

Humanization of Work

These brief observations allow us to recognize in work an unmatchable stature and dignity. It is true: it is also a weight, exertion, sweat. But on the other hand, it allows man to fulfil himself, to respond to his vocation as the lord of creation, since it gives him the possibility of forming and transforming matter. And above all it furnishes him with the way to procure sustenance and a dignified life for himself and for his dear ones: a typically human end, without which one would place one(self) only on the level of a machine or a robot. Precisely this ever greater humanization of work is particularly close to my heart; furthermore, as you know, I always try to promote it.

True Prosperity

This, therefore, is also the wish I make to your factory, to each one of you, directors and workers, and consequently to your families. May the work you do truly serve your human development, be a source of true satisfaction for you, be the opportunity for Christian witness, the place and reason for the affirmation of justice, and may it thus contribute to everyone's social well-being, as well as to your personal prosperity in the widest sense of the word.

50. Work Plays an Irreplaceable Role in the Personal Growth of the Worker[59]

Common Good, Economic Laws and Profits, Human Rights/Dignity, Leisure, Meaning of Work, Unemployment, Work and Prayer, Work and the Worker.

[An address on May 21, 1983 in Sesto San Giovanni, Italy, to a group of workers.]

To this reason for pride of a specifically Christian nature are added others which are on a more directly human level. They are reasons arising from the awareness of the irreplaceable role which work plays as much in the growth of the person as in the building up of society. In fact, just as the nation derives its own well-being from its citizens' activity, individual workers find in the daily dedication to their tasks an effective school of professional seriousness, of personal responsibility, of courageous attachment to the fundamental values of civil coexistence.

Work's Role in Personal Growth

In this regard, how can we not recall the lofty witness of civic conscience offered forty years ago by this city's workers in December 1943, when the workers of all the factories crossed their arms as a sign of protest against the dictatorship's abuses.

Work is the school of humanity, and man, when he learns to be himself, learns also to defend the values in which he believes.

Negative Aspects of Human Work

This observation, which is confirmed by the experience of what happens in many parts of the world, does not exhaust every facet of that complex phenomenon which is human work. Alongside positive values, it does not lack elements, also considerable, which seem to contradict the optimistic evaluation just now proposed.

Work is monotonous and tiring. Not only that, it seems to entail humiliation of the needs connected with man's spirituality. Work, especially that of the laborer, seems to require the human being's subjugation to his work: the machine and the ever more sophisticated technical organization of production impose objective laws on the individual's services and often obstruct the realization of his personal inventive and expressive abilities.

Moreover, the work of an office worker and of an administrative or organizational employee is not substantially different from that of a laborer: technological innovation, and today especially that of cybernetics, often reduces to zero the professional capacities previously acquired and necessitates beginning anew to reacquire one's professional qualifications in obedience to the changed characteristics of the organization of work.

Alienation of Worker from Work

Besides, the general law of the separation of the worker from his own work remains: the man who works is not dedicated directly to an activity intended for his own moral and spiritual edification, but he renders a service to the common good, a service whose effective advantage for the common good is nevertheless conditioned, and at the same time threatened, by the complex network of all economic relations. This circumstance also contributes to creating an impression of the worker's being extraneous to his own work.

Human Limitations Call for the Transcendent

For all these reasons work appears to be a reality much less positive and free than a superficial consideration of it would lead one to believe. In addition, there is another complex facet of work to be considered. Work is also the proof of human limitation, the limitation of the individual, who needs the participation of everyone else in order to acquire the fundamental needs of his own life, and also the limitation of the collective undertaking of men, which can never achieve the objective of creating everything that is indispensable to the life of each one. In fact, man does not live only by what his hands can produce. He bears in himself expectations and hopes that no earthly reality can ever completely satisfy. This is indeed the truth: man finds the full meaning of life only beyond and above life itself. He finds it in God who, in Christ, approached him in order to save him.

With this, I do not mean to say that an ever fuller liberation of man from conditions which today still oppress him in various forms should not be promoted with every reasonable means. What is being stated is the fatal "incompleteness" of every similar effort if at the same time one does not open himself to the transcendent dimension of faith.

Work and Rest

Man's freedom and hope, in his participation as worker in the collective work, are guaranteed only if he finds rest in the faithful consideration of God's work. Do we not find here the profound reason for the Biblical precept which requires man to suspend his work weekly in order to enter into God's rest and to offer to him, by participating in the Eucharist, "the fruits of the earth and the work of his own hands?" Through this pause man can more easily place himself in harmony with the Lord's plan and find in reflection on his creative work, which is the only work that is completed, the basis of a "hope which does not disappoint."[60] In fact, there is an explicit promise by God in this regard: "Happy are you who fear the Lord, who walk in his ways!"; only he will be able "to eat the fruit of his handiwork," since that work will be accompanied and made fruitful by God's blessing.[61]

Right to Employment

What need there is for God's blessing in today's world, weighed down by so many and such grave threats! Among the many distresses which trouble mankind today I want to recall here only one to which you are especially exposed: unemployment. I well know how much this problem afflicts the world of work, caught these past few years in the coils of an economic crisis which threatens every attempt at recovery.

One of the reasons for today's visit is precisely this: to attest to my participation in the sufferings of those who have lost their places of employment and in the anxieties of those who see their security threatened. The problem of unemployment is a fundamental problem, as I wrote in the encyclical *Laborem Exercens*, especially if it is considered in relation to young people "who, after appropriate cultural, technical and professional preparation fail to find work, and see their sincere wish to work and their readiness to take on their own responsibility for the economic and social development of the community sadly frustrated."[62]

Certainly, it is a question of a complex problem which is influenced by numerous factors connected with new developments in technological, economic and political conditions, as I recognized at the beginning of the aforementioned document.[63] Nevertheless, there are not missing among its causes culpable delays, lack of solidarity, blameworthy egoism. For its part, the Church does not tire of "calling attention to the dignity and rights of those who work, to condemn situations in which that dignity and those rights are violated."[64]

Therefore I also take this opportunity to renew a passionate appeal to all those who have the power of economic or political initiative, that they unite their efforts in a coordinated and responsible action which, within the framework of sacrifices equitably distributed among the citizens, will open new perspectives in this fundamental sector of social life. In fact, the harmonious commitment of everyone will bring about that progress in justice and well-being which constitutes the common aspiration of the various parts of the social whole.

Respect for the Dignity of All

With the wish that these expectations be finally satisfied, I lift my prayer to the Father of all men and all peoples that he enlighten every person of good will and direct their commitment towards the goal of an ever more mature respect for the dignity of the person, the subject and end of every work activity, for the building up of a society that is just, free and at peace.

---

51. Work Contributes True Nobility for the Human Person[65]

Common Good, Dialogue and Cooperation, Dignity of Work, Meaning of Work, Work and Prayer, Work and the Worker.

[An address on October 10, 1983 in Rome, to members of the Italian National Federation of the Knights of Labor.]

Being qualified "Knights of Labor" means that the modern world considers work a true and authentic "nobility" for man, in that it corresponds to the dignity of the human person. Work is a good thing for man. And – as I wrote in my apostolic exhortation on human labor – "it is not only good in the sense that it is useful or something to enjoy; it is also good as being something worthy, that is to say, something that corresponds to man's dignity, that expresses this dignity and increases it. ... Work is a good thing for man – a good thing for his humanity – because through work man not only transforms nature, adapting it to his own needs, but he also achieves fulfillment as a human being and indeed, in a sense, becomes 'more a human being.' "[66]

I hope that all citizens acquire an ever clearer awareness of the duty which they have of offering this personal contribution of their work, day after day, so that in mutual trust and sincere dialogue, conflicts might be overcome, and the ideal of solidarity, justice, peace, concord and the union of everyone's efforts for the common good might be ever more affirmed.

Ora et Labora

In 1962, my predecessor John XXIII, of venerated memory, gave St. Benedict the Abbot to your Federation as your Patron Saint. With this gesture, he wanted not only to offer you a protector in heaven, but also to present you a shining and great example of profound Christian faith and of tireless activity on behalf of the brethren and for the progress of the various communities. You must continuously model yourselves on your saint, whose undisputed and historic influence was happily synthesized in the motto *"Ora et Labora"* ("Pray and work"), in fulfilling your daily commitments – familial and professional – that you might live a worthy life in the light and the strength of the Christian message.

52. The Meaning of Work Depends on the Meaning of Leisure and the Celebration of the Eucharist[67]

Collaboration with God, Dominion over the Earth, Fair Wage, Human Development/Progress, Human Rights/Dignity, Leisure, Meaning of Work, St. Joseph, Unemployment.

[An address on March 24, 1985 in Fucino,
Italy, to workers from forty-six countries.]

I listened with great attention and vital interest to the addresses made by your representatives, dear workers, grasping their important elements: the land of Marsica is a land of much suffering, made sometimes hard by especially tragic events; but a land that you have transformed radically, making a marshy territory fertile, promoting communications in places where the mountains imposed isolation on the individual communities, creating workplaces where forced emigration was the painful destiny of so many young people.

Obstacles in Work

I should like to show each one of you my solidarity in the aspiration which you have expressed and which gives force to your daily work, to overcome whatever makes man dissatisfied with his condition; denouncing openly whatever comes from egoism, domination, or cheating workers of their just interests; committing yourselves to work for an effective social promotion, for the respect of man's dignity in the world of agriculture, industrial and artisans' work. You have spoken very clearly of your problems. As you say, one must defeat the modern forms of slavery, and promote laws that are ever more just and adequate, in order to overcome, with the commitment of all, the worrisome amount of unemployment. It is equally urgent to return the fruits of the earth to their providential destination, to dispel the hunger of man. In a world in which so great a part of humanity is tried by hunger, and the means of conservation and of transport of the nutritional products become constantly more efficient, it is a source of deep bitterness that one must have recourse to the destruction of produce in order to save businesses. Defending the fruits of the ground, we may increase the return to agriculture which many young people already feel to be a healthy program for their future and for their cultural needs.

The ministry which has been entrusted to me, and which has brought me to you here, urges me to make myself the echo of your requests and to encourage with renewed vigor all of your suggestions of a generous commitment to overcome the obstacles which still confront you.

Work as Gift and Burden

I have come here in remembrance of St. Joseph, patron of workers, who found the meaning of his daily work in the living presence of Christ beside his workbench. Thus he became the model of the Christian worker. He helps us to understand the profound sense of the word of God about human work: "Fill the earth; subdue it and dominate it;"[68] "It will produce thorns and thistles for you. ... You will eat bread in the sweat of your brow."[69] These two affirmations of God at the beginning of the Bible, on the threshold of history, enlighten with power and truth the drama of man's work. They indicate above all God's intention to entrust to man the task of realizing himself, acquiring with his work a true dominion over the world. They announce beforehand, too, the reversal that followed sin, reducing man to the necessity of supporting as a burden what had been offered him as a gift. The drama is resolved, not in the defeat of man – as if work were a curse for him – but in the salvific love of God, who reaches out His hand to man to take up again the project that had been broken.

Collaboration with God the Architect

"The Church is convinced that work constitutes a fundamental dimension of man's existence on earth": this is what I wrote in the encyclical Letter about work.[70] Even on the purely human level, we know that man can become himself and reach the goal of his life by means of the assiduous undertaking to transform himself, and by his hard work that has its object in the world that surrounds him: overcoming obstacles, planning new conditions of existence, producing the goods necessary for body and spirit, bread and culture. But human experience, subject to disappointments and deformations, receives a formidable support from the Christian vision. We are struck by the fact that in the Bible God manifests himself for the first time to the world and to the eyes of man as Creator, that is, as one who constructs the world with wisdom and goodness. God himself appears as a worker, in the form of the architect[71] or in that of the artisan.[72] Far from being the jealous master of His creation, God gives it to man joyfully and without reservations, and entrusts him with the task of prolonging God's work in accord with a progress that is never finished. In this way – and not through a static and frightened resignation – man can disclose to his own consciousness and to that of all creatures that he bears in himself the seal of a divine origin and destination. His work, every form of work, becomes in a certain manner the prolongation and completion of God's project.

A Just Reward for Collaboration

Work is an assignment that God makes to man; but it can turn out to be difficult, and the worker may not see the fruits of his own efforts.

It happens often that the painful toil of so many men and women is not sufficiently recognized and justly remunerated.

The social teaching of the Church – as you well know – forcefully affirms the worker's right to have a just reward and, at the same time, proclaims the primacy of man in relation to work. Man must become, not the slave, but the master of his own work; that is, he must see his own dignity respected in work.

The consequences of this principle are enormous: man may never be treated as an instrument of production; men who work have the right to solidarity among themselves and to support from society, so that their participation in the growth of the social good may be safeguarded, along with the right to a just salary, and to the security of the persons of the workers and of their respective families.

In this context, turning my thoughts to so many unemployed, especially to the young people in search of their first job, aware of the need of a cultural and educative process for those who encounter today the world of work which is continually exposed to higher and higher levels of specialization, I cannot do other than implore those who have political and social responsibilities to contribute with all the resources of their intelligence and good will to the resolution of these problems that so particularly involve the dignity of the person, with the participation of the workers themselves, with realism, courage and breadth of vision.

The Importance of Rest for Understanding Work

But the dignity of the workers would be too little recognized, and the truth and force with which the Christian revelation is charged would be impoverished, were I not to say in a loud voice that, to realize man's vocation, work is not enough, and that there exists another task which the person takes on as the soul of daily toil. Within the very system of work there resounds the commandment of the Lord, a commandment that shines out from the very beginning in the repose of the seventh day:[73] "Remember the sabbath day, to make it holy: six days you shall toil and do all your work, but the seventh day is the sabbath in honor of the Lord your God: you shall not do any work ... because in six days the Lord made heaven and earth and the sea and all that is in it, but on the seventh day He rested. Therefore the Lord has blessed the sabbath day and declared it sacred."[74]

Work and the Eucharist

With the resurrection of Jesus on the first day after the sabbath, the day of the Lord has become Sunday. It is the precious moment in which the one who works – sometimes doing hard work – can rediscover the sense of his work, expressing thanks to God for the labor of his own hands, sharing in a more extended way the company of those dear to him, from whom work risks keeping him far away, and visiting persons who are sick and needy. In particular, every Christian is called to share in a festive banquet, the Sunday Mass. Gathered together to form the Christian community, workers are enabled to sense the share in a reality that should give them strength. After having explained the Word of God, the celebrant raises the bread and the wine to God, proclaiming, "Blessed are You, Lord God of all creation. From Your goodness we have received this bread (and this wine), fruit of the earth and of the work of man, and we present it to You, so that it may become for us the food of eternal life (the cup of salvation)." God gives us in Jesus Christ the grace to perceive the true meaning of our work. Even if the work is sometimes united to tribulations, it is no longer a curse, but is a sharing in the redemptive sacrifice of Christ. As happened for Jesus, the toil – sometimes heavy – of work becomes a sacrificial prayer for deliverance from the evil in one's own heart and that of others, and at the same time is transformed into the capacity to see, in the ever better construction of the city of man, a prophecy, an anticipation, of what will be the definitive Kingdom of God.

Work and Reconciliation

Concluding my dialogue with you, dear workers of Marsica, I wish to add to this invitation to make your work a prayer united to the sacrifice of Christ, the appeal suggested by the forthcoming Italian Ecclesial Assembly which has as its theme "Christian Reconciliation and the Community of Men;" I entrust to you the task of bearing witness to Christian reconciliation, the gift of God, in the world of work, and in the wider world of society.

Solidarity of Workers

Beside us is this great center for telecommunications, built by the I.R.I., a center that bears witness to the possibility of making use of the most modern technologies to facilitate the diffusion of knowledge and information even by means of communications through space.

Here, before Telespace an expression of the most advanced science and of how much man has been able to realize with his work, I should like to address greetings and good wishes to all the workers of the world, calling down on them the protection of St. Joseph.

I greet all the workers of the world, with warm sympathy and great affection. Yes, dear worker, I wish to assure you that the Church is near you, that she is your ally, your friend. May you have confidence in her! She is beside you, to defend your legitimate aspirations and the dignity of your work, convinced that "work is a good of man – a good of his humanity – for, by means of work, not only does man transform nature in adapting it to his own needs, but even more, he realizes himself as man and even, in a certain sense, becomes more human."[75] This is the plan of God; these are my greetings; this is what you must aim at.

May work be held in honor! And above all, may all the workers of the world be held in honor!

The installations of this Italian center for diffusion of television allow the transmission everywhere in the world of this meeting on this Sunday that follows the feast of St. Joseph: they remind us that there can be a rich hope in this new technological stage in the sphere of communications. I wish that these media may always make a true contribution to agreement among men and to the progress of humanity.

"Dialogue of Salvation" with the World

The Church proclaims her deep desire to be close to all the workers of the world. She wants to be part of your lives, and to speak to you about the supreme relevance that the Gospel of Jesus Christ has for you in the ordinary circumstances in which you find yourselves every day.

The Church wants to speak to you about the dignity of your work, and how it contributes to your human and Christian advancement, to the betterment of the family and the nation, and to the very transformation of the world. As the Church points out your rights and duties, she proclaims that your work is a sharing in the activity of God the Creator. All of this she declares in the name of Christ, who looks with love upon human work and who himself belonged to the "working world."

Yes, the Church wants to hold with you workers a "dialogue of salvation," and she wants to do this in every diocese and in every parish church, for it is at this level that you must live and act as Christians. It is in these situations that you are called to apply the teaching of Christ, and through the honesty of your work and the uprightness of your lives to bear witness before your co-workers to the power of the Gospel. In all this, St. Joseph is your example and patron and friend.

Work is not Servitude but a Right

I greet you heartily also, German-speaking workers and employers. Joseph, the patron of workers, whose feast we have kept last week, reminds us of the value and the dignity of all human work, whether it makes demands more on our physical strength or on our intellectual strength. Work does not mean servitude, but is rather a commission and vocation to an active cooperation in the shaping of creation and of human society. Work is a basic right and a basic duty of man.

Therefore, work may not divide you from one another into two groups; instead, work obliges us to mutual solidarity and fraternity – the employers and the employed, those who do physical work and those who do intellectual work, those who have work and those who cannot find a place of work. Only through common endeavors, which include sacrifices for one another, can you master the great problems in the modern world of work with success and to the benefit of all. Those among you who are Christian are called in a special way, in the spirit of the Gospel, to recognize their neighbor in the underprivileged and the needy, and to come to their aid with sympathy and practical deeds.

May God bless the world of your work! May He bless the work of your hands and of your intellect!

---

53. Collaboration with God Achieves the Priority of the Person[76]

Collaboration with God, Common Good, Culture of Work, Economic Laws and Profits, Fair Wage, Human Development/ Progress, Humanization/Dehumanization, Gospel of Work, Worker Participation.

[An address on May 5, 1984 in Pusan,
South Korea, to Korean workers.]

The Son of God became man and worked with human hands. Work, then, has a dignity of its own in God's plan for creation. We hear in the very first page of the Book of Genesis that man was created "in the image of God ... male and female." Entrusting the whole universe to him, God told him to "be fruitful, to multiply, and fill the earth and subdue it."[77]

So we know, not only by reason alone but through Revelation, that by his work man shares in the Creator's work. He continues it and, in a sense, perfects it by his own work, by his toil, by his daily effort to wrest a livelihood from the earth or from the sea, or to apply his energies to the many different processes of production.

How noble is this mission that only man – by his work – can realize!

Collaboration with God

Indeed, we Christians are convinced that the achievements of the human race – in art, science, culture and technology – *are a sign of God's greatness* and the flowering of His own mysterious design.

Jesus himself gave particular emphasis to this truth: that through his work man shares in the activity of the Creator, for Jesus was himself a working man, a craftsman like Joseph of Nazareth. Jesus clearly belonged to the "working world." So did most of His disciples and listeners: ordinary fishermen, farmers and workers. So, when He speaks about the Kingdom of God, Jesus constantly uses terms connected with human work: the work of the shepherd, the farmer, the doctor, the sower, the householder, the servant, the steward, the fisherman, the merchant, the laborer. And he compares the building up of God's Kingdom to the world of harvesters and fishermen.

Priority of the Person over the Product

From Jesus' own teaching we can clearly see that the man who works is much more important than the product of his work. Human work comes from man; it is intended to benefit man, to promote his God-given dignity. Even the biggest city, the most complicated computer, the greatest nation, is only something made by man and is meant to serve man, to benefit man. Never the other way around.

That is why the Second Vatican Council, speaking of the value of human work, declares: "A person is more precious for what he is than for what he has. Similarly, all that people do to obtain greater justice, wider brotherhood and a more humane ordering of social relationships has greater worth than technical advances. For these advances can supply the material for human progress, but of themselves alone they can never actually bring it about."[78]

Nevertheless, this order of values is not always respected. Today's society, so taken up with developing a one-sided materialistic civilization, often treats work as a special kind of merchandise. Man is often treated as a mere instrument of production, like a material tool that should cost as little as possible while producing the maximum. In these cases the worker is not respected as a true collaborator of the Creator.

Work Must Transcend Ideologies

Unfortunately, the whole issue of work has often been looked at from the viewpoint of conflict between "capital" and "labor": a conflict that has vast social, ideological and political implications. This conflict has been a great tragedy for humanity and a source of suffering for untold millions of individual human beings and families.[79]

I well realize that the relationship between employers and employees in the context of your Korean cultural and social traditions has its own special characteristics, and that it is not true that the way to better relationships is to be found in a simplistic application of standards and methods devised elsewhere, still less by imposing alien ideological systems which have allowed flagrant injustices to persist, or have created new ones, threatening the very peace of the world.

Participation Is a Key to Justice

Justice requires that ways be found to give workers a greater share in the organizational aspects of production and in profits, and I am pleased to know that initiatives have been taken in this direction.

Justice also requires that the workers themselves benefit from the success of the enterprise in which they work, and that they have the satisfaction of knowing that through diligent and conscientious work they are thereby contributing to the social development of their country.

The Gospel of Work

Of course, we know that work is not all fulfillment and satisfaction. Yes, work involves toil and struggle and you have all experienced this. Work has been profoundly affected by sin, as we read in the Book of Genesis: "In the sweat of your face you shall eat bread."[80] That is why we can never fathom the full meaning of work without looking to the

Paschal Mystery of Jesus Christ in which He conquered sin and transformed all work. His work, His suffering, His obedience unto death receive their full meaning in His Resurrection: This is the "Gospel of Work" contained in the life and teaching of our Redeemer.

Work and Suffering

So we Christians find in human work a small share in the Cross of Jesus Christ. We must learn to live this human experience with Christ's attitude. By uniting our work with the mission of our Savior, we help bring about the new earth where justice dwells,[81] and we contribute mightily to the coming of the Kingdom of God.

Dear workers, farmers and fishermen, I realize that, in solidarity with millions of your fellow workers, you have had to suffer much and are continuing to suffer for the birth of this "new earth" in your land. Often in the face of indifference, misunderstanding, and even harassment, you have, as Christians consciously committed to promoting the rights and welfare of fellow workers and farmers, patiently and bravely borne the cross. All of us must work together in fraternal love to show that a more just sharing of the world's goods means access to these goods especially through a just wage.

Christ the Answer

Take heart from the words of the Gospel! The Beatitudes and the woes you have just heard are the very words of the Lord appealing on behalf of the poor and oppressed against every form of injustice and social and personal selfishness. Take courage, "for the Kingdom of God is yours!"[82] And as you rightly demand justice for your cause and for your lives, make sure that your own "works of faith"[83] always promote justice for your neighbor.

Beloved brothers and sisters of Korea, my friends: you do, indeed, have a special place in the heart of Jesus and of His Church. I know that the proportion of Christians among industrial workers, farmers and fishermen is small: herein lies a great challenge for the shepherds of the Church in Korea and for yourselves. Be certain that the life and teachings of our Lord Jesus Christ, the carpenter of Nazareth, can supply answers to the doubts and questions of working men and women. Only Jesus Christ can sustain your hopes and dispel your anxieties. He alone can show you the meaning of your daily toil. In His name and together with His Church continue, through peaceful and upright means, to pursue human dignity, promote human rights and create a better world for yourselves, your children and your children's children.

May Jesus bless your work! May He bless your families and friends, and give you His peace in overflowing measure! And through His grace may all your activities be linked to prayer, so that you may bring forth abundant "works of faith," leading to justification and eternal life.

---

54. Labor Derives Its Value from the Dignity of the Person[84]

Collaboration with God, Gospel of Work, Human Development/Progress, Human Rights/Dignity, Leisure, Meaning of Work, Spirituality, Unemployment, Work and Family.

[An address on October 18, 1985, in Sardinia, Italy, to miners of the Monteponi Mines.]

I come to you, dear brothers, prompted by the liveliest sentiments of fraternal solidarity and moved by the conviction that, despite difficulties of every sort, the type of work you do must not be an obstacle to the realization of the great objectives that give meaning and dignity to life. Prior to the advent of Christianity, physical labor, like every other form of sacrifice and suffering, was considered only an unavoidable fate tied to our existence, without light on the horizon. In particular, the ancient Romans considered the mines places of condemnation; with the harshness of the Latin expression *damnare ad metalla*, they indicated that they saw them as a destiny without escape. It pleases me to recall, at this point, that one of my predecessors, Pope St. Pontianus, the first Pope to set foot on Sardinian soil seventeen centuries ago, was sent there as one condemned to the mines because of his fearless profession of the Christian faith. And today the Church, venerating him as a martyr, intends to pay homage to a man who witnessed to the Faith to the extent of making the ultimate sacrifice.

Called to Subdue the Earth

The conditions under which you carry on your work today are fortunately no longer those of that time. They remain very arduous, however, and you merit special gratitude on the part of the entire society. In fact, thanks to the work carried on in the dark depths of the earth, the community is able to make its own new riches which were hidden there, and to put them to use for the sustenance and growth of the whole human family.

This is in fact God's design: to call man to collaborate, through the efforts of his mind and his strength, in the magnificent work of "subduing the earth." And thus, dear workers of Sardinia, you are always present to the heart of the Church which, by virtue of her fidelity to Christ, looks upon you with eyes of special love and sincere concern.

Work, Solidarity and Humanization

From the very beginning of the so-called "social question" in the last century consequent to the phenomenon of massive industrialization, the Church has committed herself to following its development at each step of the way, choosing to stay close to those who suffer the most and are defenseless, and raising her voice at the proper moment against the systematic violations of the dignity of the human person, the exploitation of workers, the appearance of growing sectors of misery and even of hunger.

With numerous interventions in the course of the past decades, the Church has claimed for workers the right to a job that is dignified and fairly recompensed for the worker and his family, and has called for "new movements of solidarity among and with workers."[85]

Avoiding a narrow view of the question, the Church sees human work in the totality of its major components, under the religious, human, family and social aspects. She is aware that only the Faith gives full meaning to work, placing man – who is by nature a worker – at the center of the universe and relating him to God. Only in this way is there laid the transcendental foundation of a justice that is no longer left to the whims of special interests or of ideological interpretations. Human activity of any sort thus becomes a factor of humanization, of evangelization and of authentic progress.

Work Is More than Economics

Dear workers, in harmony with the teachings of the Popes who have preceded me, I never tire of repeating to everyone, to executive groups and to those with social force, that the value of human work cannot be reduced to the simple process of production or considered solely in relation to its economic end.

Conceptions of this kind have unfortunately created the premises for great injustices, with very negative consequences for the moral and civil evolution of society. Using such premises, in fact, one profoundly alters the true notion of work, deprives the worker of his prerogatives and distorts the very truth about man, who is left humiliated in his most profound dignity.

The human person is not limited to temporal reality, much less to his work. A sign of this preeminence of man over the logic of production is certainly to be seen in the right to the Sunday rest; this is to be understood not merely as the interruption of economic-productive work and the recuperation of physical energies, but also as free time not geared towards the economy, time which allows the human person to tend more assiduously to family, cultural, social and religious life, to rediscover himself, turning to the superior values of love, friendship, prayer and contemplation.[86]

A Spirituality of Work

We all know that it is not difficult for a man to degrade himself because of work; every day we actually witness the harsh reality that there are various ways of exploiting human work in order to make it a means of human oppression. But, on the other hand, we also know that when man is placed in the right perspective as a protagonist of the world in which he works he can, through his work, realize himself as man and even, in a certain sense, become more human.[87] Man's dignity is not measured by what he does, by his capacity to transform and develop products of the earth, by the quantity of his material profit, but by what he is.

And I will go even further: through work he can realize himself as a Christian and, in a certain sense, be more Christian. This becomes possible when man, giving work the meaning that it has in God's eyes, lets himself be guided by faith, hope and charity. Then he comes closer to God, enters into the work of salvation, and his work becomes an exercise of faith and a stimulus to goodness and prayer.

This consideration is not surprising if one reflects on the fact that the whole man, body and spirit, participates in work, regardless of whether it is manual or intellectual. Thus, the Church rightly recalls the duty to develop a spirituality of work in the Christian sense of the expression.[88]

This is why Sacred Scripture presents for our consideration two scenes, very rich in content, which I would like simply to recall here. In the Garden of Genesis the first man, created by God, was also the first worker. In the New Covenant, at Nazareth, next to Mary's house stood a little carpenter's shop, where first the worker Joseph, and then Jesus, having also become a worker, labored in order to earn their daily bread – like you, like all workers throughout the world – by the sweat of their brow, in order to support the family.

The family! It represents the vital link which gives work its impulse of love. Universal mover, love animates the social aim of work and transforms it into service for the construction of a society of brothers and sisters: the civilization, precisely, of love.

Work Must Be Seen in Light of the Cross

Dear brother workers, I must still bring to mind another aspect of this matter, in order to enrich the image that the Christian view proposes.

The Book of Genesis teaches that the painful experience of labor performed "with the sweat of your brow"[89] is a consequence of the sin committed by man in the beginning. Sin, my dear friends, is a tragic reality not to be forgotten; it stands at the origin of society's evils and man's suffering. The Church, committed to eliminating injustices from the working world, is no less committed, under the guidance of God, to combatting sin and reducing its consequences. Still, the Church is realistically aware that, despite these efforts, suffering will continue to have a place in the life of the world.

Leo XIII, the great Pope who with such farsightedness analyzed the problems of work, wrote on the subject words which, today, in the light of historical truth, appear prophetic. He exhorted mankind not to let itself be deceived by those who want to "totally eliminate suffering from the world. Those who claim that they can do it and promise miserable people a life free of suffering and pain, all peace and delight, delude the people and lead them along a path that brings greater sufferings than those of the present."[90]

Chrisuans often accept the weight and the pain of labor as expiation for sin, as purification of the soul, a return to lost innocence. But this penitential conception of work, which certainly has an importance that cannot be neglected, does not mean the renunciation of efforts to change unjust situations, nor of the duty to improve society in a concrete way. It simply means conscious participation in the mystery of a divine plan of love which asks man's collaboration for the salvation of all humanity and the ennobling of the world, transforming the common and widespread element of suffering into an instrument of grace. Without this evangelical perspective, it is impossible to understand the sacrifice of the cross and to associate oneself with its immense value.

In speaking to you, dear workers, who have gathered in such numbers from various parts of Sardinia in order to hear once again some of the basic elements of the social teaching of the Church – so rich in ferment and potential – it is clear that I wish for you, for workers throughout this island, Italy and the world, and in particular for those who, like you miners, face more harsh environmental situations, improvement in the conditions of life and courageous legislation which will increasingly free you from the danger of being enslaved by purely productive work. I assure you that this prospect, for me, once a laborer like yourselves, is one of the objects of my daily prayers and my constant pastoral solicitude. And I fervently desire that my exhortation may stimulate you in an effort to grow humanly and spiritually.

The Scourge of Unemployment

Still, while my gaze falls upon various sectors of this assembly, my thoughts cannot help but run towards another scene, one which so saddens the hearts of all of us. It is the spectacle, effectively evoked by the man who spoke on your behalf, of a mass of young people of this tenacious and industrious island who, due to a lack of work, are forced to remain idle.

It is a known fact that the phenomenon of unemployment is today striking, with a percentage that keeps increasing, in nearly all the countries of the more industrialized world. But it is a cause of great pain and concern to note, when glancing at the statistics, that Sardinia is one of the areas hardest hit.

Without a doubt, as I have several times pointed out, the phenomenon can only be resolved in a satisfactory way through a just and rational coordination of initiatives within the framework of the national community, and also through recourse to treaties and agreements of international collaboration.[91] At this moment, however, I wish to appeal to all national and regional authorities, to all those with political and social force, who have the true good of man at heart, in order that, with a sense of great priority, they might multiply their efforts for the purpose of stimulating initiatives, of planning coordination, so that the widespread scourge of unemployment will be effectively faced, within a short period of time and little by little finally eliminated.

---

55. Work Is a Path for Growing in God's Image[92]

Collaboration with God, Dialogue and Cooperation, Dignity of Work, Fair Wage, Human Rights/Dignity, Humanization/ Dehumanization, Leisure, Private Property, Professional Training, Selfishness, Solidarity, Universal Destination of Goods, Work and Family, Work and Women/Mothers.

[A homily on July 3, 1986 in Bogota, Columbia, to Columbian workers.]

I feel happy to find myself among you, men and women of Bogota, you who work in this populous metropolis, whose flourishing life and urban growth depend to a large degree on your tenacious hard work. Today my words are intended for all the workers of Colombia, in their diverse professions and tasks, who are trying to construct a more humane city, one more welcoming for people and families, one which contains hope of a better tomorrow.

Constructing a Humane City

I have no need to tell you how near I am to your joys and sorrows, your fears and hopes, for my heart – as you very well know – is equal to yours in being the heart of a worker. As we listen to the parable of the talents, which has just been proclaimed, we confidently raise our faces to Christ, for with his own activity he sanctified work and to him we shall have to render account for the gifts we have received.

Sufferings and Anxieties

Among you there will be many who find great satisfaction in their work. A safe job, with a wage sufficient to support one's family, the happiness of being able to offer one's children a well-provided table in a decent and comfortable home, to be able to clothe them well and give them a good upbringing with a view to a better future. For this, always show God a grateful heart. There will also be not a few with great difficulties. I mean those of you who suffer the sorrow of seeing your children deprived of what is necessary to feed, clothe and educate them or you who live in the straitened conditions of a humble district where the essential services are lacking, far from your work places, with work which is sometimes ill rewarded and uncertain, in anxiety at the insecurity of the future. And unfortunately many among you are victims of unemployment. You suffer because you have no work after having looked for it in vain and even though you are capable of doing it. These difficult situations move me deeply. They are linked with a whole series of factors that affect the complex phenomenon of the world of labor.

The Meaning of Work

In the encyclical *Laborem Exercens* I considered human labor as the essential key to the whole social question, since a gradual solution to this question calls inevitably for greater humanization of work and of the worker's life. This evening I therefore call upon you, dear fellow workers, to reflect together with me upon some aspects of human work from the point of view of the Gospel, the source of light and hope which ennobles and dignifies all authentically human activity.

In God's plan work constitutes a fundamental dimension of the person. Through work, indeed, man shares in the Creator's work, while he grows in his own being; his perfection is achieved, as he subjects material to his service.

So man is responsible for all the goods that God has entrusted to him from the beginning. You too have this responsibility, men and women of Colombia. The Creator was pleased to endow this land of yours providentially with immense resources. The responsibility therefore falls upon you of causing them to bear fruit and serve the well-being of all. No one must forget that the goods which God has entrusted to man have a universal destiny. Consequently, they must not be the exclusive property of a few, whether these few be individuals, groups or nations. Therefore, those who bear the responsibility of administering the goods of creation have to take account – in accordance with the divine will – not only of their own needs, but also those of everybody else, in such a way that no one, but above all the poorest, shall be barred from access to such goods.

Work Is a Human Necessity

You need work in order to meet your vital necessities. Yet much more than a biological necessity, work is a moral necessity. Man realizes himself through creative activity. Through it he gains a better perception of his condition of being in God's image, the master and lord of creation. Through work he turns himself more into man. For these reasons, it is necessary that work also be a path of liberation. Work must be liberated from everything impeding the development of man as God's image. Work must always elevate the person in his dignity and never degrade him.

Since man needs work for his self-realization as such, he has a right to it, that is, to a worthy occupation contributing to his perfection. It has already been seen how grave and central is the problem that there are not jobs for all and the fact that, despite your professional dedication and capacities, not all of you have access to jobs.

The solution to this very grave problem is not easy. But it should be sought by proper initiatives being set in motion by the public authorities and persons and organisms that can contribute to creating jobs permitting the unemployed to find worthy and justly rewarded activities. As my venerated predecessor Paul VI pointed out in his discourse to the International Labor Conference in 1969, there is a need for "organic participation" by all social forces and all associations engaged in finding ways to solve such excruciating problems.

Cooperatives and organizations or artisans deserve the particular attention of those with responsibility. With sufficient aid in credits and professional training, they could make a valuable contribution to alleviating the grave problem of unemployment.

Dignity is in the Worker, not the Work

All you who work to win your daily bread ought to praise God for the fact you can do so worthily and honestly. Work always bears the seal of the dignity of man. It is not superior or more worthy for being objectively more important or better paid. The more humble and more fatiguing kinds of work also have personal dignity. Do not forget, therefore, that the dignity of work does not depend so much on what is done as on who does it, and that, in man's case, is a spiritual being who is intelligent and free. For the same reason, reject those jobs that degrade man or woman and likewise those which are contrary to the moral law, those which attack the lives of people, including the unborn.

Solidarity

On this firm base of this dignity common to all, the church's social doctrine reminds us that solidarity is a prior requirement of love and of justice. Man must not shut himself up in his egoism, turn his back on the needs of others and the requirements of society, as the recent "Instruction on Christian Freedom and Liberation" teaches: "The church's doctrine is opposed to all forms of social or political individualism." Yes, beloved workers, all egoisms, such as that of the lazy servant, of which the Gospel reading tells us, are symptoms of a weak or non-existent faith. True faith arouses awareness, in all its dramatic urgency, of the demands of love and justice, an acknowledgment of the right of the human person to be more a person and to grow in dignity, individually and collectively.

The principle of solidarity requires that particular interests submit to the general interest. This principle is valid also in regard to work and its special circumstances, both regarding pay levels and the urgency to create new jobs and acknowledge the right of those already holding jobs.

Problems in Agriculture

In the encyclical *Laborem Exercens* I sought to make reference to the whole range of human activity in its broad and diverse sectors which you too represent in Colombian society. I now want to address myself in a particular way to the peasants, to whom the church dedicates special pastoral care. Men and women of the land, you perfectly accomplish the Lord's command to subject the earth extracting from it the goods necessary for the sustenance of all. How many of you spend your lives in the hard work of the fields with insufficient wages, without hope of obtaining even the least bit of land as your own property and without benefits ever coming to you from properly programmed bold and effective agrarian reform. And you who are small land owners, how many difficulties you must face in order to obtain sufficient credit at long-term and moderate interest. What insecurity there is for the crops and risks for the very lives and integrity of persons! But these problems are aggravated even more when the scourge of unemployment reaches the countryside.

You are then assailed by the seductive temptation of the cities. There, not rarely, unfortunately, you find yourselves obliged to accept even more dehumanizing living conditions. That is no solution. With the united collaboration of all, moved by the Christian spirit, with the support of intermediate authorities and the necessary aid of state bodies, it is necessary to propose the creation of effectively functioning organizational structures. These, inspired by a will to give service free of all influences likely to distort their purposes, should dedicate themselves to seeking and putting into practice forms which defend, and safeguard assistance to the world of the peasant, and to augment the presence of major services, such as education, housing, health, security and so on.

True Human Progress for All

Men and women of industry, building, commerce, the services, your labor is the object of the pope's concern and deserves a word of consideration and stimulus. Many of you are organized into labor unions, and I feel singular pleasure at that because here in Colombia generations of labor leaders have been formed in the church's bosom. This entails particular demands, those of Christian commitment, for bringing the "Gospel of Work" to the world of work and labor.

In this respect I want to encourage you warmly to delve more deeply into the church's social doctrine and to put all your confidence in its orientations. These have no other aim than the good of each one in particular and society in general, as well as the dignifying of your persons and your work, recognition of your lawful rights and obligations, a just wage as concrete verification of the justice of the socio-economic system. Through these you can attain the goods which the Lord has created for all; necessary harmony and collaboration between capital and labor; and many other goods which are part of social justice and the common good, in view of integral material, spiritual, economic, social, personal and community progress for all members of the community.

Just Wage and the Family

The church's social doctrine inspires Christian praxis in its noble struggle for justice, but it excludes, because it is extraneous to the Gospel, programmed class struggle which leads to fresh forms of servitude. That social doctrine teaches that there should not be odious discrimination regarding the work men and women may do, and they should have just remuneration for it. But it likewise teaches that a just family wage ought to allow a woman who is a mother to dedicate herself to her irreplaceable tasks of caring for and bringing up children without finding herself obliged to look outside the house for a complementary income, with prejudice to her maternal functions. These ought to be socially revalued to the good of the family and society itself.

You well know that there are many children in your country who are obliged to work from a very early age so as to contribute their modest earnings to maintaining the family and themselves. Much of this work is done in scarcely healthy physical and moral conditions. It prejudices and impedes their education and physical, psychological and moral development. Solutions to such grave problems are urgently needed.

The Moral and Spiritual Order of Work

Beloved brothers and sisters, the church considers it its duty to speak on work from the viewpoint of its human value and the moral order. Through work you can grow close to God, the Creator and Redeemer, and share in his plan for salvation for man and the world. Christ spent the greater part of his life dedicated to manual work in his humble carpenter's shop and was even known as "the carpenter."[93] In union with him you can contribute to the good of your families and all other members of society and ensure that the Creator's work shall develop better every day through your efforts.

Just like the rich man in the parable we have just heard, God has entrusted a certain number of "talents" to us, and they have to be made to bear fruit. In the first place they are the "talents" of divine grace ordered toward attaining eternal life, "talents" of intelligence, of the virtues, of the energies needed to honestly and competently carry out our work. On the other hand, together with the need to work, Holy Scripture also teaches the need for rest. My venerated predecessor John XXIII recalled how rest is a right and a necessity.[94] Learn how to take your rest for the benefit of body and spirit, honest diversion and the unity of your families. And remember especially that as creatures and children of God, as people of God, we are urged to gather each Sunday to celebrate holy Mass as a family. Every day we receive all from God's hands; his providence protects us; his goodness loves us; his mercy pardons us. How can we not gather every Sunday to give thanks for these benefits and to ask pardon for our sins, to hear the Word, to celebrate his mysteries, and eat the bread of sons and daughters, "the true bread from heaven," which the Father gives us?[95] Do not depreciate the Sunday invitation to celebrate the Eucharist in common. It is the source of immense spiritual benefits. And bear in mind that Sunday ought to contribute to the unity of the family, not to its breakup. Uproot the terrible plague of drunkenness from among you – it brings many ills to individuals, families and society – and live in loving fidelity in your homes.

Make Work a Means to Christian Perfection

Like you, Christ belongs to the world of work. As a worker, Jesus is the most eloquent "Gospel of Work" for us. Is it not really consoling and stimulating and encouraging to see the Son of God made man gaining his living with the work of his hands? He was God, "but he emptied himself and took the form of a slave"[96] to redeem work from within.

Make your work lives not only a means of gaining a livelihood and an instrument of service, make them rather a way of perfection. All work involves fatigue. This, when united with the sufferings of Christ, the redeemer of man, becomes salvific for one and all. "Do it in the name of the Lord Jesus, give thanks to God the Father through him."[97] In this fashion you, too, as the good and faithful servants of the gospel parable we have been listening to, will be able to enter into the joy of the Lord because you will have caused those talents which God gave you "to bear fruit."

56. Dialogue and Cooperation Must Support Solidarity with All Workers[98]

Christian Witness/Mission, Dialogue and Cooperation, Dominion over the Earth, Human Rights/Dignity, Humanization/ Dehumanization, Solidarity, Technology, World Community.

[An address on November 26, 1986 in Sydney, Australia, to Australian industrial workers.]

I thank you for the way you have endorsed the kind words of welcome addressed to me, and I trust you can see that I am very happy to be here with you. You may know that I, too, was a worker for some years in a quarry and in a factory. These were important and useful years in my life. I am grateful for having had that opportunity to reflect deeply on the meaning and dignity of human work in its relationship to the individual, the family, the nation and the whole social order. Those years allowed me to share in a specific way in God's creative activity and to experience work in the light of the cross and resurrection of Christ.

Dedication to Ordinary Work

One of my reasons for coming here is to tell you, and all the workers of Australia, how much I admire faithfulness and dedication to ordinary work. Australia is a great country because working people like yourselves go about their tasks day after day with both cheerfulness and seriousness, earning their bread by the sweat of their brow, producing goods and services for their fellow citizens, and thus gradually bringing to perfection a world that was created by a good and loving God.

No doubt many of you have reflected from time to time that Jesus Christ himself, although the Son of God, chose to be an ordinary worker for most of his earthly life, toiling away as a carpenter in Nazareth. There is no shortage of lessons to be learned from the life of Jesus the worker. It is only right, then, that this Church should bring his message into the working world and to workers. In the past, the Church has consistently opposed ways of thinking which would reduce workers to mere "things" that could be relegated to unemployment and redundancy if the economics of industrial development seemed to demand it. The students among you can consult the writings of my predecessors – going back to Leo XIII almost 100 years ago – who treated at length topics such as the rights of workers, ownership, property, working hours, just wages and workers' associations.

Technology and Training

Perhaps you have heard that five years ago I, too, wrote an encyclical letter on human work. My aim was to cast new light on the whole area of human work, an important subject where there are always fresh hopes but also fresh fears and dangers.

Among the many new elements that affect human work I wish to mention today the rapid development of technology. There is an aspect of this we can admire: in technology we can see ourselves as more than ever "subduing the earth"[99] and gaining dominion over it. Technology itself is the work of human hands and human minds, and it enables us to produce other beautiful and useful things. This is admirable if the human person is clearly the master. But in large factories or on extended work sites, the number, size and complexity of the machines used can make the worker seem merely a part of the machine, just another cog in the whole process of production.

Many machines these days require operators with specialized training. But after being trained for a highly skilled job, the worker may suddenly discover that a new invention has made his machine obsolete and uneconomical. He may be too old to be trained a second time, or perhaps the firm employing him may go out of business. The result is that whole industries can be dislocated, and individuals and families reduced to poverty, suffering and despair.

Despite the complexity of the problem we cannot give up. All the resources of human inventiveness and good will must be brought to bear, in order to help solve the social problems of our day connected with work. It is important to have clear ideas of the principles and priorities to be followed. In this context I wish to proclaim again my own profound conviction "that human work is a key, probably the essential key, to the whole social question, if we try to see the question really from the point of view of man's good."[100]

The Human Need for Work

People need to work, not just to earn money for the necessities of life, but also to fulfill their calling to share in the creative activity of God. The human satisfaction that comes from work well done shows how profoundly the Creator has inscribed the law of work in the heart of man.

The goods of the world belong to the whole human family. Normally a person will need to work in order to have a necessary share of these good things. In the early Christian community, St. Paul insisted that willingness to work was a condition for being able to eat: "If a man will not work, let him not eat."[101] In special situations, society can and must assist those who are in need and cannot work. Yet even in these special circumstances, people still have a desire for personal fulfillment, and this can be achieved only through some form or other of worthwhile human activity.

Thus those who are forced to retire early, as well as those who are still young and strong but cannot find work, may experience profound discouragement and feel that they are useless. These feelings may lead some to seek consolation in alcohol, drugs and other forms of behavior harmful to themselves and to society.

We all need to feel that we are truly productive and useful members of our community; it is our right. And since the pace of technological change is likely to increase, it is vital for us to face all the serious problems that affect the well-being of workers.

The Human Person Is the Purpose of Work

No one has a simple and easy solution to the problems connected with human work, but I offer for your consideration two basic principles. First, it is always the human person who is the purpose of work. It must be said over and over again that work is for man, not man for work. Man is indeed "the true purpose of the whole process of production."[102] Every consideration of the value of work must begin with man, and every solution proposed to the problems of the social order must recognize the primacy of the human person over things.

Dialogue and Cooperation

Second, the task of finding solutions cannot be entrusted to any single group in society: people cannot look solely to governments as if they alone can find solutions, or to big business, or to small enterprises, or to union officials, or to individuals in the work force. All individuals and all groups must be concerned with both the problems and their solutions.

The Church is profoundly convinced that "the rights of the human person are the key element in the whole of the social moral order."[103] She has long recognized the right of workers to form associations. The purpose of such associations is to promote social justice by defending the vital interests of workers and by contributing to the common good. It is important for the members to play an active and responsible role in these associations. Hence you must make sure that the leaders of your workers' associations really have at heart all the material and human needs of the members. They must also remember that the solution to any dispute must be fair to all sides, must serve the common good of society and must take into account the economic and social situation of the country. Only if the economy as a whole is healthy will it be possible to make sufficient work available for workers, especially the young.

Achieving the Common Good through Solidarity

People are realizing more and more clearly that what happens in one part of the world has effects elsewhere. Worldwide problems demand worldwide solutions through the solidarity of all. No country can isolate itself from the common challenge. Union leaders and leaders of employer associations, as well as government agencies, need to work together in order to face the wide range of challenges. Every partner in this common endeavor should act on the conviction that everyone has a basic right to work in order to have a fair share of the world's goods. It must also be stressed that all the partners have a duty to work for solutions that respect the dignity of the individual and the common good of society. Economic problems cannot be separated from the ethical and social aspects of life in society.

Dialogue and Cooperation

On the national and local level industrial relations also require a spirit of understanding and cooperation rather than one of opposition and conflict. In all disputes, a just and peaceful solution will only be possible if all parties are, and remain, ready to talk. Always keep open the lines of communication, and remember that if disputes are not solved quickly, it is above all the weak and needy who suffer.

Fortunately for Australia, your most cherished traditions place great value on equality and mutual support, especially in difficult times. The word "mate" has rich and positive connotations in your language. I pray that this tradition of solidarity will always flourish among you and will never be looked upon as old-fashioned.

Australia also has a long and proud tradition of settling industrial disputes and promoting cooperation by its almost unique system of arbitration and conciliation. Over the years this system has helped to defend the rights of workers and promote their well being, while at the same time taking into account the needs and the future of the whole community.

I make a special appeal to you workers to be always honest in your work and generous in your collaboration with others. I appeal to you to be especially conscious of all those in need, to give them practical help and to offer them your solidarity. I have been told that you have an organization for promoting development in poorer countries. For this I congratulate you and I thank you. But you must be active too in helping the needy in your own midst, who include the unemployed, many young people, aboriginal people, the sick, the disabled, the refugees and the new settlers.

Workers More Important than Profits and Machines

I began by making reference to the new questions and problems, fears and dangers that surround us because of the development and rapid use of the new technology. This technology is part of the accumulated wealth of the human family and a part of it belongs to you too. It is to be judged by the help it gives you in your work and lives. Always remember that the worker is always more important than both profits and machines.

Dear friends, workers of Australia: it is up to you to make use of the new technology and press on the task of building a society of justice and fraternal love – a society that extends well beyond the boundaries of Australia. It is God himself who strengthens your arms, enlightens your minds and purifies your hearts for this great work.

Work: A Sharing in Christ's Mission of Service

Those of you who believe in Jesus Christ and accept his Gospel as the blueprint of your lives know that work has an even deeper meaning when it is seen in its relationship to the Lord's cross and resurrection. United with Christ in baptism, you are called to share through your work in Christ's mission of salvation and service to humanity. When offered to God in union with the work of Christ, your own work takes on an even greater value and higher dignity. Jesus Christ, the Son of God, who during his earthly life belonged so fully to the "working world," looks forever with love on human work.

And for all of you in this vast land, whatever may be your religious convictions or the nature of your work, I pray that you may experience the uplifting and exhilarating awareness of working with the Creator in perfecting his design and plan for the world. All of this is part of the dignity of human work, the dignity of man and the dignity of each and every worker in Australia!

57. Unemployment is an Evil That Must Be Combated through Training[104]

Collaboration with God, Cooperation and Dialogue, Human Development/Progress, Humanization/Dehumanization, Professional Training, Work and Family, Work and Women/Mothers.

[An address on November 27, 1986 in Hobart, Australia, to trainees at an employment training center.]

I am very happy to be with you, the young people of the Wilson Training Center. You are here to improve your skills so that you may be better equipped to find work. I encourage you with all my heart. I greet the staff of Centacare, which for over a quarter of a century has been providing services for family and social needs, particularly in recent years, in relation to the problem of unemployment. I am aware of the important assistance given by the government and the whole community for the running of this center. I sincerely trust that your efforts will be rewarded and your hopes fulfilled.

The Human Problem of Unemployment

The nature of this center leads me directly to the theme of our meeting today: the very serious question of unemployment, or rather the situation of the men and women who are suffering the effects of unemployment.

It is precisely as a human problem, a problem affecting the life and dignity of human beings, a problem with a decidedly ethical and moral character, that the church approaches the question of unemployment. The Church has a mission of service to the whole human family. It is above all a religious and moral mission, linked to the redemption of the human race through the cross and resurrection of Jesus Christ. The Church knows that the call to accept the redemption reaches human beings in the actual circumstances of everyday life. And man's eternal destiny is closely connected with all the elements that affect human freedom, human rights and human advancement. Work – or the lack of work – is one such element, a most important one.

Unemployment is the privation of all the values that work represents and contributes to individuals, families and society. Work is a right and a duty. Elsewhere I have said that "man must work, both because the Creator has commanded it and because of his own humanity, which requires work in order to be maintained and developed. Man must work out of regard for others, especially his own family, but also for the society to which he belongs, the country of which he is a citizen and the whole human family of which he is a member, since he is the heir to the work of generations and at the same time a sharer in building the future of those who will come after him. All this constitutes the moral obligation of work."[105]

Work Humanizes and Redeems

When we speak of the moral obligation to work, we mean that everyone has the duty to share in some real way in the great task of "humanizing" the universe, that is, of making the world a more hospitable place and a better instrument of personal and social development. It is also true that "work is a good thing for man – a good thing for his humanity – because through work man not only transforms nature, adapting it to his own needs, but he also achieves fulfillment as a human being and indeed, in a sense, becomes 'more a human being.' '[106]

The sweat and toil which work necessarily involves in the present condition of the human race mean that the Christian can share in the work that Christ came to do. Christ saved the world by suffering and dying on the Cross. By enduring the toil of work in union with Christ, the Son of God, man collaborates with him for the redemption of humanity. He shows that he is a true disciple of Christ by carrying the cross of work every day in the activity that he is called upon to perform.[107]

Work and Family

Work has other implications. It is an important condition of family life, since the family needs the means of subsistence, the money which is usually earned through the work of one or more of its members. In fact, the family is a community made possible by work, and at the same time it is the first school of work, within the home, for every person.[108]

Today the presence of women and mothers in almost every sector of the working world is a fact that has to be considered. They should be able to exercise their gifts and abilities in various forms of employment, but at the same time due respect must be given to their obligations and aspirations. Work should be so structured that women do not have to bargain for their advancement at the expense of their own dignity or at the expense of their role inside the family.

The mother's role needs to be socially reevaluated. Her tasks in the home require a great commitment, they demand much time and love. Children need care, love and affection. This attention must be given if children are to develop into secure, responsible persons with moral, religious and psychological maturity. While the responsibility for family development rests on both mother and father, still very much depends on the specific mother/child relationship.[109]

Society can take credit when it enables mothers to devote time to their children and bring them up in accordance with their progressive needs. The freedom of women as mothers must be clearly protected, so that they are free from psychological or any other form of discrimination, especially by comparison with women without family obligations. Mothers must not be financially penalized by the very society which they serve in a most exalted and necessary way.

Work and the Disabled

A further point I wish to make concerns the disabled. They are citizens with full rights, and they should be helped to have a real share in the life of society. It would be radically unworthy of man and a denial of our common humanity to deny disabled people access to the full life of the community in accordance with their possibilities and potential. To do so would be to practice a serious form of discrimination. Here is a clear case in which work, in the objective sense, should be subordinated to the dignity of man, to the person who works and not to economic advantage.[110]

Generosity towards Immigrants

Since World War II, Australia has shown great generosity in opening its doors to immigrants from other countries and to refugees seeking a new homeland. In return, these new Australians have contributed their own culture and working skills toward the development and enrichment of their new land. It is important that in the matter of working rights, those who began their working lives in other lands should not be put at a disadvantage in comparison with other workers. This matter too calls for generosity on the part of Australian society. The value of work should not be measured by differences of nationality, sex, religion or race.

The Scourge of Unemployment

In a sense, unemployment is a modern phenomenon. Demographic and technological changes have produced a situation in which there is not sufficient work for all those capable of it. It is a worldwide phenomenon. It is particularly serious in the Third World countries which have not yet reached an adequate stage of economic development and in which there are large numbers of young people looking for work. But it is almost as bad in many industrialized nations, for very complex reasons which it is not possible to analyze here.

In Australia, too, the pain of unemployment is suffered by many of you and your fellow citizens, and not just the young, but also by men and women who are breadwinners for their families. Even when social services help to provide the bare necessities of life, being unemployed cuts into their dignity as persons and seriously curtails their chances and opportunities in life.

Training Is a Key to Sustained Employment

Unemployment brings many evils to a community and to a nation. It causes economic and social inequality. It can cause such stress to the family and society that there follows a real breakdown of the institutions that should ensure human advancement. Those who have work may forget those who do not.

The problem calls for cooperation in planning and positive action by all agencies. Government departments, large companies and small businesses, employers' federations, unions and their alliances – all of these have a crucial part to play in finding solutions. The media too can provide positive support and information by promoting programs for the unemployed. Justice demands a concerted effort by everyone. Christ's commandment of love urges all Christians to act together on behalf of the unemployed.

Retraining programs are already under way in this country. Governments and private organizations sponsoring them are to be congratulated. Such programs are of special importance since they acknowledge the needs of the young upon whom the future social, economic and family life of the nation will depend.

But the needs of the older unemployed must not be overlooked. There are indications that in recent years the numbers of unemployed have increased as well as the average duration of unemployment. This means that many people can be excluded from the labor market for almost their whole working lives with little hope of regaining regular employment.

Some statistics present a bleak picture for thousands of people who would be only too happy to work. Powerful efforts must be made to find new means of meeting this situation so that older workers' skills may be reused, or new skills taught to them. Most of all they need the practical help that will rekindle their enthusiasm and motivation to be engaged in creative work.

In programs of training and retraining, it is important to follow the principle of self-help. This policy safeguards the individual's dignity. All are encouraged to use their abilities to the full, and to realize that their unemployed status is not a matter of personal failure.

Above all, efforts must be made to create new jobs. This is a most difficult point. We all recognize that the creation of new work in our modern society has become a most complex matter. Very often it is no longer merely a matter of local or even national willingness and capability. It requires a reordering and adjustment of economic structures and priorities on a global level.

The Human Dimension of Unemployment

The Church does not have technical solutions to offer nor the means to resolve such problems. But in her service to humanity she has a most important task: to remind those involved at every level of economic activity that unemployment cannot be treated solely as an issue of economics. Unemployment is a human problem of vast dimensions.

The Church can and does offer a social teaching. It is based on the inviolable dignity of every human person. Work is seen as collaboration with the Creator and is a condition of the self-development which is the right of every individual. The Church seeks to motivate and educate so that qualified and faith-inspired Christians will help to find solutions to the urgent problem of unemployment.

Sometimes the local churches are in a position to start or collaborate in concrete programs of service to the unemployed. Centacare, the Catholic Church's family agency in the Archdiocese of Hobart, which established and administers Wilson Training Center, is a praiseworthy example of this kind of endeavor. Other worthy forms of service elsewhere also deserve great support.

Young people of this center, friends of Tasmania and of all Australia: in your efforts to combat unemployment and to find work, know that the Church is with you. She understands your aspirations, and she appeals on your behalf and on behalf of all the unemployed to the conscience of the world. The Church appeals for a new vision of work, centered on the value and dignity of the human person. She appeals for a reordering of the economic order so that it will truly serve the integral well-being of the human family.

To all of you – the staff at Centacare and the Wilson Training Center, and you young people training for work – to the unemployed, to all who are seeking solutions to the problem of unemployment in Australia, to those serving the needs of individuals and families suffering from unemployment – to all of you I offer my encouragement. Do not lose heart! The Church will work with you and for you. And she will continue to call for the solidarity of all in this matter that so closely touches your lives. Be assured of my prayers and support. In the name of Jesus Christ I invoke upon you strength and courage.

58. Faith Helps Us Recognize the Dignity of Work[111]

Collaboration with God, Culture of Work, Environment, Gospel of Work, Human Development/Progress, Humanization/Dehumanization, Justice, Meaning of Work, St. Joseph, Service, Technology.

[An address on March 19, 1987 in Civitavecchia, Italy, to Civitavecchian workers.]

I wish to take in all of you in an embrace of brotherhood, since I am aware of your problems and anxieties, but also of your pride in the dignity that is yours in the various spheres of your activity, for every worker is a witness to the value that his work has, because work is a reality that is closely united to man and to his identity. Work permits each one to be himself, because it sets him free from poverty, guarantees his livelihood more securely and enables and encourages him to have a valuable and conscious share in social responsibilities, far removed from all oppression, and sheltered from situations that are an offense to his dignity. In work, a culture comes to development – I mean the awareness that one has a responsible role within the sphere of material and spiritual values, with the possibility and the advantage of having more, in order to be more.

Good Work Leads to Authentic Human Fulfillment

I wish to assert this today, on the feast of St. Joseph, who worked beside Jesus for so many years, a partner in the same professional work carried out by the Son of God made man, a witness to the humility and the physical labors of Jesus within the walls of the house of Nazareth. Joseph was the first to receive the substance and the sublimity of the "Gospel of Work" from the direct testimony of the Lord, and he was therefore able to discern in the hard work of Jesus the human, religious and salvific meaning of daily toil. "Jesus, the incarnate Son of God, the Redeemer of all men, was a worker for so many years of his life. The work of Jesus the worker belongs in this way to the work of the redemption of man, of the divine redemption of man."[112]

The Transcendent Nature of the Person

In the light of Christ, the Redeemer of man and of human work, with the example before our eyes of St. Joseph, the humble carpenter who realized his own dignity as one who was free and responsible precisely in his daily toil, the Pope speaks to you today, men and women workers, to tell you of all the esteem that the Church has for you and for the contribution which you make to social well-being. In her dialogue with the world of work, the Church feels it to be her own mission – one that is particularly urgent today – to assert strongly and clearly the dignity and the centrality of the value of the person. For this reason, she warns against every attempt to reduce man to a simple cog in the great machine of production. Man has his place within the process of production, but he is not reducible to this: he transcends it, because man is not only matter, but is also spirit; as such, he bears a destiny that points him beyond the horizon of time, towards eternity.

It is, accordingly, with lively hope that the Church encounters today, in all the sectors of human life – including that of work – numerous signs of a new hunger and thirst for transcendence and for the divine. The world of work seems each day to discover more of the importance of God's place in life, and seeks to become a community based on solidarity and brotherly love.

Dignity of Work Derives from the Dignity of the Person

It is only if the world of work fully recovers awareness of the vertical dimension of man that it will be able to affirm fully the dignity of work and to defend this dignity against the attacks that are made against it from various quarters. The dignity of work does not depend on the activity in which the work is expressed, but on the subject who carries out the activity and puts into the activity something of himself, of his own intelligence and creativity. We defend the dignity of work, therefore, by defending the dignity of man. The dignity of man has its basis in the fact that he is made "in the image and likeness of God." To recognize this divine reflection that shines out in every human being means to establish the basic source of all the social claims that are made necessary by the safeguarding of the rights of the worker.

Divine Justice

Men and women of the world of work, I speak to you with great openness: God is on your side! Faith in him does not suffocate your rightful claims, but rather gives them a basis, an orientation and a support. God remains the supreme guarantor of your rights. It is therefore before his tribunal that every person must appear one day to render account for the injustices perpetrated against his fellows.

If one believes in God, therefore, one will be ready even today to ask questions about oneself and about one's own way of entering into relationships with others in every sphere of life, but especially in the sphere of work. Faith does not deaden awareness. Rather, it stimulates it to seek continually the conditions that are more in keeping with the innate dignity of a being endowed with intelligence and liberty, and therefore capable of living his own life responsibly.

This innate dignity of man must find its principal expression in work. This has to be said with special force today, when the ever more rapid progress of technology risks the suffocation of the worker, isolating and marginalizing him. One can see on the horizon the danger of a new slavery of work, the consequence of a productive structure in which the person, with his capacity of initiative and responsibility, is ever less involved. The solution to this problematic tension is not to be sought in a slowing down or even a halting of technological development. It will be found rather in the continual commitment to give the worker new skills and to create ever greater areas in which he can play a conscious and responsible part in the direction of the firm.

In this battle to safeguard the dignity of the worker, believers must be in the front line, since they recognize the primordial design of God in his dealings with man. Do we not read on the first page of the Bible the commandment to "fill the earth and subdue it?" Man is called to be God's collaborator in the work of creation. Every productive activity must therefore be structured in such a way that it is worthy of a "collaborator of God!"

Stewardship of Resources

Among the problems that assail man today, you are aware here at Civitavecchia in a particularly vivid manner of the problem of the provision of energy. We see a constant increase in the demand for energy, caused by the growth of industrialization and by a higher individual consumption that is connected with the expansion of the population and the improvement in living standards. This is a problem that is the direct responsibility of the public authorities and also involves the field of scientific research.

It falls to me to underline the duty – incumbent on all of us – to have respect for the goods which God has created and willed to put at the service of all. In point of fact, however, truly frightening and disturbing levels of pollution of the natural environment have been reached. This situation, which obviously concerns the whole world, risks finding its first victims precisely among the workers. It is necessary to call into being a new type of collaboration among scientists, to avoid an irreversible development which would entail mortal risks for all mankind. Our planet would very soon be uninhabitable if we were to refuse to look diligently for means to correct the negative effects of the various technologies. It is necessary to display, in responding to the questions about safety, a commitment equal to that displayed hitherto in the promotion of the interests of energy and production, in order to guarantee the respect and the conservation of all the possibilities and beauties of the universe.

We live in a world that must be appreciated and respected, and we must not yield to the temptation to alter its balance. Scholars and scientists everywhere, no matter what their specific interests, should feel themselves profoundly challenged by the growing demand for energy which is urgently posed by the needs of modern society; but they should also pay due attention to the vital requirement that the essential balance of nature should not be disturbed; this is the first condition that guarantees the construction of a world of justice and peace, in which man can be the conscious subject and artisan of technological progress in a harmonious relationship with the cosmos.

Creation Reveals God's Order

Every workman, everyone who works in industry and the production of energy, is also a human being continually in touch with the reality of creation and with its laws. The world which surrounds us and on which we act with our work, together with the impressive energies within nature, continually reveals to us the marvelous order willed by God. Out of this daily contact, even though it takes place in hard toil, man comes to know the physical world, but is also brought to meditate on the relationship that it has with God, and to recognize the infinite power of the Creator and Lawgiver of the universe. Every worker can thus see himself as a sharer in a divine plan, and can accept with gratitude the sublime mission to "subdue and dominate what is created" in order to employ all the riches of the cosmos for the advantage of man. We can say that a religious context is disclosed here, in which every worker discovers the presence and the value of a serious and binding moral commitment; the commitment to use all technologies and discoveries for the greater good of humanity. In contact with the forces of the universe, which reveal themselves to be ever more surprising and precious, every worker senses how great is the responsibility of all to act in accordance with the order established by God.

Work is a duty given by God, and a necessity imposed by the many needs of existence; but it is also a way to set out on a common path, collaborating with love and respect for the good of all. Men and women workers of Civitavecchia, open your hearts to brotherhood and solidarity, following the model of Christ! Accept the message which the pages of the Gospel continually address to you!

---

59. Work Is Humanized by Safeguarding the Dignity and Solidarity of Workers[113]

Christian Witness/Mission, Community of Persons, Culture of Work, Dialogue and Cooperation, Economic Laws and Profits, Gospel of Work, Human Rights/Dignity, Humanization/ Dehumanization, Justice, Materialism and Consumerism, Selfishness, Solidarity.

[An address on April 10, 1987 in Buenos Aires, Argentina, to workers.]

I have said on another occasion that the years I spent as a laborer in a chemical plant gave me a new lesson about the Gospel. It is true, because in that environment, in that period of forced labor, I realized the profound relationship of solidarity that exists between the Gospel and the problems connected with human work in our times. It is not a new theoretical observation; it is a joyful human and Christian reality which the Church, now on the threshold of the third millenium, is seriously bound to spread. Then it can be known and experienced by men and women of the world of labor. I encourage you today, that each worker make the "inner effort in order that work may be given the meaning which it has in the eyes of God."[114]

Bringing the Gospel to Human Work

Work is like a "vocation" or a call, which elevates a person to become a sharer in the creative action of God. It is the means that God offers to man to "subdue" the earth, discover its secrets, transform it, enjoy it and in this way, enrich his own personality. His model is Christ, the Redeemer of man, who did not refuse to spend a great part of his life in the carpenter's shop, and thus redeemed the effort and the dignity of work, transforming it forever into an instrument of redemption.

In the letters that many of you sent to Rome in connection with this pastoral visit, you stated in clear terms the circumstances, desires, and sad situations, as well as the hopes that lie in your hearts.

In my frequent meetings with workers from all over the world, I sometimes hear reasons for sadness, discouragement and despair; these come, to a great extent, from the growing problem of unemployment. Certainly the world of labor gives us serious reasons for worry; I know them well. However, it is no less certain that such reasons should not lead you to feel defeated, to assume an attitude of passivity or hopelessness. Our Catholic faith provides us with enough reasons as to why we should never despair, no matter how difficult or hard any situation may seem.

Work Contributes to the Spirit

In the encyclical *Laborem Exercens*, I pointed out to the world of production a concrete and clear objective: that human activity consider, above all, personal values. "If this is not done, incalculable damage is inevitably done throughout the economic process, not only economic damage but first and foremost damage to man."[115]

Furthermore, I am inviting you today not to conform to an impoverished and deformed vision of work; but my wish is that you enter deeply into the profound richness that can contribute to the life and spirit of each person. The manner in which you understand this point determines considerably not only the meaning of your life, but also the range and the results of your labor organizations and union involvement.

Profit Cannot Be the Only Motive

You are aware of the fact that when the socio-economic world is organized for the exclusive motive of profit, proper human dimensions suffer a loss. Such a situation could lead to a lack of interest in the quality of work, and thus prejudice the greatly desired cohesion and solidarity of the workers. Some claim that the only reason for your life is money and consumerism; if you allow yourselves to be polarized by this exclusive motivation, you are unable to discover personal satisfaction and service which the exercise of your profession includes.

Build a Community of Work

This is why I insist that you cannot conform to certain short-term objectives, whose purpose can be reduced to collective bargaining about wages and lessening of working hours. In the face of the problems of modern society, do not allow the greater effort of labor organizations to be made sterile by ineffective political disputes, which often make your aspirations tools to achieve advantageous positions. Justice requires that there be honest union debate, but it should lead to the attainment of objectives proper to the world of labor, and be directed to the strengthening of solidarity and the raising of the level of the material and spiritual life of the workers. Certainly the intimate relationship between the world of labor and political life, the so-called indirect employer, demands constant contact and dialogue between workers and politicians. It should always be a constructive dialogue, which should consider not only the interests of the group, but the welfare of the great Argentinean family, in the Latin American perspective and even in that of the whole world.

Your country, your society, enjoys a strong and dynamic labor organization which, as you know, constitutes an "indispensable element of social life."[116] That element, however, even if it is indispensable, cannot be identified with the struggle of social classes; such an idea is ideologically and historically unsatisfactory, and its worst consequences lead to the disadvantage of men and women workers.

"It is characteristic of work that it first and foremost unites people. In this consists its social power: the power to build a community."[117] In the same way, the fruits of your organization should always be constructive, so that its total effectiveness is placed at the service of the person, the family and the whole society, and they are not used against the community or the individual.

Promote the Dignity of the Person

The great goal of the union must be the development of the person, of all workers: therefore new "movements of solidarity in the sphere of work can be necessary."[118] The Pope encourages you to make a further step in solidarity; he wants to inspire you to make ever greater efforts to promote the inalienable dignity of man, of every man, of every worker, and always contribute to his personal fulfillment. This is the only way that you will fulfill your mission to promote and defend "the vital interests of those employed in the various professions."[119] It would be a shame if solidarity among workers breaks down when the working conditions become degrading or when there is an increase in abuses and arrogance in those who, from their positions of advantage, appropriate rights that in no way belong to them. Neither should there be a lack of solidarity in those wide areas of misery and hunger, which would be the same as the inhuman treatment of workers and their families. Thus the organizational strength of workers should reach even those places in order to attain certain conditions that will free the persons from their miserable situation.

Wherever there is a father or a mother of a family who, because of circumstances, cannot fulfill the responsibility to earn enough to live in dignity with his or her loved ones, the solidarity of working men and women should also reach those situations.

Say "Enough!" to Injustice

Does it seem logical to you that the solidarity of workers be reduced to inactivity, or that it only proposes and considers short-term goals, when the needs of so many workers are urgent? No Christian should remain insensitive to the needs of others, because he knows that before God the value of his behavior depends on the love that he offers others.[120] Now, if charity is the greatest commandment for us, how can one remain uninvolved before injustice, if justice is the fundamental motive and the first fruit of charity?

The service that your organizational strength can give to man, and with him to the community, demands a serious commitment from each one of you, that will lead you to say "enough!" to everything that may be a clear violation of the dignity of the worker.

Enough, to a reductive conformism, which proposes monetary remuneration and less working hours as the only objectives for the labor organization, silencing every dialogue that may have the person and his dignity in life and profession as the central issues.

Enough, to certain situations in which the rights of labor are harshly subordinated to economic systems, which seek exclusively the greatest profit, without considering the moral quality of the means that are used to obtain it.

Enough, to a labor system which obliges mothers of families to work long hours outside their homes, thus neglecting their functions in the home; which does not value sufficiently work in agriculture; which marginalizes less capable persons; which discriminates against immigrants.

Enough, to the practice in which the right to work is at the discretion of transitory economic or financial circumstances, which do not take into consideration the fact that the full employment of the work force should be the primary objective of every social organization.

Enough, to the manufacture of products that endanger peace and seriously threaten public morality, even including the health of specific sectors of the population.

Enough, also, to the lack of solidarity in the world distribution of food; to the lack of systematic recognition of labor organizations in many countries of the world; and in this International Year of the "Homeless," enough also to the pressing situation of the lack of dignity in the physical living conditions of workers in so many suburbs of the great cities.

However, do not forget that this commitment acquires its strength, above all, from an attitude of personal solidarity. You must overcome the tendency to remain unknown in human relations; you must make a positive effort to transform "solitude" into "solidarity," looking for occasions for exchange, understanding, confidence, mutual help, and fostering friendship.

Solidarity Is the Fundamental Structure of Work

The fundamental objective of your involvement should be to humanize economic activity and the world of work. Therefore you should achieve, little by little, the gradual harmonization of work relationships with what I called in the encyclical *Laborem Exercens* "the fundamental structure of all work,"[121] which is a structure of unity, collaboration and solidarity.

A basic principle of this action of solidarity in labor organization consists in the conscious decision "to consider man not according to whether or not he is useful in his work, but to consider work in its relation to man with every man, to consider work according to whether or not it is useful to man."[122] Solidarity, precisely, is to make room for persons in society, in labor activity, so that in these environments of basic life, everyone can conduct himself with the awareness and responsibility of acting as persons.

The strength of labor is very great; and, when it is used positively, it is capable of transforming itself into a basic factor for the construction of a community in which the principal social questions are answered according to the principles of justice and equity.

In your efforts to practice solidarity, you will succeed little by little in containing the effects of degradation or exploitation, and the unions will be strong factors in the construction of social justice, in the recognition of the just rights of workers and of the dignity and the true welfare of society.[123] Therefore, without confusing your action of solidarity with political activity, you will influence society more effectively than if you tried to act directly in political life solely from the union organization.

As you know very well, this is why you should not allow your efforts to be transformed into a kind of group or class "selfishness." Even when the purpose of a specific action is to safeguard the rights of a person or a working class, that objective must not be in opposition to the common good of the whole society. Neither should you forget solidarity with those persons who, for various reasons, are not members of your organizational force. Your support of those who are weaker will be proof that your solidarity is authentic.

In the Gospel of Work we find the most convincing example of solidarity: Almighty God, whose greatness transcends man completely, became flesh out of love, out of solidarity, and worked just like any other person. Jesus Christ is the best example of the unlimited solidarity which workers are called to imitate. Wherever a man or a woman develops an activity, works and suffers, Christ is present there.

Human Work Is Fundamental to the Plan of God

The Church, faithful to her divine Founder, has respected and always promoted the dignity of labor. She has done this by restoring the fundamental role that belongs to human work in the designs of God. She has done it by extolling the achievements of human intelligence, particularly in the field of science and technology; she has done it by showing her special love for all workers and in particular those who are more severely tried by fatigue, like manual laborers and farmers. She has done it by listening to their complaints and safeguarding their interests and their legitimate aspirations. She has done it by drawing closer to the world of labor, both in the shanty-towns and the humble "ranchitos," or in their comfortable residences, in order to help them both materially and spiritually, warn them of so many dangers, preserve their moral and social values and raise their living conditions.

Today, it is the Pope who comes to you to honor in you all those who are serving in the great task to which all of us are called, that is, to transform the world according to the designs of God. I come to discover in your faces the features of the face of Jesus of Nazareth, and to exhort you to respond with a deep sense of responsibility to the mission to which God has called you, that you may become the builders of the Argentina of today and of tomorrow.

---

60. Human Persons Have a Responsibility for the Care and Wise Use of the Earth and Its Resources[124]

Collaboration with God, Dominion over the Earth, Environment.

[An address on January 9, 1988 in Rome, to youth attending the Italian National Congress of The Proprietor Farmers' Organization.]

In young people the Church always sees the future, creativity, and the hope of a better world, placing particular confidence in movements which are clearly and generously inspired along the perennial lines of great Christian principles.

Nature Is God's Gift

In this regard I warmly encourage you never to lose sight of this fundamental principle: God has given nature to humanity as a gift.

God created the earth, the waters, creatures of the sea, earth and air, the rivers, mountains and plains with immutable laws, and through many yet unexplored directions of physics and biology. It was God who formed the human person, placing him, as Scripture marvelously expresses it, in a garden, so that he could "cultivate and care for it."[125] What God had made was very good.[126]

Human Persons Are Collaborators but Not Masters

The human person, therefore, is a collaborator and craftsman, but not the absolute master, neither of himself nor of things, which he is called in turn to mold so that the garden may become more bountiful. The earth which he has received as a gift must be subjected to the "dominion" of the human person in the framework of the divine plan, or else his role as collaborator will be compromised.

For these reasons the Church has always been close to farm laborers and has never ceased to raise her voice, in her social documents, against the injustices, both open and hidden, which are so frequently committed against the rural workers in regard to those who work in other sectors. For the same reasons, in my encyclical on human work, I paused to emphasize the "fundamental importance" of agricultural work in the context of the development of the social community.[127]

Dear young people, I am confident that the very mention of these basic considerations can be a stimulus and light for you in the course of your thorough discussions in this congress.

Human Responsibility for the Resources of the Earth

The earth and natural elements do not constitute merely a factor of production that is indispensable to the maintenance of physical life, the sustenance of families, and economic and social prosperity, but also one of the instruments capable of giving security and impetus to the growth of the individual as a human person.

The resources spread about on the surface and wisely hidden by God in the depths of the earth should be discovered and evaluated in the service of the person, family and society in an organic way. The human person has the task of intervening in the natural environment to adapt it to proper higher demands and to care for it as a source of income, without ever compromising its characteristic as an instrument of human and community development.

For this reason the rational care of the environment is necessary. Wherever this does not occur, the human person abdicates his role as regards nature, according to the clear design of God, and uncontrollable selfishness and unbridled material interests triumph.

Unfortunately this happens all too often today. The use of resources with no consideration for the environmental and human context mars the beauty of the countryside, upsets the vital dynamic equilibrium, and causes pollution and breakdown, harming natural processes, and threatening the survival of living things.

The earth thus loses its face, created by God a garden at the service of the human person, to become merely a source of economic exploitation, an abandoned desert.

Dear young people, in thanking you for your visit, your demonstration of homage and devotion, I hope that your reflections will bring about concrete ideas for the spread of an environmental culture and plans for collaboration with the forces of good will. May the earth flourish again as a garden for all; may the Lord see that people also make good things.

---

61. Family and Work Are Fundamental Dimensions of Human Existence[128]

Dignity of Work, Human Rights/Dignity, Meaning of Work, Technology, Work and Family, Work and Women/Mothers.

[An address on June 5, 1988 in Piacenza, Italy, to agricultural workers.]

"The family and the world of work": these are two interrelated themes which, in this first decade of my pastoral service in the See of Peter and his successor, I have always borne in mind, indeed favored. I wish to return to them at this meeting of ours as well. I know that your diocesan synod is dealing with them. Hence I, too, would like to make my contribution to a pastoral matter of such importance.

Family and Work Are Interdependent

Our essential point of reference here is the solemn divine imperative that includes the account of the creation of the world and of man in the first chapter of Genesis: "Be fruitful and multiply, and fill the earth and subdue it."[129] In the wondrous context in which these words are pronounced, they express, in the light of God's revelation, the relation existing between the primordial human family ("Be fruitful") and work ("Subdue the earth"). The growth of the human family to the point of filling the earth and "subduing" the earth through work are intimately connected objectives which proceed together historically, in reciprocal interdependence. The divine command thus shows itself to be intrinsic to man's specific nature and worthy of the unique value of the human person.

In speaking of work, I mean to refer to all the dimensions in which it has developed and been transformed through the centuries: work in the various areas of agriculture, craftsmanship, industry, technology, professional life, culture and art. We are dealing with a "fundamental dimension of man's existence on earth."[130] The vocation to work is inserted in him from the beginning as a natural predisposition. Speaking in Fiorano, I referred mainly to the industrial and technological sector; here in Piacenza, my attention turns rather to agricultural work, in relation to the necessary revitalization of the rural world.

The Value of Agricultural Work

Still, even among you there can be noted, as an element almost of imbalance, the marked concentration of residents in tertiary activities, especially in the areas of public administration and commerce. It is not pointless, then, to call attention to the lack of appreciation, from the social point of view, for farm work.[131] So prevalent is this attitude that it makes farmers feel like second-class citizens. It thus becomes more difficult to resist the temptation to abandon rural areas for anonymous urban industrial agglomerates and administrative centers.

It is therefore necessary to regenerate the civic conscience and the awareness of the primary value of agricultural work. I wish to reaffirm in your presence what I wrote in the encyclical Letter *Laborem Exercens*, so as to encourage those who have remained faithful to the earth and those who are recovering the taste for rural work: "The world of agriculture, which provides society with the goods it needs for its daily sustenance, is of fundamental importance." It is necessary "to restore to agriculture – and to rural people – their just value as the basis for a healthy economy, within the social community's development as a whole. Thus it is necessary to proclaim the dignity of work, of all work but especially of agricultural work, in which man so eloquently 'subdues' the earth he has received as a gift from God."[132]

Work Is for Man and for the Family

God says: "Be fruitful and multiply, and fill the earth and subdue it."[133] There is in fact an intimate relation between work and the fruitfulness of man destined to fill the earth. Indeed the human person, the active subject of the process of work, is not an isolated entity, but is always placed in the context of his family, which forms his constant point of reference. This is a dynamic force of the human conscience, to whose voice workers are particularly attuned. What they sense most of all is precisely that bond that unites work and family. Work is for man and for the family, because the family is first of all man's proper place. It is the vital world in which he is conceived and born and in which he matures. It is the environment for which he assumes his most serious responsibility: the place of earthly happiness and human hope, which opens out to eternal hope.

The Real Meaning of Work and Family

The intimate connection between work and family, these two fundamental dimensions of human existence, becomes fully evident if they are considered in their precise meanings. On the one hand, work is to be understood as the activity through which the person realizes himself and thus fulfills the vocation that is his by reason of his very humanity. Work, then, is an experience in which one discovers his dependence on the Giver of all the resources of creation and his "interdependence" with others, and the consequent laws of "solidarity."[134]

On the other hand, the family is to be understood as the project of God's love for the love between man and woman, and thus as their vocation from "the beginning."[135] The human person, who cannot live if love is not revealed to him, if he does not encounter love, discovers in this way that his very work is ordered to the expression of love. Work is for the family inasmuch as work is for the person, who is ordered to the family.

Technology Must Respect the Dignity of the Human Person

It is therefore necessary that the process of production adapt itself to this objective structure of human existence.

In Europe we are perhaps witnessing the conclusion of what history will recall as the age of industrialization: new forms of work, such as computer science and satellite communication, will give a new appearance to the activity of production. However, it must not be forgotten that in its early stages industrialization was often a brutal and dehumanizing social phenomenon. It was a time of cruel exploitation, even where the ruling ideologies preached the liberation of the oppressed.

The technological revolution now advancing has already reached a point of great turbulence in the field of genetic technology, in which the very structure of living things, including man, is at stake.

To avoid the repetition of the errors of the first industrial revolution, or even worse errors, it is absolutely necessary that technology does not proceed devoid of spiritual and transcendent values, but that it let itself be guided and permeated by them. It is absolutely essential that biomedicine and related technologies accept the directives of right reason, directives which the Magisterium of the Church proposes concerning respect for the sacredness of human life.

Women and the Gospel of Work

Finally, there is a theme that is particularly close to my heart: that of women and work. the Gospel of Work has a particular value for women: it seeks to attach new esteem, on the social plane, to the motherly tasks specific to women, to the toil and risks inherent in them, to the needs of children for care and love in order that they may develop as responsible, balanced and mature persons.

It is not a question, as some have insinuated, of binding women to the role of housewife; nor is it a question of excluding them from work outside the home or of assigning them only family duties. Since man and woman enjoy equal dignity, both having been created in God's image,[136] the whole gamut of human activities is and must be open to women, whether in the economic, social, cultural or political realm. However, for women there is a specific activity that regards her as "mother of all living."[137] In that activity, woman reaches her highest self-expression; so it is just that the state and society sustain her in the performance of that task specific to her with the social provisions from which women working outside the home benefit.

Mutual Collaboration of Women and Men

Still, I repeat that it is not a question of shutting the woman between the four walls of the home or of charging her with the entire educational duty within the family. Within the conjugal community the equal personal dignity of the man and the woman must be recognized in full and mutual love. The constant collaboration of the parents is thus necessary in the education of the children. The active presence of the father is of great help in their formation; but the presence and care of the mother, of whom little children have a special need, must be safeguarded. Her presence in the home must be facilitated, without neglecting, however, her legitimate social advancement.

It is not a question, then, of schematic role divisions, but of mutual collaboration in the family and in society, according to the various conditions and circumstances, with full equality and responsibility, and with attention to the needs of the family – the school of humanity and the foundation of society.

Workers Are Witnesses to the Gospel

Much remains to be done to assure human work of its full dignity. I charge you, Christian workers, to be witnesses to the Gospel in your work settings: proclaim the name of Christ in your factories and offices, and on your farm. Draw your inspiration from Him who became a "worker" for us.[138]

Act in such a way that work becomes an effective means of developing in yourselves a strong and generous personality, and of establishing firm bonds within your families, which constitute the primary purpose of your labors. May the family truly become for you the "domestic Church," in which daily labors find their justification and meaning; may the Spirit of God fill you with ardor for this great mission!

62. We Must Be Enlightened and Respectful Managers of Nature and Persons[139]

Common Good, Culture of Work, Dominion over the Earth, Human Development/Progress, Spirituality.

[An address on October 10, 1988 in Strasbourg, France, to French boatmen and dock workers.]

Man has received from God the power and mission to dominate the earth, to master its elements. When we look at all that has been accomplished along the Rhine, we admire the ingenuity and efficiency of human activity. The water flow has been regulated to protect the land from flooding and to facilitate navigation. Cities, cultures and industry have profited from the abundance of water. The energy of the previously reduced water levels has become useful and productive energy.

Care of Natural Resources

It is true that the very life of the river and the quality of its water have suffered from a sometimes imprudent or excessive use. We must learn lessons from the pernicious effects of certain industrial activities. I wish that you may continue these positive efforts already undertaken to fight against the pollution of the Rhine. Nature is put at our disposal; may we be capable of being the enlightened and respectful managers of a good which must keep its fruitfulness for the generations to come.

The Importance of the Rhine River and Those Who Work on It

Throughout Europe the Rhine follows a path traced throughout history by the soldiers and merchants of various countries in their time. As its juridical status recognizes, its waters are a common patrimony par excellence. There is nothing more obviously international than the waters of such a river, to the point that at a very early stage the nations reached an agreement to regulate navigation together and to create the historically most ancient European international organization. In continuing to develop its activity, you give a good example of cooperation in this continent which is in the process of progressing towards unity.

By the efforts of the boatmen, which were for a long time accomplished amid very hazardous conditions, the Rhine represents for several countries a source of multiple material and cultural riches. The transportation and trade of merchandise are naturally accompanied by intellectual, artistic and spiritual exchange. Is there not a true relationship between the cities of the Rhine, even if history has sometimes found them in opposition to one another?

Craftsmen of International Bonds

Dear friends, boatmen and port workers, you are the effective craftsmen of international bonds which this great river affords. Your many tasks complement one another and allow you to help to create a vast economic network. By being involved in it, you constitute an attractive human environment and you manifest a precious solidarity which frontiers do not stop.

You also experience the numerous difficulties of boatmen: your family life is marked by ceaseless displacements, separations, difficulties in the education of your children. The modernization of the boats and their maintenance shortens the shifts. However, the number of jobs is diminishing, and you are not assured of regular work. Progress obtained does not always benefit people at the same pace.

No Economic Progress without Social Progress

That is why I want to recall the Church's conviction that there is no economic progress without social progress. Your activities are often designated as "services," and they are indeed services for those who receive material or merchandise from them. However, do we give enough thought to the people who effectively render these services, the boatmen and the dock workers?

The Church's social teaching speaks of the "civilization of work." This implies a solidarity on the part of all those who participate in economic circles in view of the common good. It is also helpful to remember that the phrase "the common good" does not denote an abstract or personal entity. It involves the true good of all the people, sought in solidarity for the entire community. The common good surely implies sacrifice and a great sense of collaboration; however, it also requires that it is always lived with concern for justice and the equal dignity of all.

Development of the Person Is the Aim of the Economy

The Bishop of Rome would like to tell you once again of the Church's esteem for all types of work in your profession and her profound desire to see the human dimension always respected. You know that social doctrine demands that the chief aim of the economy should be the integral development of the person in conditions which allow this professional life to be compatible with the personal flowering of each person, and his family life as well. This supposes that people do not allow themselves to be hemmed in by a pragmatic materialism. It presumes that economic agents, at all levels of responsibility, pursue the ideal of a society based on solidary where the values of service to one's neighbor, and openness of the person to the transcendent in his personal relations with God the Creator and Savior, are placed in the forefront.

63. Professional Life Must Be Compatible with the Personal Growth of Each Person[140]

Collaboration With God, Economic Laws and Profits, Humanization/Dehumanization.

[An address on June 25, 1989 in Gaeta, Italy, to sailors, fishermen and port workers.]

The sea, to which the history of your people is closely connected, is, as you know, God's creation, a manifestation of the greatness of him who guides all our destinies in the course of time. However, the very image of the sea, not always calm and peaceful, and sometimes terrifying, also serves to remind us of the trials to which God sometimes subjects us in order to test the strength of our faith and the firmness of our hope. Nonetheless, we know that there is no storm in life from which God cannot save us, to lead us to the harbor of security and peace.

Christ Is Your Courage in Difficult Times

With its many aspects the sea therefore reminds us that our life needs a guide and support to accompany us along the billows of our existence. The moving Gospel passage which presents Jesus in the boat with his disciples in the midst of the sea immediately comes to mind: "Suddenly a violent storm came up on the sea, so that the boat was being swamped by the waves; but (Jesus) was asleep. They came and woke him, saying, 'Lord, save us! We are perishing!' He said to them, 'Why are you terrified, O you of little faith?' Then he got up, rebuked the winds and the sea, and there was a great calm."[141]

This scene needs no commentary: Jesus is the true Lord of history; he has dominion over events which at every moment depend on his omnipotent will. He can direct and sustain the ship of our existence even in the most difficult and darkest times.

Collaboration in the Redemption

The words which I wrote in the encyclical letter *Laborem Exercens* are quite fitting for you, people of the sea, to your concerns and hard work: "Sweat and toil, which work necessarily involves in the present condition of the human race, present the Christian and everyone who is called to follow Christ with the possibility of sharing lovingly in the work that Christ came to do. This work of salvation came about through suffering and death on a Cross. By enduring the toil of work in union with Christ crucified for us, man in a way collaborates with the Son of God for the redemption of humanity. He shows himself a true disciple of Christ by carrying the cross in his turn every day in the activity that he is called upon to perform."[142]

Civilization of Work

This Christian view of work, far from weakening our awareness of the person's intrinsic dignity and the legitimacy of his just claims, rather contributes towards strengthening it in its deepest and truest core.

Besides the worker's duties to society, the Church constantly recalls those of society to the working person. Despite the acclaimed recognition of the rights of every worker, it is not rare today to find cases of patent violations of basic rights in the world of work.

This is why the Church never tires of emphasizing the need for a "civilization of work" and that which is its foundation and soul, social solidarity. There cannot be a civilization of work if there is lacking the solidarity towards all those who take part in the economic process in view of the common good, of that good which is not reduced to an abstract or impersonal entity, but which involves the real interests of all persons, pursued in solidarity by the entire community. The Church proclaims that the main objective of the economy is the integral development of the person, in such conditions that professional life may be compatible with the personal growth of each person and with his or her family life.

Sanctification of Work

Within this perspective it is your right to demand that your work should not prevent you from fulfilling your religious duties. It is necessary to do so in such a way that professional demands are compatible with the sanctification of work through participation at Mass on Sundays and holy days, a regular sacramental life, and an active insertion in your ecclesial communities.

With the help and intercession of St. Erasmus, patron of sailors, uphold the treasure of faith which has been jealously passed on to you by your parents, by ancestors whose memory is held in blessing. Be "of one heart and mind,"[143] even when you are far from home, on the immensity of the sea, in order to share your worries and tribulations, joys and hopes, between yourselves and your loved ones.

64. *Technology Developed without God Is Destined to Turn against Human Persons*[144]

Christian Witness/Mission, Dignity of Work, Economic Laws and Profits, Humanization/Dehumanization, Materialism and Consumerism, Solidarity, Technology.

[An address on October 29, 1989 in
Martina Franca, Italy, to farmers and artisans.]

Today, we know, the economy of this territory is not lacking in difficulties, to the point where small family farms are seeking to take on new activities, artisan and other. Agriculture and craftsmanship are experiencing a complex evolution, not only and not so much in terms of the structures and methods of production, but in the relationship of dependence between demand and supply, which imposes limits on the quantity and ever more demanding conditions on the quality and novelty of the products. No sector of production can any longer consider itself self-sufficient.

Growing Interdependence

In the agro-industrial and agro-alimentary chain, agriculture is the link in the economic system of the country and, with craftsmanship, is the mirror of an interdependence which is ever more marked as things develop. Precisely for this reason your work, too, is exposed to the risk of a new slavery imposed by the employer of "indirect" labor. I spoke of this in *Laborem Exercens*, warning against a policy of work which is not correct from the ethical point of view, precisely because it overlooks such a system of conditioning, conducted at times by the State itself.[145] I am here to encourage and to seek efforts toward economic policies directed to the safeguarding of the specific rights of workers, particularly of the South.

Solidarity

I have often spoken of solidarity. This is both a source and a fruit of peace with God and with the whole created order. It grounds and nourishes that peaceful and harmonious relationship of human beings with one another and with the cosmos, which has been the fertile tradition of rural civilization, as well as of the culture of the workshops which are genuine schools of life.

Respect for the Environment

Citizens of Martina, I cannot help sharing with you my concern for one of the most urgent challenges of our generation: how to reconcile the economy of development with human ecology, with the quality of life.

Scientific research, suggestions and initiatives of professional associations and, above all, the responsibility of those in charge of the economy should establish the "human" compatibility between the technologies of production, transformation and commerce, and respect for the balance of the natural environment. "When it comes to the natural world, we are subject not only to biological laws but also to moral ones, which cannot be violated with impunity."[146] This is a task which involves every citizen.

In this land of yours which is still relatively immune to the pollution of the larger urban and industrial areas, the Pope exhorts you to farsightedness with respect to goods like clean air and clear water, green forests and cultivated soil. Only in this way will you deliver whole to future generations the heritage of these natural riches of yours. Only in this way will you pass on the genuine meaning of creation and of brotherhood to your descendants and to those who tomorrow will inhabit this land which is dear to you.

Quality of life is not only the result of a healthy and clean environment, but it is also the fruit of the integral promotion of the economic, cultural and moral values of a people.

The Need for Generous Revitalization

Such values must always be reoffered, redeemed and rendered harmonious through evangelical wisdom.

In particular, the quality of moral and religious life which has always been the soul and leaven of your civilization involves all of you in a work of generous revitalization. The original expressions of popular piety and of social commitment which characterize your history stimulate you now to a new sowing, wherever this is possible; in religious associations and in places of formation, in the apostolate of charity, in confraternities and in other organizations. Knowing that "to each is given the manifestation of the Spirit for the common good,"[147] be joyful and industrious "workers in the vineyard," in order that Martina Franca – which has given the world people of genius and culture, cardinals, bishops and priests, religious and lay persons, well-deserving of society and of the Church – may continue to bear abundant fruits of cooperation and of solidarity even in our own times.

---

65. Christians Must Integrate the Worlds of Work and Faith[148]

Christian Witness/Mission, Collaboration with God, Common Good, Dialogue and Cooperation, Dignity of Work, Dominion over the Earth, Human Development/Progress, Human Rights/ Dignity, Gospel of Work, Justice, Materialism and Consumerism, Selfishness, Service, Solidarity, Unemployment, Universal Destination of Goods, Work and Family, Work and Society, Work and the Worker.

[An address on May 26, 1990 in Malta,
to workers gathered at St. Margaret Square.]

To all of you I repeat the Church's great esteem for the world of work. Work is a fundamental part of our life here on earth. It often involves heavy fatigue and even suffering, but it can also be the forge of strong character and vigorous personality, the means by which we build up the world according to the values in which we believe. For the Christian, work is our way of taking an active and responsible part in the marvelous work of the Creator which surrounds us everywhere and completely fills our being.

Esteem for the World of Work

But why should the Pope talk about work? Perhaps some people may think that he has no right to do so; they think that work has little or nothing to do with religion. I might answer by saying that my own personal experience of work was one of the most interesting and formative periods of my life. I have expressed the richness of that experience in some of my writings. Today I have come to you, the workers of Malta, as a friend who shares the concerns and hopes of the men and women who – in the words of the book of Genesis – earn their bread by the sweat of their brow.[149] I have also come as the Bishop of Rome, the Successor of Peter, and therefore as a messenger of One who was known as a carpenter and the son of a carpenter.[150]

Jesus Christ and Work

Yes, the world of work is not alien to the Gospel of Jesus Christ. The Lord understood perfectly the reality of human labor. His words were filled with references to workers and their various occupations: the farmer who plants the seed and the laborer who harvests the crop, the vinedresser and the shepherd, the one who mends the nets beside the sea, the builder and the domestic servant, the merchant and the housewife, the soldier and the state official. They all had a place in Jesus' interest and teaching. And the Apostles he chose to carry on his redemptive mission were workers and fishermen.

In every age the Church continues to present Jesus' teaching about work, and especially today when economic relations and production processes are complex and increasingly impersonal, and threaten to turn against man himself. The Church preaches a social doctrine because the great questions affecting society, not least the question of labor, have a powerful impact on people's lives and cannot be separated from the moral and ethical responsibilities of everyone involved.

Social Justice Based on the Dignity of the Human Person

Unfortunately, it is the experience worldwide that the history of labor relations, especially during the last two centuries, has often developed as a social struggle between workers and employers. Only with great difficulty has the ideal of social justice made headway. Today, with the opening of so many previously closed frontiers and the determination of peoples to live in freedom from ideological oppression, it is becoming clearer that although the quest for justice can be opposed and delayed, it cannot be suppressed. It is a fundamental aspiration of the human spirit. Systems built on untruths about the spiritual nature of man and of human relations cannot last. The dignity of the human person is the only solid basis of a social system capable of giving the right direction to human relations, and of fostering mutual understanding, dialogue and cooperation. In an increasingly interdependent world, there can be no other way forward. In Malta, too, this is imperative.

Work Commanded by God

Even though there are many kinds of work, in a sense all work shares the same nature. Its purpose is to transform and organize reality in a way that is useful and productive. Work is the implementation of God's original command, recorded in the first pages of the Bible: "Fill the earth and subdue it."[151] Whether through physical, intellectual or spiritual effort, "each and every individual takes part in the giant process whereby man 'subdues the earth' through his work."[152]

Gospel of Work

This is the beginning of what I call the "Gospel of Work" which the church wishes to transmit to the modern world. Whoever hears this "Gospel" and lives by it can no longer look upon labor as mere commodity to be bartered in exchange for pay. In a wider and more noble view, work must also be seen as the path to self-development and as the normal means for people to create the conditions that permit a healthy cultural, social and religious life.[153] Because the nature and organization of labor affects people so totally, Catholic social doctrine insists that the human person is the center and norm of all economic processes. That is why the Second Vatican Council made this earnest appeal: "The entire process of productive work must be adapted to the needs of the person and to the requirements of his life, above all of his family life."[154] A change of priorities is needed in the world economic order if the reality of work is truly to serve people and not oppress them in new forms of slavery. This is especially evident in the condition of workers in the developing countries of the South, but also in the industrialized countries of the North. Maltese society too is called to strive for those changes which are necessary for promoting a development which embraces all sectors.[155]

Unemployment

The "Gospel of Work" holds that all honest labor, competently carried out, has an innate dignity and confers dignity on those engaged in it. That is why unemployment is such a deadly thing. It leaves its victims without adequate economic support, but more than that it deprives them psychologically and socially. For that reason, I urge you: do not abandon the unemployed, especially young people seeking a livelihood. The unemployed and their families have a right to the effective solidarity of the State, of business interests and of workers' organizations themselves.

Rights of Workers

Workers are the subjects of rights and duties. People who work, especially dependent workers, have a right to he treated for what they are: free and responsible men and women, called to have a share in the decisions that concern their lives. A society that seeks the true well-being of its members will make appropriate provision for family support. It will make it possible for mothers to give their primary attention to their children and homes, and, where necessary, it will provide for the special needs of working mothers. And particular classes of workers need the special attention and protection of society. Agricultural workers, for example, often feel that their contribution to society is not fully appreciated. The "Gospel of Work" then, preaches that economic, social and political systems must be sensitive to the complete well-being of individuals and to the needs of their families.

Duties to the Common Good

But workers and their organizations also have solemn duties towards the common good. The first of these duties is to work well, to contribute effectively to building a better society. This too is part of the "Gospel of Work," proclaimed two thousand years ago in the life and activity of Jesus of Nazareth, the Incarnate Son of God. The value which Jesus placed on work during the long years of his hidden life was not lost on the early Christians. Saint Paul boasted of the fact that he worked day and night in order not to be a burden to others,[156] and he summed up the spirituality of work in these works: "Whatever your task, work heartily, as serving the Lord and not men, knowing that from the Lord you will receive an inheritance as your reward."[157]

Human Workers Cooperate with the Creative Intention of God

These words are an invitation to integrity and competence on the part of everyone, workers and employers, people engaged at every level of economic and productive activity. At the same time, the Apostle is calling us to widen the horizon of human activity to include God's plan for the world and for our eternal salvation. The world of work must not be seen as a part of reality somehow opposed to faith and religion, as if in conflict with God and his Church. Work can be a source of satisfaction and development, as well as of cultural and spiritual growth, only if society sees it as cooperation in the creative intention of God and respects each person's unique dignity and higher aspirations, including the rights of conscience, as inalienable gifts of the Creator.[158]

Solidarity and Responsibility

The outstanding virtue of the working men and women of Malta should be solidarity: a commitment to the common good and a rejection of selfishness and irresponsibility. We must become responsible for one another. What are needed are concrete acts of solidarity: between employers and employees, between working men and women themselves, with special sensitivity for the poor and the defenseless. In all of this, workers' unions have a specific part to play. It is their task to defend the rights of their members through the legitimate means at their disposal, keeping also in mind the rights of other categories of workers, the general economic situation of the country and, in short, the common good. In the present state of technological progress and social development, they are being challenged to adopt a broader view of their social function and responsibilities. Their great task is to harmonize the quest for material progress with the cultural and spiritual advancement of society. In other words, a great wave of social solidarity, not conflict, is the proper response to the increasingly interrelated and interdependent nature of today's problems.

Vertical and Horizontal Dimension of Work

But solidarity, dialogue and cooperation must be built on a firm foundation. These values demand a "readiness, in the Gospel sense, to 'lose oneself' for the sake of the other instead of exploiting him, and to 'serve him' instead of oppressing him for one's own advantage."[159] Thus the essence of the "Gospel of Work" is also the heart of the Christian message itself. Jesus Christ sums up his teaching in these familiar words: "You shall love the Lord your God with all your heart, and with all your soul, and with all your mind. This is the great and first commandment. And a second is like it, You shall love your neighbor as yourself."[160] The first direction of work, then, is vertical, towards God: your work itself is an unfolding of the Creator's intention and a contribution to the realization in history of the divine plan.[161] The second direction of work is horizontal: it is an effective way of putting into practice love of neighbor. Your work, insofar as it brings benefits of all kinds to society, is a magnificent form of service to others.

Integrate the Worlds of Work and Faith

The task then which the Pope leaves to the workers of Malta is to integrate the world of work into the world of faith. There can be no separation between the traditions of the Catholic faith, manifested at Sunday Mass, and the sense of commitment, honesty, justice and brotherhood shown in the workplace during the week.

Dear friends, it is in this spirit of the "Gospel of Work," which was proclaimed by Jesus Christ two thousand years ago and continues to be proclaimed by the Church in our day, that I invite you to:

Say No to injustice at every level of society!

Say No to the individual and class selfishness that seeks its own interests without concern for the common good of the whole of society!

Say No to the materialism that deadens conscience and the spiritual dimension of life!

Say Yes to a new solidarity between all the members of the work force, and between workers and employers, between the world of work and the whole of Malta's people!

Say Yes to the full material and spiritual development of every inhabitant of these islands, with special provision for the poorest and neediest!

Say Yes to God's plan for creation and to his Truth written in the nature of all things and in the depths of the human heart!

The carpenter of Nazareth and the workers of Malta ought to be of one mind and one heart. Remember the words of the Scripture reading we heard at the beginning of our meeting: "Whatever you do, whether in speech or in action, do it in the name of the Lord Jesus."[162] In union with Jesus Christ, your work and your efforts to transform the world take on the quality of a sacrifice pleasing to God. By offering "what earth has given and human hands have made," you prepare the way for God's kingdom. That is the deepest meaning of your labor.

Dear brothers and sisters, may Christ's kingdom of truth and life, of holiness and grace, of justice, love and peace, take possession of your hearts, for the true progress and prosperity of Malta. God bless you all.

66. Christian Workers Have a Responsibility to Proclaim the Church's Social Doctrine[163]

Christian Witness/Mission, Human Rights/Dignity, Meaning of Work.

[An address on March 18, 1991 in Rome, to delegates representing the International Confederation of Christian Workers.]

Truly, in your quality as committed Catholic workers, you bear living witness to [the Church's social teaching], fully conscious of your responsibility to your companions at work and to the Church herself. Indeed, you represent a group of organizations which want to identify themselves as Christian. In that, you are the heirs of the teaching of *Rerum Novarum* and of its illustrious author who, as you know well, affirmed the importance and necessity of associations of Christian workers and who defended their right to existence and freedom.

During this brief meeting, on the vigil of the feast of St. Joseph, model of craftsmen and workers, I want to recall two things which seem important to me for the fulfillment of your vocation as Christian workers grouped in an organization such as yours.

Call to Holiness

In the first place, be more conscious of your dignity. To be a worker is in itself a source of pride because by your work, whatever it may be, you make the life of men and women in society easier and happier by devoting your energy and skills to them. What is more, by being a Christian worker you set out to imitate Jesus Christ who himself freely chose to be a worker.[164] Thus you make your life and condition an offering pleasing to the Lord. The call to holiness is not something added on or marginal to your status as Christian workers, but it reveals its entire meaning. Do not be afraid to profess your faith openly, individually or as members of a confederation which bears the very name that identifies you.

Bearers of the Church's Social Doctrine

In the second place, as you have recalled, I have chosen to proclaim this centenary year of Leo XIII's encyclical the Year of the Church's Social Teaching. Now, that directly touches your vocation as Christian union members. As such, you are the witnesses and, one could say, the bearers of that doctrine which is still all too often ignored or misunderstood.

During these difficult times which are confused in many ways, your mission is to proclaim, and especially to incarnate, social doctrine in the very exercise of your life as workers, members and leaders of your organizations. Indeed, it is a question of knowing this doctrine well, of making it known to others, especially to young people. But most of all it is necessary to put it into practice in dialogue with your colleagues at work, with business leaders and with leaders of other union organizations which are not specifically Christian. The Church's social doctrine in fact is meant to be lived and applied in the concrete life of men and women in all dimensions of life in society and with all the responsibilities that involves, from one's own family to the life of the nation and the international community.

---

67. True Human Progress Respects the Special Role of Women and Mothers[165]

Work and Women.

[An address on March 19, 1991, in
Matelica, Italy, to women factory workers.]

Certainly the entrance of women into the work-place helped change the traditional life-style of your city; in part it took from the female role of wife and mother the traditional tasks of raising the children and keeping house, once almost exclusively her role. The rhythms of work regulated by the needs of the company, prolonged absence from the home, greater economic and psychological autonomy, did not fail to have a profound effect on the mental attitudes and behavior that prevailed only a few decades ago. All this did not have totally positive repercussions: all too often the woman has ended up paying a heavy price for modern progress. It is necessary that, in the changing social context, women commit themselves to rediscover and reaffirm the deepest reasons for their femininity.

Personal Dimensions of Motherhood and Virginity

Woman's personality, as I wrote in *Mulieris Dignitatem*, bears two dimensions, motherhood and virginity, which are the two paths of her personal vocation and justify and complement one another. Only by deepening our knowledge of the truth about the human person "who can fully discover his or her true self only in a sincere giving of self," will a person open up "the path to a full understanding of women's motherhood."[166] In this motherhood, joined to the man's fatherhood, we have a reflection of the eternal mystery of generation which is in God himself. Although both of them, father and mother, are the parents of their child, "the woman's motherhood constitutes a special part of this shared parenthood, and the most demanding part."[167] It is the woman, in fact, who "pays directly for this shared generation which literally absorbs the energies of her body and soul,"[168] and a man owes a special debt to his wife. In the light of these considerations it seems obvious that no program of the equal rights of women and men is valid if it does not bear in mind what has been mentioned above. In fact, it would end up being detrimental and unjust to those, the women, whom it claims to want to promote and protect.

Times are changing, and so are the ways of organizing society. The pace of productivity is accelerating, but the dignity and order of love must remain immutable. The woman represents "a particular value by the very fact that she is a human person and, at the same time, this particular person, by the fact of her femininity"; her dignity "is measured by the order of love which is essentially the order of justice and charity."[169]

Risks from Rapid Change

When the changes in the work-place are so rapid that they do not allow for a proper preparation for change on the part of the subjects who work there, it can happen that the productive needs take precedence over consideration for the person. At that point moral principles and the indispensable ethical references to the care of the person are put in crisis, and respect for his or her intangible dignity is diminished. This is probably not the case in your firm, where you seek to adapt the work schedule to your commitments as women and mothers of families, but we all know that today there are occupational contexts where the dignity of the woman is threatened. It is necessary for her to regain her special role, avoiding the risk of being considered almost as an object of productivity.

True Role of Women

Work, that personal participation in the transformation of creation and source of a dignified living, must not take away from the woman, spouse and mother, the possibility of fulfilling the social and family functions which are proper to her, because only in this manner can she fulfil her human vocation in its feminine aspect as well. A job that would restrict the woman's environment and end up taking her away from her role of love, preventing her real fulfillment, would deprive the human and Christian community of an indispensable protagonist in its evolution and the growth of civilization.

How necessary, then, is the new evangelization and an expert, effective apostolate to the world of work in order to respond concretely to the demands placed upon the modern organization of work! Only thus will it be possible to reclaim and promote a true space for the role of woman, spouse, mother and teacher. Only under these conditions will the family not suffer from the absence of the feminine function and the children will not be deprived of a mother's affection and support, which are indispensable for the harmonious growth and balanced development of the domestic cell.

Progress, as it has developed, favors some people, while it marginalizes others. There is the danger of seeing a gradual and imperceptible loss of attention to the person and all that concerns him or her. Still very timely is the observation I made at the conclusion of *Mulieris Dignitatem*: "In this sense, our time in particular awaits the manifestation of that genius which belongs to women, and which can assure sensitivity for human beings in every circumstance: because they are human! and because the greatest of these is love!"[170]

68. The Christian Vocation Is a Call to Activity in Many Areas of Social Life[171]

Christian Witness/Mission, Collaboration with God, Common Good, Culture of Work, Economic Laws and Profits, Human Development/Progress, Human Rights/Dignity, Meaning of Work, Selfishness, Solidarity, Spirituality, Technology, Universal Destination of Goods.

[An address on December 7, 1991 in Rome, to the Christian Associations of Italian Workers.]

The decision to call your associations "Christian" was a clear affirmation that the life of those who believe in Christ does not only regard the personal choices of the members, but it involves the way of thinking and of acting of the whole movement. For each of you, being Christian means accepting in faith and joy Jesus Christ, the Son of God made man, risen and living, who frees us from sin, who communicates his own divine life and calls us to collaborate in his mission of salvation.

Christian Mission of Collaboration

Certainly, a movement is Christian because its social and economic union and political choices are inspired by the Gospel and by the social doctrine of the Church; but it is Christian also because, as a movement, it intends to shape the mentality and educate the spiritual life of its members so that they may find in Christ a sure guide in facing the problems of modern life within the particular competence of various temporal sectors. Christian formation, therefore, must constitute the main objective of the whole movement, and it must find its logical connection with the ecclesiastical structures of the social apostolate and with work.

In the effort to be an authentic Christian movement you have before you numerous and serious problems which require great competence, solid faith and generous love for every person but especially for those in need.

Value of Life

Fortunately, today people have a heightened awareness of the value of the life and health of every person, with an ever more effective system for the prevention of accidents at work and of assistance during illness. On the other hand, however, the protection and the promotion of life from conception to natural death have been given a grave blow from a mentality and civil legislation which permits abortion; likewise the fight against drugs, AIDS and the pollution of the environment appear to be indecisive and inconstant.

The working world has particular reasons and motives to support vigorously this action on behalf of life, aiming principally to eliminate the moral, cultural and social causes of these sad phenomena. The problems of life concern every upright human conscience; every Christian, and therefore every Christian worker, should feel personally challenged and involved in solving these problems.

Technology for the Common Good

The Christian appreciates technological innovations, but he knows that he must strive to avoid making them "idols"; he must see to it that they are used for the common good, under the control of all components of society.

The changes that they bring about in employment, in the method of working, in the times of work and in human mentality, create a series of problems which you must face daily together with other social forces, in open dialogue with the persons responsible for introducing these changes, without ever forgetting the ultimate aim, which is the integral development of every person.

The problems of the economy and of the market are connected with technological problems. A precise knowledge of the workings of the market will help you to join with the work of those with social power and of the State, so that the market may effectively serve the common good.[172] This good certainly requires the existence of free enterprise, but it requires that it be realized for man and in a human manner. From this derives the duty to promote free enterprise and an economic policy which finds work for the unemployed, especially young people.[173]

What you do for the education of youth, for the realization of justice and of a progress that is not only economic but also social and moral, represents an important contribution. A serious study of the problems of work and all its aspects will help you to understand the relationship between work and migration, between work and unions, between social and political activity.

Business: A Community of Work

I know that you pay particular attention to the business as a community of work.[174] Every business must become a true community, even while maintaining the distinction of roles. Everyone, in fact, has precise rights and duties, which must be coordinated so that they may prepare the way for ever greater forms of participation. In fact this is the only way in which a shared responsibility in labor and economic problems can be established.

The presence of immigrants will give you the chance to realize this orientation and to put into practice a positive and cordial welcome with a type of dialogue that is also open to the proclamation of Christ. Thus the "authentic culture of work,"[175] so important for the development of human civilization, is progressively formed.

Marriage and the Family

The crisis of modern society will be overcome if marriage and the family recover their true physiognomy and precise function; and this can take place fully when the family is founded on a single indissoluble marriage, which Jesus Christ raised to the dignity of a sacrament; when the social, economic and working order does not hinder it, but promotes it in conjugal communion, in the procreation and education of children; when the woman's role of wife and mother receives concrete economic support as well as being appreciated from the cultural point of view; when the family itself is respected in its rights and in its educative duties against unjust penalization of its free educational and scholastic choices; when within it spiritual life is cultivated and the growth of the married couple proceeds together with that of the children. In this way the working world becomes a place where the family can find its nature and function.

Fight against Selfishness

One must have the capacity and courage to change what needs to be changed. But even more courage is needed to fight every form of personal and social selfishness. Be prepared therefore, for every sacrifice to strengthen moral values in yourselves and in social life. They are the foundation of every civilized way of life and of all social activity.[176] Open your life to Christ, foundation and strength of the freedom which welcomes truth.[177] A truly civilized state cannot ignore the need for moral values. Your formation and your presence in society must express a strong testimony which helps everyone to return decisively to the path of moral seriousness.

United Activity Especially for the Poor

For its part, a Christian movement which acts in the social sector is sure to find in the defence and promotion of ethical values which reflect the full truth of man as manifested in Jesus Christ a powerful impulse towards that united activity of Catholics, which has so contributed towards the good of Italy.[178]

While seriously working for the common good, remember above all the poorer people who have a right to your solidarity on the basis of the principle of the universal purpose of the earth's resources: with the measure of this solidarity the Lord judges you, your actions and the community to which you belong.

Spirituality of Work

Dear workers of the ACLI, I cannot end these reflections, which I entrust to your responsible commitment as Christians working at this great moment in history, without recalling the spirituality which must be profoundly present in your daily work. To this spirituality I dedicated the last part of the encyclical *Laborem Exercens*, knowing well that the Church "sees it as her particular duty to form a spirituality of work which will help all people to come closer, through work, to God, the Creator and Redeemer, to participate in his salvific plan for man and the world and to deepen their friendship with Christ in their lives by accepting, through faith, a living participation in his threefold mission as Priest, Prophet and King, as the Second Vatican Council so eloquently teaches."[179]

In fact, as the Pastoral Constitution *Gaudium et Spes* affirms, "by work a person ordinarily provides for himself and his family, associates with others as his brothers, and renders them service; he can exercise genuine charity and be a partner in the work of bringing divine creation to perfection. Moreover, we believe by faith that through the homage of work offered to God man is associated with the redemptive work of Jesus Christ, whose labor with his hands at Nazareth greatly ennobled the dignity of work."[180]

May he, Jesus Christ, be the light and the strength of your commitment to inspire your work and the entire working world with the Gospel!

---

69. *Work is the Key to Social Justice* [181]

Dignity of Work, Human Rights/Dignity, Meaning of Work, Private Property/Co-Ownership, St. Joseph, Spirituality, Work and the Worker, Unemployment, Work and Prayer

[Delivered as an address on March 19, 1992 in Castellammare di Stabia, Italy, to shipyard workers.]

Ethical recovery at the personal and social levels are closely interrelated. Social injustice and evil, in authentic structures of sin or social sins, as I already mentioned in the Apostolic Exhortation *Reconiliatio et Paenitentia*, are due to the accumulation and concentration of many personal sins.[182] Just as "structures of sin" exist, there can and must be "structures of good," of justice, solidarity, mutual respect, and peace, the result and concentration of personal actions.

May political leaders and public administrators never forget that by a special vocation they are called to promote the common good. It is a responsibility which consists first of all in the appropriate use of the resources of nature, culture, history and the human resources present in the area in order to contribute to solving the social problems the city suffers from; this is to be done in an attitude of true service.

A key, or rather, probably the most important key to these problems is *work*, as I said in *Laborem Exercens*.[183]

The feast of St. Joseph, patron and model of workers, which I wanted to celebrate with you this year, offers us the opportunity to reflect on the *true meaning of work*. In fact, it is not enough just to work, even though it is already quite a feat to satisfy that basic human right. It is necessary to know the why and wherefore of working, beyond the immediate benefits which derive from it. "By means of his work man commits himself, not only for his sake but also *for others* and *with others*. Each person collaborates in the work of others and for their good. Man works in order to provide for the needs of his family, his community, his nation, and ultimately all humanity."[184]

St. Joseph: An Enduring Model for Workers

Let us now look at the figure of St. Joseph, the just man, the spouse of Mary and Jesus' foster father. The Gospel presents him to us as a worker. In fact, in defining Jesus' social identity, it was said of him: "Is he not the carpenter's son?"[185]

For him his work as a carpenter was not merely a way of contributing to the support of the Son of God and his Virgin Mother, but created the environment for the life of the Holy Family itself. Thus work entered into the mystery of the incarnation, becoming an instrument of redemption. "At the workbench where he plied his trade together with Jesus, Joseph brought human work closer to the mystery of the Redemption."[186]

This must be our starting point if we want to understand the deepest meaning of human work. God himself wanted to make it his own.

In recent years surprising things have been happening before our very eyes and nevertheless, today, like never before, history is revealing its ambiguity: contrasts of light and darkness, great progress in technology and growing masses of poor people. The Marxist system which promised equality and justice, uprooting God from human hearts, has fallen in Eastern Europe, while new problems are looming on the horizon for those peoples. No one can be sanguine in the face of a capitalistic system when it is closed in on a "radical capitalistic ideology ... which refuses even to consider" the "reality of human alienation" and "which blindly entrusts its solution to the free development of market forces."[187]

The Human Person Gives Meaning To Work

In the face of all the dangers of human alienation which are found in the culture and economy of today's world, the Church does not hesitate to declare her choice: she is always on the side of the human person, but especially when the person is neglected, mistreated and scorned, because the human person seen in the light of Christ is the Church's principal way.[188]

Human work is understood by the Church according to this logic. As I pointed out in the Encyclical *Laborem Exercens*, before considering human work in its objective aspect as a production process within a technical and economic perspective, it should be seen in its subjectivity: it is the human person who gives meaning to work.[189] Workers are not, nor can they ever be, mere wheels in the machinery. Through work they fulfill their existence as the image of God, live their vocation to collaborate with the Creator, and experience the saving power of the paschal mystery.

In work and through it a man and woman fulfill their specific human vocation. The state and society, all of us, are obliged to recognize this dignity and nobility.

Right to Work

Dear friends, the workers, I know how extremely anxious you are about the future of your work and the problem of unemployment for young people which has so many of your families in its grip. The problem is a very serious one, especially for the effect it has on juvenile delinquency and particularly on the grievous, disgraceful phenomenon of organized violence.

In *Centesimus Annus* I wrote: "A society in which (the right to work) is systematically denied, in which economic policies do not allow workers to reach satisfactory levels of employment, cannot be justified from an ethical point of view, nor can that society attain social peace."[190] In this regard, we must recognize that we are facing a worrisome situation which challenges the whole of society. Therefore, I appeal to all those responsible for public affairs, the politicians and administrators, that they do everything in their power to solve these serious problems. I particularly invite businessmen to make their indispensable contribution, reminding them that "just as the person fully realizes himself in the free gift of self, so too ownership morally justifies itself in the creation, at the proper time and in the proper way, of opportunities for work and human growth for all."[191]

The appeal is all the more pressing since some of you are in precarious situations of need and the more insidious and widespread is the tendency of those who are comfortably well-off to believe, without foundation, that they have done everything possible.

Spirituality of Work

Dear friends, the obligation we have of earning our bread by the sweat of our brow, according to the divine command,[192] which Jesus himself chose to fulfill, can be satisfied in a fully human way only within a spirituality of work in the Christian sense of the word. To put it more simply, it is necessary for us believers to make our work a real process of sanctification. In imitation of the carpenter of Nazareth, therefore, make your work a liturgy, an act of worship in which you joyously offer God your work, which is often hard, maintaining an attitude of service and dedication towards the family and society.

To the human, spiritual, economic, social and cultural dimensions of work, then, you should add the Christian dimension, which finds a living example in St. Joseph, the Virgin Mary, and Jesus Christ, himself a worker: rather, it finds its ultimate reference in the creator himself who, as Genesis teaches us, "was finished with the work he was doing" and, as St. John states, "is at work until now."[193]

Therefore, no one can succeed in properly understanding the dignity of work, on the part either of the worker or of society, unless they consider it in this light. That is why in the Church's tradition it has constantly been associated with prayer: "*ora et labora.*"

Dear friends, helped by these reflections, may we find additional spiritual energy to give work its just value in our life.

May each of you feel responsible for the whole community in a spirit of solidarity and fraternity.[194] In particular, may those who have more and can do more feel that they have a greater responsibility than those who are less fortunate or who have nothing. May my encouragement accompany you in this task; I strengthen it with a special Blessing.

The Theology of Work Culminates in the Cross of Christ

In conclusion, I want to thank all of you once again for the various gifts I have received, but most of all for this gift, the most significant one, the crucifix made by one of your fellow-workers. It is a gift which says much to us; I would say that it explains the whole theology of work because the theology of work culminates in the cross of Christ.

We are working to build a better earth, an earth which is our home, a human world, in the various countries and continents; however, we must never forget that we must also build a home for ourselves, one in which the cross of Christ plays a leading role. By his sacrifice Christ showed us that he is close to each of us, that he is the true Emmanuel who at Nazareth began by being close to Joseph, and ended on the cross. Thus he remained in the history of all people, and in the history of all peoples, for all centuries. His cross represents for us – presents to us – a transcendent dimension, and tells us that we are all involved in this transcendency of the cross of Christ. Therefore the gift of the crucifix made for me in this office, in this shipyard, is a most precious gift to me. It is not only a work of art, but is also a profound expression of your lives.

Notes

1 The translation was taken from *L'Osservatore Romano*, July 14, 1980, p. 17.

2 Lk 10:5-37.

3 The translation was taken from L'Osservatore Romano, August 25, 1980, p. 18.

4 Lk 2:19.

5 The translation was taken from *L'Osservatore Romano*, September 8, 1980, pp. 1-2.

6 Gen 1:28; 2:15; 3:19.

7 2 Thess 3:7-12.

8 *Gaudium et Spes*, n. 67.

9 Wis 15:1,5.

10 The translation was taken from *L'Osservatore Romano*, January 19, 1981, p. 18.

11 *Gaudium et Spes*, n. 38.

12 Jn 13:14.

13 *Gaudium et Spes*, n. 38.

14 The translation was taken from *L'Osservatore Romano*, March 30, 1981, pp. 5-7.

15 Mt 13:55.

16 Gen 1:27.

17 Gen 1:26.

18 *Gaudium et Spes*, n. 67.

19 Address on June 29, 1979, in the Sanctuary of the Holy Cross at Mogile.

20 *Redemptor Hominis*, n. 14.

21 Mt 5:6.

22 The translation was taken from *L'Osservatore Romano*, April 5, 1982, pp. 9-11.

23 *Redemptor Hominis*, n. 16.

24 *Laborem Exercens*, n. 14.

25 *Dives in Misericordia*, n. 12.

26 *Familiaris Consortio*, n. 49.

27 Col 3:14.

28 The translation was taken from *L'Osservatore Romano*, July 5, 1982, pp. 9,10.

29 *Laborem Exercens*, n. 1.
30 Gen 1:28.
31 *Laborem Exercens*, n. 20.
32 Gen 1:26.
33 The translation was taken from *L'Osservatore Romano*, June 28, 1982, p. 10-12, 20.
34 *Laborem Exercens*, n. 1.
35 Address to ILO, 10 June 1969, n. 15. AAS 61, p. 498.
36 *Laborem Exercens*, n. 6.
37 *Laborem Exercens*, preamble.
38 Gen 1:28.
39 Address to ILO, 10 June 1969, n. 11. AAS 61, p. 495.
40 *Laborem Exercens*, n. 8.
41 *Populorum Progressio*, n. 3.
42 The translation was taken from *L'Osservatore Romano*, February 21, 1983, p. 4.
43 *Laborem Exercens*, nn. 6, 7, 25, 26.
44 *Laborem Exercens*, n. 6.
45 *Laborem Exercens*, n. 26.
46 *Gaudium et Spes*, n. 34.
47 The translation was taken from *L'Osservatore Romano*, February 21, 1983, p. 10.
48 1 Thess 5:19.
49 1 Jn 4:20.
50 *Laborem Exercens*, n. 13.
51 "The Italian Church and the Prospects of the Country," 1981, n. 16.
52 Is 2:4.
53 Is 11:6.
54 Zech 9:10.
55 Hab 2:3.
56 Jer 29:11.
57 Papal message for the World Day of Peace, January 1, 1982, n. 3.
58 The translation was taken from *L'Osservatore Romano*, April 25, 1983, p. 4.
59 The translation was taken from *L'Osservatore Romano*, June 13, 1983, pp. 11-12.
60 Rm 5:5.
61 Ps 128; Gen 1:28.
62 *Laborem Exercens*, n. 18.
63 *Laborem Exercens*, n. 1.

64 *Laborem Exercens*, n. 1.

65 The translation was taken from *L'Osservatore Romano*, December 19, 1983, p. 8.

66 *Laborem Exercens*, n. 9.

67 The translation was taken from *L'Osservatore Romano*, April 29, 1985, p. 6.

68 Gen 1:22.

69 Gen 3:18-19.

70 *Laborem Exercens*, n. 4.

71 Gen 1.

72 Gen 2.

73 Gen 2:1-3.

74 Ex 20:8-11.

75 *Laborem Exercens*, n. 9.

76 The translation was taken from *The Pope Speaks*, Fall 1984, pp. 225-228.

77 Gen 1:27-28.

78 *Gaudium et Spes*, n. 35.

79 *Laborem Exercens*, n. 11.

80 Gen 3:19.

81 2 Pt 3:13.

82 Lk 6:20.

83 Jas 2:17.

84 The translation was taken from *The Pope Speaks*, vol. 31, Spring 1986, pp. 10-15.

85 *Laborem Exercens*, n. 8.

86 *Gaudium et Spes*, nn. 61-67; *Populorum Progressio*, n. 20.

87 *Laborem Exercens*, n. 9.

88 *Laborem Exercens*, n. 24.

89 Gen 3:19.

90 *Rerum Novarum*, n. 27.

91 *Laborem Exercens*, n. 18.

92 The translation was taken from *Origins*, July 17, 1986, pp. 309-313.

93 Mt 6:3.

94 *Mater et Magistra*, n. 248ff.

95 Jn 6:32.

96 Phil 2:7.

97 Col 3:17.

98 The text was taken from *L'Osservatore Romano*, December 1, 1986, pp. 19-20.

99 Gen 1:28.
100 *Laborem Exercens*, n. 3.
101 2 Thess 3:10.
102 *Laborem Exercens*, n. 7.
103 *Laborem Exercens*, n. 17.
104 The text was taken from *Origins*, December 11, 1986, p. 16.
105 *Laborem Exercens*, n. 16.
106 *Laborem Exercens*, n. 9.
107 *Laborem Exercens*, n. 27.
108 *Laborem Exercens*, n. 10.
109 *Laborem Exercens*, n. 19; *Familiaris Consortio*, n. 23.
110 *Familiaris Consortio*, n. 22.
111 The translation was taken from *L'Osservatore Romano*, April 6, 1987, p.
112 *Insegnamenti*, p. 1906.
113 The translation was taken from *L'Osservatore Romano*, May 18, 1987, p. 8.
114 *Laborem Exercens*, n. 24.
115 *Laborem Exercens*, n. 15.
116 *Laborem Exercens*, n. 20.
117 *Laborem Exercens*
118 *Laborem Exercens*, n. 8.
119 *Laborem Exercens*, n. 20.
120 Mt 25:33-40.
121 *Laborem Exercens*, n. 20.
122 Speech to the International Labor Organization, 15 June 1982.
123 *Laborem Exercens*, n. 20.
124 The translation was taken from *L'Osservatore Romano*, February 1, 1988, p. 7.
125 Gen 2:8-15.
126 Gen 1:31.
127 *Laborem Exercens*, n. 21.
128 The translation was taken from *The Pope Speaks*, Winter 1988, pp. 304-308.
129 Gen 1:26.
130 *Laborem Exercens*, n. 4.
131 *Laborem Exercens*, n. 21.
132 *Laborem Exercens*, n. 21.
133 Gen 1:28.
134 *Sollicitudo Rei Socialis*, n. 38.

135 Mt 19:4.
136 Gen 1:27.
137 Gen 3:20.
138 Mk 6:3.
139 The translation was taken from *L'Osservatore Romano*, November 14, 1988, pp. 17, 20.
140 The translation was taken from *L'Osservatore Romano*, July 24, 1989, p. 5.
141 Mt 8:24-26.
142 *Laborem Exercens*, n. 27.
143 Acts 4:32.
144 The translation was taken from *L'Osservatore Romano*, December 11, 1989, pp. 6-7.
145 *Laborem Exercens*, n. 17.
146 *Sollicitudo Rei Socialis*, n. 34.
147 1 Cor 12:7.
148 The translation was taken from *L'Osservatore Romano*, June 4, 1990, pp. 5-6.
149 Gen 3:19.
150 Mt 13:55; Mk 6:3.
151 Gen 1:28.
152 *Laborem Exercens*, n. 4.
153 *Gaudium et Spes*, n. 67.
154 *Gaudium et Spes*, n. 67.
155 *Sollicitudo Rei Socialis*, n. 21.
156 2 Thess 3:8.
157 Col 3:23-24.
158 *Gaudium et Spes*, n. 35.
159 *Sollicitudo Rei Socialis*, n. 38.
160 Mt 22:37.
161 *Gaudium et Spes*, n. 34.
162 Col 3:17.
163 The translation was taken from *L'Osservatore Romano*, March 25, 1991, p. 8.
164 Mk 6:3.
165 The translation was taken from *L'Osservatore Romano*, March 25, 1991, p. 6.
166 *Mulieris Dignitatem*, n. 18.
167 *Mulieris Dignitatem, n. 18.*
168 *Mulieris Dignitatem, n. 18.*

169 *Mulieris Dignitatem*, n. 29.
170 *Mulieris Dignitatem*, n. 30.
171 The translation was taken from *L'Osservatore Romano*, January 15, 1992, p. 4.
172 *Centesimus Annus*, n. 35 and *passim*.
173 *Centesimus Annus*, n. 43.
174 *Centesimus Annus*, nn. 35-37.
175 *Centesimus Annus*, n. 15.
176 *Centesimus Annus*, n. 46.
177 *Centesimus Annus*, n. 46.
178 Address to the Ecclesial Congress of Loreto, April 11 1985, n. 8.
179 *Laborem Exercens*, n. 24.
180 *Gaudium et Spes*, n. 67.
181 This translation was taken from *L'Osservatore Romano*, March 25, 1992, pp. 1-2.
182 Reconiliato et Paenitentia, n. 16; cf. also *Sollicitudo rei socialis*, n. 36.
183 Laborem Exercens, n. 3
184 *Centesimus Annus*, n. 43.
185 Mt 13:55
186 *Redemptoris Custos*, n.22.
187 *Centesimus Annus*, n. 42.
188 *Redemptor Hominis*, n. 13; *Centesimus Annus*, n.53.
189 *Laborem Exercens*, n.6.
190 *Centesimus Annus*, n. 43
191 *Centesimus Annus, n.43*.
192 cf. Gen 3:19.
193 Jn 5:17
194 cf. *Sollicitudo Rei Socialis*, n. 38.

CHAPTER 4: ADDRESSES TO GENERAL AUDIENCES

70. The Cross Is Essential for Understanding Human Work[1]

Gospel of Work, Human Rights/Dignity.

[An address on June 9, 1979 in Nowa Huta, Poland, to Catholics of Nowa Huta.]

The new cross that sprang up not far from the ancient relic of the holy cross in the Cistercian Abbey proclaimed the birth of the new church. This birth is deeply engraved on my heart and, when I left the See of St. Stanislaus for the See of St. Peter, I took it with me as a new relic, a priceless relic of our time.

The new cross appeared when the land of the old countryside near Cracow that became the site of Nowa Huta saw the arrival of new men to begin new work. People did hard work here before that. They worked in the fields. The land was fertile and so they worked with pleasure. Some decades back industry began, great industry, heavy industry. People arrived here, coming from various places; they came to expend their energy here as workers in the iron industry.

It was they who brought with them the new cross. It was they who raised it as a sign of their will to build a new church, this very cross before which we are now standing. It was my good fortune, as your archbishop and cardinal, to bless and consecrate in 1977 this church that was born from the new cross.

The Mystery of the Cross Is Engraved on Human Work

This church was born from the new work. I would make bold to say that it was born from Nowa Huta. For we all know that man's work has deeply engraved on it the mystery of the cross, the law of the cross. In it comes true what the creator said after the fall of man: "By the sweat of your face shall you get bread to eat."[2] Both the old work in the fields, which makes wheat grow, but also thorns and thistles, and the new work in the blast furnaces and the new foundries are always carried out "with the sweat of one's brow." The law of the cross is engraved on man's work. It was with the sweat of his brow that the farmer worked. It is with the sweat of his brow that the ironworker works. It is with the sweat of his brow – the terrible sweat of death – that Christ agonizes on the cross.

The cross cannot be separated from man's work. Christ cannot be separated from man's work. This has been confirmed here at Nowa Huta. This has been the start of the new evangelization at the beginning of the new millennium of Christianity in Poland. We have lived this new beginning together and I took it with me from Cracow to Rome as a relic.

Human Dignity Is at the Foundation of an Understanding of Human Work

Christianity and the church have no fear of the world of work. They have no fear of the system based on work. The pope has no fear of men of work. They have always been particularly close to him. He has come from their midst. He has come from the quarries of Yakrzowek, from the Solvay furnaces in Borek Falecki, and from Nowa Huta. Through all these surroundings, through his own experience of work, I make bold to say that the pope learned the Gospel anew. He noticed and became convinced that the problems being raised today about human labor are deeply engraved in the Gospel, that they cannot be fully solved without the Gospel. The problems being raised today – and is it really only today? – about human labor do not, in fact, come down in the last analysis – I say this with respect for all the specialists – either to technology or even to economics but to a fundamental category: the category of the dignity of work, that is to say, of the dignity of man. Economics, technology and the many other specializations and disciplines have their justification for existing in that single essential category. If they fail to draw from that category and are shaped without reference to the dignity of human labor, they are in error; they are harmful; they are against man.

This fundamental category is humanistic. I make bold to say that this fundamental category, the category of work as a measure of the dignity of man, is Christian. We find it in its highest degree of intensity in Christ.

The Cross Dignifies Work

Let this suffice, dear brothers. It was not on one occasion alone that I met you here as your bishop and dealt more abundantly with all these themes. Today, as your guest, I must speak of them more concisely, but remember this one thing: Christ will never approve man's being considered, or of man's considering himself, merely as a means of production, or that he be appreciated, esteemed and valued in accordance with that principle. Christ will never approve of it. For that reason he had himself put on the cross, as if on the great threshold of man's spiritual history, to oppose any form of degradation of man, including degradation by work. Christ remains before our eyes on his cross, in order that each human being may be aware of the strength that he has given him: "He gave (them) power to become children of God."[3]

71. Work Requires Gratitude, Stewardship and Generosity[4]

Collaboration With God, Dominion over the Earth, Economic Laws and Profits, Environment, Spirituality, Universal Destination of Goods.

[A homily on October 4, 1979 in Des Moines, Iowa, to 350,000 persons consisting mainly of American farm families.]

Here in the heartland of America, in the middle of the bountiful fields at harvest time, I come to celebrate the Eucharist. As I stand in your presence in this period of autumn harvest, those words which are repeated whenever people gather for the Eucharist seem to be so appropriate:

"Blessed are you, Lord God of all creation, through your goodness we have this bread to offer which earth has given and human hands have made."

As one who has always been close to nature, let me speak to you today about the land, the earth, and that "which earth has given and human hands have made."

The Land Is God's Gift and Man's Responsibility

The land is God's gift entrusted to people from the very beginning. It is God's gift, given by a loving Creator as a means of sustaining the life which he had created.

But the land is not only God's gift. It is also man's responsibility. Man, himself created from the dust of the earth,[5] was made its master.[6] In order to bring forth fruit, the land would depend upon the genius and skillfulness, the sweat and the toil of the people to whom God would entrust it.

Thus the food which would sustain life on earth is willed by God to be both that "which earth has given and human hands have made."

To all of you who are farmers and all who are associated with this agricultural life when he described God his Father as "the vinedresser,"[7] you cooperate with the Creator, the "vinedresser," in sustaining and nurturing life. You fulfill the command of God given at the very beginning: "Fill the earth and subdue it."[8]

Here in the heartland of America, the valleys and hills have been blanketed with grain, the herds and the flocks have multiplied many times over. By hard work you have become masters of the earth and you have subdued it. By reason of the abundant fruitfulness which modern agricultural advances have made possible, you support the lives of millions who themselves do not work on the land, but who live because of what you produce. Mindful of this, I make my own the words of my beloved predecessor Paul VI: "It is the dignity of those who work on the land and of all those engaged in different levels of research and action in the field of agricultural development which must be unceasingly proclaimed and promoted."[9]

What then are the attitudes that should pervade man's relationship to the land? As always we must look for the answer beginning with Jesus, for, as St. Paul says: "In your minds you must be the same as Jesus Christ."[10]

In the life of Jesus, we see a real closeness to the land. In his teaching, He referred to the "birds of the air,"[11] the "lilies of the field."[12] He talked about the farmer who went out to sow the seed.[13] He referred to his heavenly Father as the "vinedresser,"[14] and to himself as the "good shepherd."[15]

This closeness to nature, this spontaneous awareness of creation as a gift from God, as well as the blessing of a close-knit family – characteristics of farm life in every age including our own – these were part of the life of Jesus. Therefore I invite you to let your attitudes always be the same as those of Christ Jesus.

Three attitudes in particular are appropriate for rural life.

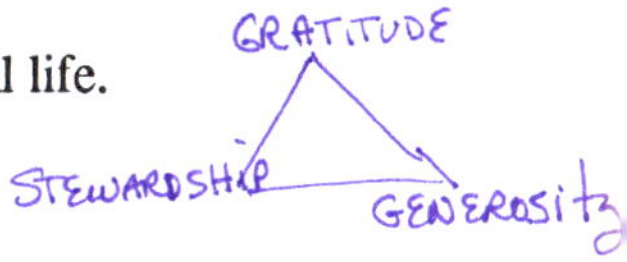

Gratitude

In the first place: gratitude. Recall the first words of Jesus in the Gospel we have just heard, words of gratitude to his heavenly Father: "Father, Lord of heaven and earth, to you I offer praise." Let this be your attitude as well. Every day the farmer is reminded of how much depends upon God. From the heavens come the rain, the wind and the sunshine. They occur without the farmer's command or control. The farmer prepares the soil, plants the seed and cultivates the crop. But God makes it grow. He alone is the source of life.

Even the natural disasters, such as hailstorms and drought, tornadoes or floods, remind the farmer of his dependence upon God. Surely it was this awareness that prompted the early pilgrims to America to establish the feast which you call Thanksgiving.

After every harvest, whatever it may have been that year, with humility and thankfulness the farmer makes his own the prayer of Jesus: "Father Lord of heaven and earth, to you I offer praise."

Stewardship

Second, the land must be conserved with care since it is intended to be fruitful for generation upon generation. You who live in the heartland of America have been entrusted with some of the earth's best land: the soil so rich in minerals, the climate so favorable for producing bountiful crops, with fresh water and unpolluted air available all around you. You are stewards of some of the most important resources God has given to the world. Therefore conserve the land well, so that your children's children and generations after them will inherit an even richer land than was entrusted to you.

But also remember what the heart of your vocation is. While it is true here that farming today provides an economic livelihood for the farmer, still it will always be more than an enterprise of profit-making. In farming, you cooperate with the Creator in the very sustenance of life on earth.

Generosity

In the third place, I want to speak about generosity, a generosity which arises from the fact that "God destined the earth and all it contains for all men and all people so that all created things would be shared fairly by all mankind under the guidance of justice tempered by charity."[16]

You who are farmers today are stewards of a gift from God which was intended for the good of all humanity. You have the potential to provide food for the millions who have nothing to eat and thus help to rid the world of famine. To you I direct the same question asked by Paul VI five years ago: "If the potential of nature is immense, if that of the mystery of the human genius over the universe seems almost unlimited, what is it that is too often missing . . . except that generosity, that anxiety which is stimulated by the sight of the sufferings and the miseries of the poor, that deep conviction that the whole family suffers when one of its members is in distress?"[17]

Recall the time when Jesus saw the hungry crowd gathered on the hillside. What was his response? He did not content himself with

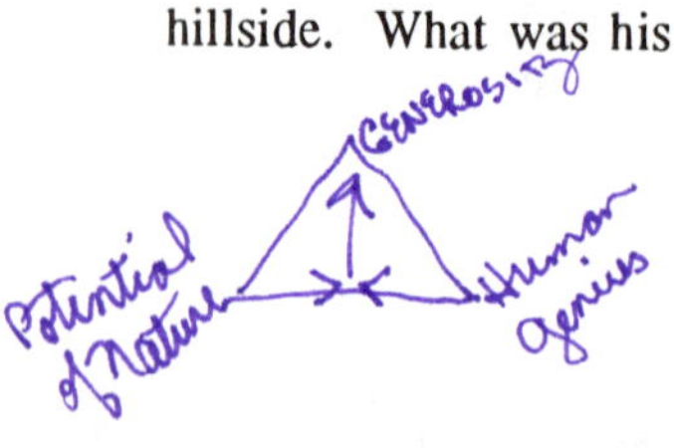

expressing his compassion. He gave his disciples the command: "Give them something to eat yourselves."[18]

Did he not intend those same words for us today, for us who live at the closing of the 20th century, for us who have the means available to feed the hungry of the world? Let us respond generously to his command by sharing the fruit of our labor, by contributing to others the knowledge we have gained, by being the promoters of rural development everywhere and by defending the right to work of the rural population, since every person has a right to useful employment.

Christ Satisfies the Deepest Hunger of Humanity

Farmers everywhere provide bread for all humanity, but it is Christ alone who is the bread of life. He alone satisfies the deepest hunger of humanity. As St. Augustine said: "Our hearts are restless until they rest in you." [19]

While we are mindful of the physical hunger of millions of our brothers and sisters on all continents, at this eucharist we are reminded that the deepest hunger lies in the human soul. To all who acknowledge this hunger within them Jesus says: "Come to me, all you who are weary and find life burdensome, and I will refresh you."

My brothers and sisters in Christ: Let us listen to these words with all our heart. They are directed to every one of us. To all who till the soil, to all who benefit from the fruit of their labors, to every man and woman on earth, Jesus says: "Come to me . . . and I will refresh you." Even if all the physical hunger of the world were satisfied, even if everyone who is hungry were fed by his or her own labor or by the generosity of theirs, the deepest hunger of man would still exist.

Bring Your Work to Christ

We are reminded in the letter of St. Paul to the Galatians: "All that matters is that one is created anew." Only Christ can create one anew, and this new creation finds its beginning only in his cross and resurrection. In Christ alone all creation is restored to its proper order. Therefore, I say: Come, all of you, to Christ. He is the bread of life. Come to Christ and you will never be hungry again.

Bring with you to Christ the products of your hands, the fruit of the land, that "which earth has given and human hands have made." At this altar these gifts will be transformed into the Eucharist of the Lord.

Bring with you your efforts to make fruitful the land, your labor and your weariness. At this altar, because of the life, death and resurrection of Christ, all human activity is sanctified, lifted up and fulfilled.

Bring with you the poor, the sick, the exiled and the hungry; bring all who are weary and find life burdensome. At this altar they will be refreshed, for his yoke is easy and his burden light.

Above all, bring your families and dedicate them anew to Christ, so that they may continue to be the working, living and loving community where nature is revered, where burdens are shared and where the Lord is praised in gratitude.

---

72. *Our Work Should Express Our Faith and Gratitude*[20]

Christian Witness/Mission, Service, Work and Prayer.

[A homily on November 9, 1980 in Rome, to Italian farmers.]

Today the Liturgy has us celebrate the commemoration of the Dedication of the Lateran Basilica, the Cathedral of the Diocese of Rome and therefore the first Cathedral of the Universal Church. Our spiritual meeting on this double occasion of "dedication" and "thanksgiving" lends itself to two reflections of fundamental importance. The first one regards the value of Christian faith. Your thanks to God, of course, springs from faith; and the first exhortation that I wish to address to you is precisely this: esteem your faith! Keep your faith firm! Today there is need of an enlightened, convinced, deep faith. It is necessary to be prepared to answer adequately the questions that modern society continually proposes, and perhaps even violently, in order never to succumb in the clash with the various and contrasting mentalities; it is necessary to update and develop one's own religious culture. Therefore, especially in periods when work is comparatively calm, attend formative meetings in your parishes: meditate on the "Word of God," particularly on feast days, in order to be really convinced "worshippers of God in spirit and truth," as Jesus says to the Samaritan woman.[21]

As St. Peter wrote to the first Christians, it is necessary to gather around Christ, the living stone, with full certainty and confidence, "and like living stones be ourselves built into a spiritual house, to be a holy priesthood, to offer spiritual sacrifices acceptable to God through Jesus Christ." Your dignity and responsibility as Christians is immense! "You in fact," – the Apostle continues – "are a chosen race, a royal priesthood, a holy nation, God's own people, that you may declare the wonderful deeds of him who called you out of darkness into his marvelous light."[22]

Gratitude

The second reflection concerns the attitude of thanksgiving that must distinguish the life of every person, of every Christian in particular. The words of the Psalmist must be ours, even in moments of distress and sorrow: "O come, let us sing to the Lord; let us make a joyful noise to the rock of our salvation! Let us come into his presence with thanksgiving; let us make a joyful noise to him with songs of praise!"[23] In his letters St. Paul instilled this constant spirit of gratitude: "Give thanks in all circumstances; for this is the will of God in Christ Jesus for you;"[24] "Be filled with the Spirit ... always and for everything giving thanks in the name of our Lord Jesus Christ to God the Father."[25] It is a "eucharistic" attitude, which gives you peace and serenity in toils, frees you from all selfish and individualistic attachment, makes you docile to the will of the Almighty, even in the most difficult moral requirements, opens you to solidarity and universal charity, makes you understand how absolutely necessary prayer is, and above all, eucharistic life through the Holy Mass, the Act of Thanksgiving par excellence, in order to live and bear witness consistently to our own Christian faith. To give thanks means to believe, to love, to give! And with joy and generosity!

Love of Work

Here is the message I entrust to you on this Day of Thanksgiving: have faith! be grateful! "Always seek to do good to one another and to all!"[26] And love your land, love your work! This is the encouragement I wish to leave you last of all. Certainly, all arts and trades are useful and valuable, and every word and occupation must be fairly evaluated, esteemed, and respected. But work in the fields is essential and we are all debtors to those who dedicate themselves to it. It calls for continuity, industriousness, appreciation and esteem for traditional values, acceptance of risk, love of labor, and a sense of responsibility. Continue to love the land; instill this love in the young people who form new families! And the whole of society must be sincerely grateful to you, for so many reasons!

---

73. Human Work Is an Essential Part of God's Plan[27]

Dominion over the Earth, Meaning of Work, Service, Spirituality, Work and Society, Work and the Worker.

[A Sunday Angelus Message on September 20, 1981
at Castel Gandolfo, Italy, to a general audience.]

"The kingdom of heaven is like a householder who went out early in the morning to hire labourers for his vineyard."[28]

These words begin the Gospel passage of today's Liturgy. The well-known parable of the workers in the vineyard contains many themes. Fundamental among them is the thought that it is God who calls man to work, and that this must serve the continual formation of the world according to the plan of God himself. Every kind of human work, every one of its variations, is understood in the gospel parable.

The parable, from its very beginning, contains man's calling to rediscover the meaning of his work, keeping in mind the salvific Plan of God.

Work Gives Meaning to Human Life

What is human work? We can give only a contracted answer to this question. It is above all a prerogative of the human person, an element of human completeness, which precisely helps man to be more man. Without work, he is unable not only to nourish himself, but also to fulfill himself or reach his true dimension. In the second place, and as a result, work is a necessity, a duty, that gives to the human being life, serenity, commitment, meaning. The apostle Paul, we recall, severely warns: "If anyone will not work, let him not eat."[29] Therefore, each one is called to carry out an activity at whatever level it may be, while idleness and exploitation are condemned. Besides, work is a right: "It is the great and fundamental right of man," as I said two years ago in Poland in Nowy Targ. So much so that it must be promoted and safeguarded by society even in the possible conflict with other rights. Under these conditions, work becomes even a service, so that man "grows in the measure in which he gives himself for others."[30] And from this harmony not only the individual, but also, and I would say above all, society itself benefits.

These are only some thoughts on the subject of the nature of human work. We put them together here, referring to the call of the householder who always goes out to hire laborers for his vineyard, as the Gospel parable says. We recall that this parable at its very beginning contains the invitation for man – whatever kind of work he performs – to rediscover his ultimate meaning in the salvific plan of God. And we pray that the awareness of this meaning may grow and deepen in every man. In fact, according to the plan of God, through work we must not only subdue the earth, but also achieve salvation. Therefore there is connected with work not only the dimension of temporality, but also the dimension of eternity.

74. Work Should Unite and Strengthen the Family[31]

Christian Witness/Mission, Work and Family.

[A Sunday Angelus Message on October 25, 1981 in Rome, to a general audience.]

We have already touched upon the question of human work several times on the occasion of our Angelus prayer on Sundays. This perennial subject, as ancient as man, as ancient as divine Revelation in the history of man, has become a particularly relevant one for us, in the current year, in consideration of the ninetieth anniversary of the Encyclical *Rerum Novarum.*

Work and the Family

Today we must turn our attention to that particular link that exists between human work and the life of the family.

In actual fact, from his very origins man has had recourse to work to dominate the earth and to guarantee his own subsistence and that of the family. The two aims are truly human, but the second one contains a particular evangelical content.

The family finds in work the support for its development and union, the central factor that conditions its life, qualifies it, gives it its rhythm and constitutes an element of cohesion and stability.

Work, therefore, belongs to the sphere of what man loves, what he lives for, that is, it belongs to the sphere of love. As I said last year in France to the workers of St. Denis, "In the years when I too was a worker, I knew what value the home, the future of their children, the respect due to their wives, to their mothers, had for me and for these men who were at the same time fathers of families." [32]

Work Should Strengthen Family Life

Work, therefore, cannot destroy the family. On the contrary, it must unite it and help to strengthen it. Let the family not become, because of work, a superficial meeting of human beings, a hotel used only for meals and rest!

It is indispensable, therefore, that "the rights of the family [be] deeply inscribed in the very foundation of every code of labor, which has its subject precisely man and not just production and profit."

---

75. Women Possess a Special Vocation to Contribute to the Progress of Society[33]

Common Good, Work and Family, Work and Women/Mothers.

[A Sunday Angelus Message on December 6, 1981 in Rome, to a general audience.]

The problem of juridical equality between man and woman must be solved by a social legislation which recognizes the equality of working men and working women and at the same time, as *Pacem in Terris* states, protects the right of the latter "to conditions of work reconcilable with the requirements and with their duties as wives and mothers."[34] It is necessary to construct a society in which women can attend to the upbringing of their children, who are the hope of future society.

The Church is sensitive to this point; and, as I said at the conclusion of the Synod of Bishops celebrated in October last, "the family must be able to live in a fitting manner even when the mother dedicates herself completely to it." This does not mean the exclusion of woman from the world of work and social and public activity. On the contrary, I repeat to all women: "Be present with your creativeness in the transformation of the society. . . . Bring your contribution, illuminated by your religious feeling, to all your leaders and also to the highest authorities!"[35]

Personalistic Dimension of Work

In the encyclical *Laborem Exercens* I have already had occasion to express myself clearly on this subject. But some themes of that document should be emphasized, and above all the personalistic dimension of work. In fact, "man's work concerns not only the economy but also, and especially, personal values."[36] "The whole labor process must be organized and adapted in such a way as to respect the requirements of the person and his or her forms of life, above all life in the home, taking into account the individual's age and sex."[37] "The true advancement of women requires that labor should be structured in such a way that women do not have to pay for their advancement by abandoning what is specific to them and at the expense of the family, in which women as mothers have an irreplaceable role."[38] In a society which wishes to be just and human, it is absolutely necessary that the spiritual and material requirements of the person should occupy the first place in the hierarchy of values. It is to be hoped, therefore, that while respecting the equality of the right to work of all, both men and women, it will be made possible for every mother, "without inhibiting her freedom, without psychological or practical discrimination, and without penalizing her as compared with other women, to devote herself to taking care of her children and educating them in accordance with their needs, which vary with age."[39]

Vocation of Women to Society

The Church recognizes and praises the specific contribution, a necessary and irreplaceable one, that woman, particularly today, can and does make to the promotion of the common good in public order and in the area of work. Endowed by the Creator with an innate gift of her own, made up of deep sensitivity and a fine sense of practical matters and moderation, she is called, together with man, to contribute to the growth of a more just and more human society. Therefore I wish, today also, to invite every woman, with words of deep encouragement, to extend the exercise of her precious qualities from the sphere of private life to that of public and social life, and to do so with wise responsibility.[40]

---

76. St. Joseph Is a Model of Dedication to Christ in One's Work[41]

Dignity of Work, St. Joseph, Service.

[A Sunday Regina Caeli Message on May 1, 1982 in Rome, to the general public.]

"Whatever your task, work heartily, as serving the Lord. ... You are serving the Lord Christ."[42]

St. Joseph Is a Model for All Workers

How can we fail to see in these words from today's liturgy the plan and synthesis of the whole existence of Saint Joseph, whose testimony of noble dedication to work is proposed to our consideration by the Church on this the first day of May? Saint Joseph, a "just man," spent the greater part of his life toiling over a carpenter's bench in a humble village in Palestine. His was an existence outwardly no different from that of many other men of his time, engaged like him in the same demanding work. And yet such a singular existence is deserving of admiration and persuades the Church to hold it up as an exemplary model for all the workers of the world.

What is the reason for such a distinction? It is not difficult to recognize. It lies in the dedication to Christ that sustained Saint Joseph in all his toil. The presence in the house in Nazareth of the Word Incarnate, Son of God and son of his wife Mary, gave to Joseph a daily "raison d'etre" for turning to bend over his workbench, so as to draw from his toil the sustenance necessary for the family. Truly "all that he did," Joseph did "for the Lord"; and he did it "with all his heart."

All Work Serves Human Persons

Today all workers are invited to look at the example of this "just man." The singular experience of Saint Joseph is reflected in some way or other in the life of each one of them. However diverse may be the tasks that they perform, their activity is always directed towards the satisfaction of some human need: it is aimed at serving man. Besides, the believer well knows that Christ wished to be hidden within each human being, declaring explicitly that "whatsoever is done to one of the least of the brethren, is as if it were done to himself."[43] In every work it is therefore possible to "serve Christ," if one follows the recommendation of Saint Paul and imitates the example of Saint Joseph, guardian and servant of the Son of God.

Today, the first of May, in addressing a very warm greeting to all of you assembled here in the Courtyard of St. Damasus, my most loving thoughts go out in a special way to the workers present here and, through them, to all the workers of the world, exhorting them to renewed awareness of their own dignity. By their toil they serve their brothers: they serve man and, in serving man, they serve Christ. May Saint Joseph help them to see their work in this light, to value it in all its dignity and never lack the strong motivations which might support them in moments of difficulty.

77. Human Work: A Sharing in Christ's Kingship[44]

Christian Witness/Mission, Collaboration with God, Dominion over the Earth, Human Development/Progress, Human Rights/ Dignity, Gospel of Work, Service, Solidarity.

[An address on February 15, 1984
in Rome, to a general audience.]

"Be fertile and multiply; fill the earth and subdue it."[45] The word of God the Creator assigns man an irreplaceable task for the development of the potentials inherent in the universe. He is called to share in the work of the Creator, significantly defined by the Bible with the word "work." According to his abilities, he continues, develops and completes what God has begun.

The Gospel of Work

But the significance of human work is not exhausted in this task. It is irreplaceable also for the building of a more just society, where truth and love reign, and there is visibly manifested, therefore, the promise of the Kingdom, that promise contained in the Redemption of Christ. "For this reason," I said in Guadalajara during my apostolic journey to Mexico, "work must not be a mere necessity, but it must be considered a real vocation, a call from God to build a new world in which justice and brotherhood dwell, a foretaste of the Kingdom of God, in which there will certainly not be shortages or limitations. Work must be the means for the whole of creation to be subjected to the dignity of the human being and child of God."[46]

Work Can Open Us up to Christ

Deepening our reflection under the guidance of the Second Vatican Council, we "know through faith that by offering his labor to God a man becomes associated with the redemptive work itself of Jesus Christ, who conferred an eminent dignity on labor when at Nazareth he worked with his own hands."[47] Indeed, work, redeemed by Christ, becomes for man an expression of his own vocation, that of being called to conform himself to Christ to live in a profound intimate union with the Son of God. In the perspective opened up by the Redemption, work becomes one of the fundamental modalities through which man is opened to himself and, in Christ, to God the Father.

The Second Vatican Ecumenical Council has taught us also that one of the principal fruits of this union with Christ is the sharing in his kingship, that is, in his destiny as Lord of the universe and of history.[48] Christ exercised his kingship above all in service to his brothers and sisters, a service inspired by love.[49] Sharing in this kingship, man acquires a renewed freedom to place himself generously at the service of his neighbors in the daily toil of work, work that is perceived and exercised as a manifestation and testimony of love.

Hidden in a work that is at times heavy and wearisome, love does not always immediately reveal its presence. Gradually, however, if the one who is working has faith and perseverance, love begins to manifest itself in the solidarity that is created between man and man. Performed with and for love, work is a great opportunity for man's growth, to whom, as my venerated predecessor Pius XII said, it assures "a field of proper freedom, not only economic freedom, but also political, cultural and religious freedom."[50]

Collaborating with God

In addition, work implies a "royal service," because by enduring its toil "in union with Christ crucified for us, man in a way collaborates with the Son of God for the redemption of humanity. He shows himself a true disciple of Christ by carrying the cross in his turn every day in the activity that he is called upon to perform."[51] In work conceived in this way, there is fulfilled, in continuity with Christ's mission, man's capacity to transform the world, making it homogeneous with his sublime dignity as one redeemed. The redemption of work puts man in a position to exercise his "regal duty" that is, to respond to the Creator's command to subdue and have dominion over the earth.[52] Therefore *Gaudium et Spes* can affirm that work "comes immediately from the person. In a sense, the person stamps the things of nature with his seal and subdues them to his will."[53]

The Inheritance of Work

Work has a great creative value also because it leads the individual to commit himself to the whole family, social and political community.

Every person, in fact, constantly receives help from those near him, as well as from those far away. He avails himself of the material, moral, cultural and religious goods created by whole generations about whom he has perhaps never heard. He lives from the work, the effort, the fervor, the devotion, the sacrifices that others have made. No one of these goods, the fruit of this enormous labor, is foreign to him. It would therefore be selfish to accept all this richness passively without committing oneself to respond to it by offering with his own work a positive contribution to the solution of the dramatic social situation in which we are living today.

This basic consideration throws light on the dimension of participation inherent in human work. It throws open to man the path to self-fulfillment, offering him the incomparable opportunity to communicate himself to others, in stable and firm relationships, attentive to concrete needs, above all to that supreme need to find a meaning for his existence. This dimension, opened by the Redemption of Christ, is thus revealed as an optimum antidote to the situation of alienation into which human work often spills.

The Holy Year of the Redemption is a call for each one of us to rediscover in Christ the Redeemer the most profound meaning of work and, with it, the joy that springs from the awareness of making a personal contribution to the building of a renewed world.

---

78. Christ Is the Model for the Worker[54]

Christian Witness/Mission, Collaboration with God, Dominion over the Earth, Gospel of Work, Human Rights/Dignity, Humanization/Dehumanization, Just Wage, Meaning of Work, Unemployment.

[A homily on February 3, 1986 in
Ranchi, India, to a general audience.]

Today I would like to reflect with you on the value and dignity of human work. Jesus Christ was a carpenter's son. He worked for the greater part of his life on Earth in the same trade as his foster father, Joseph. By working, Jesus proclaimed in the ordinary activities of his daily life the dignity of work. All human work is a participation in the activity of the Creator himself. Whether we work in a factory, an office, a hospital, the fields, or as a rickshaw driver or as a mother at home – whatever work we do – we all share in the creative activity of God. This gives all work its meaning and worth. "The basis for determining the value of human work is not primarily the kind of work being done but the fact that the one who is doing it is a person."[55] It follows from this that all human work, however humble it may appear, must be fully respected, protected and justly remunerated, so that families and indeed the whole community may live in peace, prosperity and progress.

Work brings joy and fulfillment, but it also entails toil and fatigue. The fulfillment and joy spring from the fact that human work enables men and women to exercise that mastery over the earth which God has entrusted to them.[56] For God said to the first man and woman: "Be fruitful and multiply, and fill the earth and subdue it. And have dominion over the fish of the sea and over the birds of the air and over every living thing that moves upon the earth."[57]

The Toil of Work

The work we do, however, may not be the type of work we would prefer or it may be hazardous, such as work deep down in the mines. The work may be hard, monotonous and exhausting. Such is our human condition. It is written in the Bible that because of disobedience man will earn his bread by the sweat of his brow and that the land upon which he labors will not easily yield its fruits.[58] Yet for a worker who places his trust in God, the toil and fatigue of work are accompanied by the joy of knowing that he or she is collaborating with the Creator.

Christ Is Our Model

For those of us who are Christians, Jesus is the perfect model and inspiration for our work. In his work, Jesus remained in deep communion with his heavenly Father. We should therefore consider carefully how Jesus faithfully performed his daily work during the many years of his life in Nazareth. This is a powerful example for all of us. The witness of Jesus in his work as a carpenter fills us with joy and encourages us to persevere in our humble service to humanity.

Furthermore, dear brothers and sisters in Christ, we must never forget the reason why Jesus came into the world. Jesus came to accomplish the work of salvation. And how did he accomplish the work of salvation? Through his suffering and death on the cross and by the victory of his glorious resurrection. All human work, no matter how insignificant it may seem, shares in this work of salvation. As I stated in my encyclical on human work: "By enduring the toil of work in union with Christ crucified for us, man in a way collaborates with the Son of God for the redemption of humanity. He shows himself a true disciple of Christ by carrying the cross in his turn everyday in the activity that he is called upon to perform."[59]

Defending the Worker

The church, seeking to be faithful to the example and witness of Christ, has a very special concern for the welfare of workers. The well-known encyclicals of the popes, starting with *Rerum Novarum* of Leo XIII, have continually defended the right of the worker to a just wage and to proper working conditions. The church's teaching is founded on the principle that every human person is created in the image of God and has a unique God-given dignity. Thus no one should be used as a mere instrument for production, as though the person were a machine or a beast of burden. The church rejects any social or economic system that leads to the depersonalization of workers. Over and above her concern for proper working conditions, the Church insists on a just wage for workers, a wage that takes into account the needs of their family. "Just remuneration for the work of an adult who is responsible for a family means remuneration which will suffice for establishing and properly maintaining a family and for providing security for his future."[60]

The Problem of Unemployment

My heart goes out in a special way to the many unemployed who want to work but are unable to find suitable employment, at times because of discrimination based on religion, caste, community or language. Unemployment and underemployment give rise to frustration and a feeling of uselessness, and cause disharmony in the family. They bring anguish and untold hardships and weaken the very fabric and structure of society. They threaten the dignity of every man and woman. There is an urgent need to take fresh initiatives to solve this grave problem, and these initiatives often require collaboration on the national and international level. It is crucially important that the negotiations and plans to overcome unemployment be marked by respect and dialogue between employers and those seeking work.

Share the Light of Christ through Work

Yes, he has called us all in Jesus Christ. Jesus Christ is the light. Indeed, he is "the way, and the truth, and the life."[61] And so he can lead us to the Father, to this God who is light and truth and holiness itself. Jesus calls us and invites us to share in his own divine life – through everything which makes up our earthly existence, through all the toil of our human work.

Accepting the light which is in Christ, we too must become "the light of the world."[62] We have to become "the salt of the earth,"[63] which gives taste to human life.

As followers of Christ, you are called to be the light of Christ here in India and with Christ to transform the world. Let your work serve the good of your neighbor. Share with the underprivileged, the sick and the handicapped. Strive to remove everything that oppresses people, and working together do all you can to solve the unemployment situation. Wherever you are, seek to radiate the presence of Christ: in your families, before your children, in your place of work, through the joyful practice of the virtues you have found in Jesus.

---

79. The Meaning of Human Life is Given in Prayer and Work[64]

Leisure, Work and Prayer.

[A homily on July 20, 1986 in Rome, to a general audience.]

The Word of God, and especially the Gospel of St. Luke that we read in today's liturgy, speaks to us of two sisters, Martha and Mary, who received Jesus as a guest in their home not far from Jerusalem. He was their guest more than once, including during the last days before the Paschal events. And we, having heard them often, know well those words addressed to Martha by Jesus, in which he compares her work and daily solicitude to the attitude of her sister, who instead sought to listen to the Word of the Lord. Those words of Jesus are very significant, very symbolic: they speak to us of the value that all of us must introduce into our lives. They lead us to understand that all our work, or, in other words, everything that is constituted by our human activity, like the fruit that comes from the Word of God, has its own value, its own meaning. Jesus said on another occasion: "Man shall not live by bread alone, but by every word that proceeds from the mouth of God."[65] In this way man certainly lives by the fruit of his labor, but at the same time he lives by what comes from the Word of God. In this way a program of Christian life was formed, constituted by the two well-known elements *ora et labora*: and this program was brought to us, as the very essence of Christian civilization and culture, especially in the West, by the great Patriarch of the West, St. Benedict. *Ora et labora*: they are his words, very simple but at the same time extraordinarily profound, explaining to us the meaning, the structure, of human life. Each of us must know how to combine the two: work and prayer, one's activity and listening to the Word of God.

We Must Live More by the Word of God

We can say that the modern world is more open to what comes from human activity. We live, especially here in the West, in a scientific-technological civilization in which man attaches much greater importance and confidence to the works of his mind and hands, and in which he is also much more committed to his activities and successes. But this attitude often creates a spiritual void, causing man to be unhappy in spite of all the successes of his work, of his temporal activity oriented exclusively toward earthly goals. And so there is a great need to counterbalance this disproportion. We must live more by the Word of God.

Encountering certain groups of young people today, we see that they are once again seeking the Word of God and prayer, because they see, they experience, the fact that they do not find in their activity, in all that makes up the activity of man and of this world, full satisfaction for their spirits.

Whence comes my wish for you: with this brief consideration based upon today's Gospel, the Liturgy of the Word, my accompanying hope for all of you, my dear collaborators, personnel of the Papal Villas, and among you the Director, is that you will be capable of making a beautiful synthesis of these two elements of human life, that you will be capable of living, certainly, by your daily work, but also of illuminating this work with the much greater light that comes from the Word of God, that which becomes ours, that is, properly man's, in prayer.

---

80. Industriousness Is a Virtue but Not an End in Itself[66]

Christian Witness/Mission, Common Good, Gospel of Work, Solidarity, Spirituality.

[An address on June 4, 1988 in Piacenza, Italy, to a general audience.]

Tolerance is a moral value of your culture, a value not to be underestimated. In my recent encyclical I pointed out "the positive and moral value of the growing awareness of interdependence among individuals . . . sensed as a system determining relationships."[67] In fact, interdependence, when it is recognized and practiced, can lead people to discover and to give a name to that form of realizing the common good which is solidarity. It would greatly benefit community life if, in addition to tolerance, which is itself so precious in a world troubled by conflict, public life had at its foundation the moral category of solidarity, which "is not a feeling of vague compassion or shallow distress at the misfortunes of so many people, both near and far. On the contrary, it is a firm and persevering determination to commit oneself to the common good; that is to say, to the good of all and of each individual, so that all might be truly responsible for all."[68]

Persons Have Priority over Work

In these days, as I have travelled through Emilia, one of the richest regions of Italy, my thoughts have turned repeatedly to the Gospel parable of the rich man who is tempted to trust exclusively in the goods that he has managed to put aside.[69]

Though even among you one encounters the sad phenomenon of unemployment – especially among the young – and other situations of social distress which the Mayor recalled in his address and in regard to which I express my sincere compassion, it is a pleasure to note that the industriousness of your population, its remarkable spirit of enterprise and efficiency, are usually rewarded by good levels of income together with a great ability to set aside savings.

However, material well-being and economic success, while they represent a legitimate desire of man, cannot constitute the one aspiration of life. The education of persons and the building up of the family presume a constant reference to transcendent values and to a culture that always gives the person priority over work and material goods.

The Practical Duty to Seek the Common Good

This is not to be interpreted as an invitation to flee one's concrete responsibilities. The Church recalls with clarity the duty to collaborate in the economic development of a territory through one's efforts and through investments, in order to help assure new employment possibilities, both for the present and the future, in a location as near as possible to home.

The [Second Vatican] Council said "the common good is seriously endangered by those who hoard their resources unproductively."[70] I myself recently recalled that "collaboration in the development of the whole person and of every human being is in fact a duty of all towards all, and must be shared by the four parts of the world: East and West, North and South."[71]

Productivity Is Not an End in Itself

Take care that your industriousness always remains a virtue, that it expresses your capacities and a proper commitment of earthly realities, but that it does not become the sole or principal value of your lives. Do not let it happen that, under the influence of a system dominated almost exclusively by productivity as an end in itself, dedication to work becomes alienation and a force destructive of the person and the family.

The Practice of Faith

The history of this two-thousand-year-old city, whose roots were sprinkled at the outset by the blood of the martyr St. Antonino, the herald of the gospel in your midst, witnesses to the efforts of persons who have developed with equal intensity the seeds of diligence and of faith, of fidelity to the homeland and love for the Church. Under the human and religious aspects, your remote and recent past, rich in saints and illustrious citizens, illustrates the fact that the principles of Catholicism belong to the historical heritage of the people of Piacenza.

May this apostolic visit likewise serve to increase that Christian humanism which inspires the conduct of your people. May no one content himself with a piety consisting only of exterior practices, traditions and mere observance; rather, may the spiritual life of each be filled with true Christian faith, willed and consistent. Since one is never a Christian by himself, do not live your faith in isolation, but in the solidarity and support of the Christian community; and offer to others, in your turn, the gift of faith that you have received. The Church of Piacenza in Synod is to continue among you the dialogue of friendship and salvation to which the Pope wishes to contribute today.

The hope and wish for a better future is entrusted to your vitality, solidarity, and faith.

Christian Witness

The Pope says to each of you: refuse to allow the marvel of a life lived in full humanity to be concealed in anonymity and silence. "No one after lighting a lamp puts it in a cellar or under a bushel."[72] Participate, increase dialogue, support the organizations charged with the common good, assist those among you and in the world who are afflicted by suffering.

---

81. Solidarity Is Realized in Service[73]

Common Good, Service, Solidarity, Unemployment.

[An address on June 5, 1988, in Castel San Giovanni, Italy, to a general audience.]

"We are all responsible for all."[74] This is true in every context and every order of human life, especially in the order of civil and social coexistence.

This interdependence can be felt as a kind of coercion, or it can be accepted and embraced as a moral duty. When it is interpreted in the second way, interdependence becomes a value: the value of solidarity. Solidarity is the firm and persevering commitment to the common good. Those who have responsibilities in the areas of government, business or the economy – but also each person in his daily toil – must question themselves and make decisions in the light of these two criteria; solidarity and common good. In this view, special attention is accorded to the weakest and poorest members of society.

Value of Accomplishments Displayed in Service

Solidarity is realized in service. Our human accomplishments are valuable to the degree that they show themselves to be instruments in the service of our fellow man.

Too often, even today, human dignity is trodden underfoot, offended, humiliated. An individualism which is often insensitive to the needs of others and exasperated by the consumerism that seems to characterize our age drives many people to make their own material well-being their greatest aspiration in life.

In the meantime, too many men and women still are without work, which should be a real possibility for all, given that it constitutes a fundamental dimension of life. Unemployment, which today strikes especially the young, is a sad reality which keeps those who are afflicted by it from realizing their human vocation.

Develop Your Abilities!

My presence in your midst, while it is meant to manifest the Church's concern for all human problems, is intended to be an appeal, an exhortation, a source of encouragement.

Aware of your human and spiritual energies, I exhort you to esteem your capacities, not to be afraid to unleash the resources of your creativity. May no one among us abdicate his responsibilities before life and its problems. Christ himself works silently in the depths of your freedom to lead you to produce, as St. Paul says, fruits of "love, joy, peace, patience, kindness, goodness, faithfulness, gentleness, self-control."[75]

It is from this perspective that I invite all of you, citizens of Castel San Giovanni, together with those who are present here with you, to put into practice and to develop the capacities of your minds and hearts, even amidst the difficulties you may encounter.

82. The Gap between Technology and Ethics Hinders Authentic Progress[76]

Entrepreneurship, Human Development/ Progress, Human Rights/ Dignity, Materialism/Consumerism.

[An address on June 5, 1988 in Reggio Emilia, Italy, to a general audience.]

I began to reflect on [your] traditions as I observed the flourishing city from the helicopter: her homes and industry, her streets and avenues, all "watched over," as it were, by the bell-towers and cupolas of the churches. As I admired fields, harvests, vineyards, the true garden of this fertile Po valley, I saw in them a clear witness to the qualities of industriousness and intelligent imagination which characterize you, dear citizens of Reggio Emilia. In spite of the destruction you suffered during the last world war, you have, in fact, been able to adjust your economy to the new situations and to reach impressive levels in the national context. You have done so through an interesting synthesis of free initiative, state-subsidized businesses and cooperatives. Through creative thinking, industrial workers have succeeded in emerging efficiently and constructively from the crisis that had afflicted that sector. Likewise, the flourishing and intensive cultivation of the land and the development of specialized animal husbandry are the fruit of the combined contribution of agricultural experts and specialists in scientific and university research.

Fundamental Values Must Always Be Defended

The level of material well-being you have attained has certainly not eliminated certain problems common to many advanced societies, problems which increase the burden of those affected. I am referring to unemployment, immigration, the phenomenon of drugs, the situations of loneliness and disadvantage in which many of our brothers and sisters find themselves. A society which wishes to be just and to respect the rights of its members must strive to see that the fundamental values proper to man's dignity are defended always and in every case. No acceptance must be given to modern projects which fail to coincide with man's true progress. There is no authentic progress, in fact, in notions that open the way to a consumer and libertine mentality and mores, thus creating a rupture between technology and ethics, between material progress and spiritual growth.

The Church has always offered her commitment and concrete efforts to help consciences mature in this direction and to lead individuals and the community towards the goal of a true humanism. Here, too, your city is heir to stimulating examples of witness. Past generations have left here meaningful signs of their noble sentiments in buildings, works and institutions that show their preferential love for those in greatest need of assistance and love.

83. Our Responsibilities and Our Solidarity Have Their Origin in God's Will[77]

Dominion over the Earth, Environment, Fair Wage, Meaning of Work, St. Joseph, Service, Solidarity, Spirituality, Work and Family.

[A homily on May 1, 1989 in Fianarantsoa, Madagascar, to a general audience.]

St. Joseph, the carpenter, and Jesus who shared his task during those long years, invite us today to reflect on the dignity of human labor, of your daily work, dear brothers and sisters of Madagascar.

Many of you cultivate the land; you know, perhaps better than others, the gifts that man receives as well as the responsibility he bears. You love the land of your ancestors; it has a special place in your life; with your hands guided by the experience of successive generations, by ever increasing knowledge, you help this soil to produce food, you watch over fertile herds.

Mission from the Creator

Quite naturally, you fulfill the mission which the Creator gave to man made in his image, to "subject to himself the earth and all that it contains, and to govern the world with justice and holiness," as the Second Vatican Council said, taking its inspiration from the Bible.[78]

In order to do this work well, every day you experience the effort and the trouble that are necessary. You also frequently experience even uncertainty or fear, because so many things do not depend on you! You must struggle against the hostile elements of nature, you must protect your fields and watch over your flocks that are often threatened. However, the beauty of the human worker is his patience, perseverance, and ability to overcome obstacles.

This is the price you pay for drawing from your work what is needed for the sustenance of your family and others. By using God's gifts better, your trained hands can offer new gifts to the human family. I am thinking not only of agriculture, but of all the professions; the true meaning of human work is "a prolongation of the Creator's work, a service to their fellow men."[79]

Man Is Responsible for Nature

In this regard, I would like to repeat how great is man's responsibility for nature, even though the Creator entrusted it to him. From the north to the south of your great island, I was able to admire its beauty, the diverse wealth of the land and its fruits. However, we know that the use which is made of it runs the risk of depleting and impoverishing the soil. Throughout the world to some small degree people are aware of the damage caused by exploitation which destroys much without considering the lives of the future generations. Today everyone shares in the great responsibility to show that they are worthy of the mission entrusted by the Creator, in assuring the protection of creation.

Economic Justice

To ensure that the worker's dignity is fully respected, the first human value which must inspire all the partners is simple justice, that is, an income adequate to support the worker and his family. In today's society, where it is impossible to live isolated in a small group, it is just that essential services be equitably assured, without deducting an excessive share of the product of labor. I am thinking of the possibilities of acquiring instruments for work without the debt becoming crushing. I am thinking of the means of transport and the conditions of marketing products. These are only simple examples. I mention them to remind you that all people are in solidarity, whatever type of activity they perform. In all these fields justice and fraternity meet; the gospel appeals for love of neighbor meet the aspirations of all.

Unemployment

Among you, as in many other countries, there is a serious concern that we cannot pass over in silence: it is becoming very difficult, especially for young people, to find a job. Unemployment causes much suffering. I know that such a problem is not solved by words. However, must not one reflect and act, since it is well understood throughout the whole of society that it is just to assure every member of the community a livelihood by the fruit of his labor? All those in positions of responsibility can contribute to this elementary respect for their brothers and sisters; they must strive to provide suitable means for professional training or for the better utilization of natural resources to the advantage of all the inhabitants. In the whole world there is still much to be done in this regard.

Primacy of the Spirit over Matter

Your people have a great sense of friendship, of sharing; in your traditional culture each one feels bonded to the whole society, giving primacy to the spirit over material goods. These are values which modern society must not compromise. On the contrary, they are indispensable for truly human progress. We have the conviction of faith that man's effort, with the help of God the Creator and Savior, can lead him to "perfect himself and bring about a more humane ordering" of the world.[80]

In creating man and woman, God called them to "fill the earth" and "be its masters."[81] That means that man has a real responsibility, but also that he must remember God when he is doing his work. In order to produce, he is using that which God created.

The Psalm of today's Mass tells us that, "if the Lord does not build the house, in vain do the builders labor."[82] One cannot forget that all activity and work are a cooperation in the divine work of creation.

Without that, it is "vain for you to rise early, or put off your rest," as the Psalmist recalls.[83]

It is necessary, therefore, to keep God before your eyes in beginning your work and in finishing it. We must remember that our responsibilities and our solidarity, in work and in other things, have their origin in God's will.

That has been taught us most of all by Jesus, the worker who worked alongside St. Joseph. That has been taught us by Joseph himself, the carpenter of Nazareth.

---

84. *Human Work Derives from and Builds on God's Creation*[84]

Christian Witness/Mission, Collaboration with God, Culture of Work, Dominion over the Earth, Gospel of Work, Materialism and Consumerism, Spirituality, Work and Prayer.

[A homily on August 20, 1989 in Oviedo, Spain, to a general audience.]

"Blessed are you, Lord, God of all creation. Through your goodness we have this bread to offer, which earth has given and human hands have made . . ."

Every day the Church repeats these words in the celebration of the Eucharist, at the offering of the bread.

Beloved brothers and sisters here present, I wish to meditate on this liturgical blessing with you. The truth regarding the sanctification of human work finds in this blessing its simplest, yet at the same time its fullest, expression.

Yes, "the work of human hands" is part of the sacrifice of Christ. Its place is there where the "source of life and sanctity" is.

Generosity of Creation

Lord, God of all creation! First of all we want to meditate on the mystery of creation, that is, the truth regarding your fatherly generosity. Creation is the first and fundamental gift. Everything that exists does so thanks to you who, being one, "are Existence itself." Thanks to you, whose name (as we know from the Book of Exodus and the testimony of Moses) is "He who is."

Furthermore, you alone, "He who is," are the beginning and the end. In you "we live and move and have our being."[85] The creation of man is a singular gift, since the human being – man and woman – has been created in the image and likeness of God, the Creator. "And God blessed them, and God said to them, 'Be fruitful and multiply, and fill the earth and subdue it'. . . . And God saw everything that he had made, and behold, it was very good."[86]

Human Work Begins with God

Thus, the beginning of human work is contained in the mystery of creation, that admirable "work" of the Creator himself. The Book of Genesis tells us that God the Creator, like man, worked for six days so as to rest on the seventh. Human work contains two elements. The first is talent; the second is effort. Each person receives talent from God through his parents, and also directly, through other people, through one's surroundings, from educators and teachers. The parable of the talents, which we have just read, tells us that the talent has to be used well: it cannot be wasted ("hidden in the ground"). To use these talents, one must face up to the effort of work.

This "effort" is none other than that required of each person in using his intelligence and will to master the gift which is gratuitously offered by the Creator and the heritage passed on by the culture to which he belongs. In this way, through industry, he develops the "talents" received; he makes them grow; he makes them correspond more and more to present and future needs. Seen from this perspective, the history of work is the creative exercise of this human "effort" in the face of a continually renewed awareness of needs which by their very nature cannot be satisfied. It is also the development of the possibilities which spring from the patrimony of "talents," that is, the things and knowledge accumulated in the past.

Furthermore, work is never the application of an anonymous force. Rather it is a dynamic expression of culture. It is here that the primordial and subjective meaning of this "effort" in dominating the earth is introduced: it is an act of a person who is an "image of God," that is, an individual "capable of deciding for himself and who tends towards the realization of himself."[87] Work should not be limited to the efficient production of things in the context of the machinery of society; it should be, above all, the humanization of nature and the growth of man in his humanity, which is a decisive element in testing the truth about man.

This ethical basis of work – verifiable according to whether or not it takes into account the dignity of persons and their relations of freedom and solidarity – condemns every attempt not to give responsibility to man, and everything which reduces him to a simple cog in a machine which moves according to the presumed inexorable laws of things. All the wisdom contained in the admirable maxim "*ora et labora*" – pray and work – is based on the correlation between "talents" and "effort," between God's sovereign initiative and man's free collaboration. Contemplation of the gift and responsible action mutually enrich each other. May work be an experience of the synthesis of beauty, truth and good, leading to an ever more human life!

Building upon Creation

The psalm of today's Liturgy says the same thing. While the parable from St. Matthew's Gospel speaks of the necessity of effort, so that human work may yield appropriate fruits, the psalm shows the help and cooperation of God himself, without which work could be useless. "Unless the Lord builds the house, those who build it labor in vain."[88] We all know well that a house is not built without human work. Nevertheless, at the same time, the Psalmist indicates a fundamental aspect of all "spirituality" of human work. In effect, through work man constantly builds upon that which has already been created. The work of the Creator always comes first.

Temptation to Ignore God

Certainly, the scientific and technical advances which have reduced human "effort" are extraordinary and admirable, since they perfect a person's work and multiply the goods available to satisfy his needs. In this how can one fail to see man's fulfillment of God's command to subdue and master the earth? And, notwithstanding that, the reference to God as creator and origin has been obscured in the person of today's urban-industrial society. The great "conquests" blind people, who are subject to the temptation of Genesis. The denial of his creaturely dependence corresponds to the unleashing of his desire for power.

Hence the fundamental ambivalence of the progress that has been made, where the increasingly greater dominion over things goes hand in hand with lack of clarity about the meaning of human life; where the great technical development of work does not lead to the establishment of the essential principles of dignity and solidarity, thus causing greater depersonalization, disinterest and exploitation; where man changes from being master of nature to being its destroyer. The free and responsible agent in the work of creation now wants to become the "master." He thinks he is self-sufficient; he does not believe that there is any need for the "*God hypothesis*." He separates the "*ora*" from the "*labora*." He gives into the desire for power, and he ends up faced with the fact that every society constructed without God eventually turns against man himself, the builder of "Towers of Babel." Is it not clear for all to see that societies of atheistic materialism with their collectivist-bureaucratic organization of human work are a failure? But on the other hand, it is clear that neither are there fewer problems in the neo-capitalistic society, over-concerned with reward, which alters the just balance of the world of labor, a society also affected by a growing materialistic culture.

A New Culture of Work

Therefore, the task of Christians today, for the good of all people, is to give witness, by the way they work, to an authentic humanization of nature, leaving in it a trail of justice and beauty, showing the true human meaning of work and thus giving obedience and glory to the Creator. Above all, it is a question of rebuilding in the world of work and economy a new subject, bearer of the new culture of work. It is not enough for each one to exercise well the role which society has given him: businessman, trade unionist, politician, consumer or economist; he must do new things, try new ways, new initiatives, new forms of solidarity and labor organization based on this culture.

The impulse to undertake such tasks can come solely from the sense of "gratuity" which derives, before any consideration of convenience, from an awareness of having a common destiny of freedom inscribed in the economy of Creation and Redemption. For this very reason, man's work will be judged above all by the works of today's Gospel: "Well done . . . good and faithful servant; you have been faithful over a little, I will set you over much: enter into the joy of your master."[89]

Since work has this definitive dimension, it is therefore essential to practice what St. Paul says in his Letter to the Colossians (Second Reading): "Whatever your task, work heartily, as serving the Lord . . .

in the name of the Lord Jesus, giving thanks to God the Father through him."[90]

Charity and Work

And finally: "And above all these put on love, which binds everything together in perfect harmony,"[91] because the basic and ultimate measure of the value of human work is charity. Work "with love," not only with hands and mind, but united to Christ. "Blessed are you, Lord, God of all creation. Through your goodness we have this bread to offer, which earth has given and human hands have made," "knowing that from the Lord you will receive the inheritance as your reward."[92] The value, the non-transferable and eternal value of all human work, is ultimately measured by this inheritance. Charity is the key to this inheritance.

---

85. Work Should Respect a Proper Hierarchy of Values[93]

Christian Witness/Mission, Common Good, Dominion over the Earth, Economic Laws and Profits, Environment, Gospel of Work, Human Rights/Dignity, Justice, Materialism and Consumerism, Solidarity.

[A homily on May 10, 1990 in Monterrey, Mexico, to a general audience.]

Today I wish to meditate along with you on the message which the Lord offers us in this Eucharistic celebration. "Do not worry about your life, what you will eat, or about your body, what you will wear ... look at the birds in the sky ... learn from the way the wild flowers grow."[94]

Materialism

What do these words spoken by Jesus Christ in the Sermon on the Mount mean? What was their significance for those who heard them for the first time? What meaning do they encompass for us today?

Truly these words of the Gospel seem to contradict so many criteria and attitudes which we see in the modern world. In reality, productivity, earnings, and economic progress seem to be considered as the ultimate and definitive criteria governing human behavior for humanity and today's society. And it is in relation to these criteria that persons and peoples are judged and evaluated and given a place on the social scale according to the importance paid to them and the power they possess.

If this hierarchy of values is accepted, the human being would be obliged to seek possessions continually as life's only goal. Therefore the person would be evaluated not for what he or she *is*, but for what he or she *has*.

Creator and Creatures Are above Human Productions

Jesus, the Master of the Sermon on the Mount, the one who proclaims the Beatitudes, teaches us first of all that the Creator and creatures stand above the works of man. Man and society can produce only industrial commodities which advance civilization and progress to the degree that they find in the created world the resources which allow them to carry out their work.

To you, humanity, gazing contentedly at the works of your hands, the fruits of your genius, Christ says: Do not forget the One who gave origin to everything! Do not forget the Creator! And further, the more deeply you come to know the laws of nature and the more you discover its wealth and potential, so much the more do you have to be mindful of him.

Respect Creation

Do not forget the Creator – Christ tells us – and *respect creation* Accomplish your work by correctly using the resources God has given you! Transform nature's wealth with the help of science and technology, but do not abuse it nor be usurpers or exploiters without concern for the goods of creation! Do not destroy or contaminate! Remember your neighbor and the poor! Think about future generations!

Dear brothers and sisters, Christ says this in a special way to the people of our time, who are increasingly coming to see the unavoidable need for protecting the environment they live in.

How lovingly the Master and Redeemer gazes upon the beauty of the created world! The visible world has been created for man. Therefore

Christ says to those who listen to him: Are you not worth much more than the birds in the sky and the lilies of the field?[95]

Respect for the Human Person

Certainly we are more important in God's eyes. What gives worth and value to the human being is having been created in the image and likeness of God; this is reflected in his or her nature as a person, and in the ability to know what is good and to love it.

But precisely for this reason the person cannot allow his or her spiritual being to be subjected to what is inferior in the hierarchy of creatures. People cannot take as the final goal of their existence what the earth and the temporality of created things offer them. They cannot lower themselves to serve things, as if these were the sole end and the final destiny of their lives.

On the contrary, man is called to seek God with all his strength, including by means of his work in the world. Only in God does man find confirmed his very freedom, domination and superiority over all other creatures. And if sometimes this simple and profound belief grows weak, contemplation of nature itself should make us recall that, if God takes such care of all creatures, what will he not do to see to it that we have all we need?

Seek Justice

To us human beings falls a basic task: to seek the Kingdom of God and his justice.[96] We must use all our strength in this task, because that Kingdom is "like a treasure hidden in a field, the pearl of great price," which the Gospel speaks to us about; and to obtain it we must do everything possible, even to the point of "selling all we have,"[97] that is to say, having no other desire in our hearts. In this task our work too must be part of the effort we expend in seeking God's Kingdom.

But we must be wary of a temptation: the desire to place earthly goods above God. For this reason Christ tells us: "You cannot serve God and money, for no one can serve two masters."[98] If what is represented by the Biblical symbol "money" succeeds in making itself the object of a higher and more exclusive love on the part of persons and society, then we are witnessing the temptation to ignore God.[99] Yet can we not state that this temptation, at least to some extent, exists in our world? Do we not see it especially in certain regions and people?

Isn't this ignoring of God already a reality in various forms: first in the field of human thought and next in that of its application? Has not living as though God does not exist become a program for many people of our time?

Jesus of Nazareth speaks to his contemporaries, but his words extend with awesome force even into our own days and problems. These are eternal topics for humanity, yet we frequently see that the hierarchy of values has been inverted: what is secondary and transitory is placed first: it goes to the top of the list. On the contrary, what must really occupy the first place is always God alone. It cannot be otherwise. For this reason Christ tells us: "Seek first the Kingdom and its justice, and all these things will be given you besides."[100]

Therefore, what must be done so that the search for the Kingdom may be a reality in the lives of individuals, families and society?

Service of One's Neighbor

As we see in the reading taken from the Acts of the Apostles which we heard, the true disciples and followers of Christ have tried to answer this question since the beginnings of Christianity. The Scripture passage tells us that the first disciples "held everything in common."[101] This fact is very rich in meaning. For the search for the Kingdom demands above all love, love of God and love of neighbor.[102] In this sense, the first disciples placed their earthly goods at the service of love. That is to say, they tried to direct the new life they had embraced towards serving the common good, or the service of one's neighbor. For this reason they sold their possessions and distributed them among everyone, according to the needs of each. Simultaneously an important aspect of the community was "breaking bread in their homes and taking their meals with exaltation and sincerity of heart."[103]

Responsibilities of Business Leaders

These are only a few words, but they are full of meaning! The light which they radiate must enlighten the world of production and the economy too, so that the perspective of the common good may be opened up with farsightedness and generosity. A unified effort for the sake of others is a need which seeks to enlist leaders in business and industry in the difficult tasks of administering justly the fruits of human activity. It includes creating wealth and jobs, thereby making a contribution towards raising the level of society's well-being and clearing the way for the integral advancement of persons. Solidarity appeals equally to those engaged in the world of technology which is "undoubtedly man's ally. It makes work easier, it improves it, speeds it up and augments it."[104] Finally, it appeals to every worker, to every person, who must direct his or her work towards the good of everyone else.

Poverty

Among you who are listening to me, brothers and sisters, there are many who are assured a stable job which give them much satisfaction and allows them to provide properly for their families. Thanks must be given to God for all that. But how much suffering must those endure who cannot give their children food, clothing, and the necessary education? Those who live in a poor, overcrowded area lacking the most basic services and far from their jobs, work which sometimes pays poorly and is unstable, causing them to look towards the future with anguish and discouragement?

How many children are forced to go to work at an early age, how many workers carry out their professions under unhealthy circumstances, including a lack of legal and associative structures which could offer opportune protection for the rights of workers against abuses and the many forms of manipulation?

I am deeply moved by these hard and at times dramatic situations: they affect so many persons in the world of work and are tied to a whole series of factors, not only arising from those situations themselves but also structural in nature, that is, dependent upon the socio-economic and political organizations of society. For this reason, moved by my concern for the neediest, I wish to make a new call for social justice.

Defects of Capitalism

Without denying the good results achieved by the joint efforts of the public and private sectors in countries where freedom rules, we cannot, however, be silent about the defects of an economic system which frequently has money and consumption as its main power source. This subordinates the person to capital in a way which, without taking personal dignity into account, considers him or her to be only a gear in production's mammoth machine where one's work is treated as a simple commodity at the mercy of the tide of supply and demand.

Justice

It is certain that at the root of the evils which harm individuals and groups one always finds man's sin. Therefore the Church always tirelessly preaches conversion of heart so that all, in a unified spirit, may collaborate in the creation of a social order which is more in line with the demands of justice.

The Church cannot in any way let the flag of justice be snatched up by any ideology or political current, for justice is one of the first requirements of the Gospel and the core of her social teaching. Likewise, in this area the Church has to be present in the world with something to say about the values and principles which inspire community life, peace, peaceful coexistence and true progress. Precisely for this reason she has to oppose all those forces which try to sow certain forms of violence and hatred as a dialectical solution to conflicts. The Christian cannot forget that the noble struggle for justice must not be confused in any way with the program "which views class struggle as the only way to eliminate class-based injustices which are present in society and within classes themselves."[105]

Solidarity

Seeing you here in such great numbers in this city of Monterrey, assembled by your common Christian faith to meet the Successor of Peter, I feel the desire well up in my heart to make an appeal to you for solidarity, for brotherhood without borders. Knowing that you are children of the same God and brothers and sisters of Jesus Christ has to prompt you to devote all of your unified strength under the impulse of faith to guaranteeing that this great country become more just, fraternal and welcoming. The ardent desire that your beloved country might advance materially and spiritually upon the foundations of Christian principles which have marked its pilgrimage through history prompts me to say this.

The solidarity I am calling you to must extend its roots deeply and seek its nourishment in the Holy Mass, the sacrifice of Christ who saves us. It must find its inspiration always in the word of God which enlightens the path of our lives.

The Church listens continually to that Sermon on the Mount spoken by Christ. From generation to generation she listens to the Gospel which is the Gospel of Work.

In our era this Gospel has become current in a new way in view of the numerous problems of socio-economic development; in view of the problems relating to capital, with the production and the distribution of goods being so disproportionate and unjust, especially in certain areas of the world.

---

86. The Example of St. Joseph Teaches That Sanctification Comes through Work[106]

Christian Witness/Mission, Dignity of Work, Meaning of Work, St. Joseph, Work and the Worker.

[A homily on March 18, 1991 in Camerino-San Servino Marche, Italy, to a general audience.]

St. Joseph's day is a feast dear to all because he is the patron of the Church, the guardian and example of the people born from Christ's preaching and the model of wisdom for believers. They invoke him in their difficulties and in the problems of our day which truly challenge the Christian's mission. We in turn are inspired by him to be faithful guardians of the Gospel of Christ.

The Church, proposing him as the protector of workers and craftsmen, made him a point of reference and a model for the many persons who spend a great part of their time in seemingly profane activities. The husband of Mary teaches that a person's work is never extraneous to God's plan. Sanctification comes from work when the person works in harmony with the Creator, as did Joseph, the silent worker in the home of Nazareth.

Work and the Mystery of the Cross

Sharing the daily work of the most common activities with Joseph and Mary, Jesus enlightens us about the fact that all work, no matter if it is humble and hidden, draws a person closer to the mystery of the cross: it is a redemptive activity, it is a necessity and a liberation, it is a manifestation of the opportunity which the human person has to subdue the earth. Work makes life more human when it helps to build a new, more perfect world. As such, work makes implicit the proclamation that humanity is journeying towards the new heavens and the new earth foretold by Christ's resurrection.

Work and Sanctification

I want to remind the workers present here of all this – all those in this region who constantly strive to promote new and better living conditions: those who work the land and those who work in small or large industries; those who work in the trades and those who practice ancient and traditional arts; those who are searching for work and migrants; those who have traditional work places and those who use the most modern technologies. I want to remind everyone that work, which is sometimes seen as condemnation and servitude, has rather been assumed by Christ as a moment of redemption and the proclamation of liberation. It is the path to personal sanctification and salvation. It is the constructive moment of fraternal solidarity. Every profession can thus be understood as a particular vocation which confers a superior dignity on human work and a transcendent value because of the spiritual union with Christ.

Personal Christian Witness

The Church's mission of evangelization has been entrusted by God to the free and generous collaboration of people. To each one the Lord says: "You will be my minister and witness."

Human mediation intimately touches the mystery, and with it the problem of every vocation to the apostolate: it makes fulfillment possible, it enriches and comforts people on their journey, from the moment in which they perceive its signs to the time that it is brought to its complete fulfillment. Every Christian is entrusted with the task of "naming" the fundamental vocation that flows from baptism and which is made specific in the various particular vocations. This is done through a different existential path by which people intertwine their personal history with that of God, conforming themselves with radical availability in love to the heavenly Father in service to their brothers and sisters.

Trust in the Lord

"Firm is the heart of the just one who trusts in the Lord." Thus we sang to prepare ourselves to listen to the Gospel.

Firm is the heart of those who recognize God's way in their lives who know how to trust in his promise and relive in their own life, as Joseph did, the behavior of the "just ones" which Scripture speaks of.

Those who trust in the Lord put the word of God at the center of their lives and listen to it always, as did Joseph and Mary, and docilely follow it.

Those who trust in the Lord and have no fear are not dismayed in the presence of the Most High, nor do they close themselves up in egoism.

Those who trust in the Lord are faithful and just.

Those who trust in the Lord do not fear to follow the path he has chosen for them.

Those who trust, work as God has ordained.

And this is the example given us forever by St. Joseph, husband of the Mother of God upon this earth.

Amen!

---

87. Obedience to God Is Shown in the Family and in Work[107]

Community of Persons, Dominion over the Earth, Materialism and Consumerism, Meaning of Work, St. Joseph, Service, Work and Family.

[A homily on March 19, 1991, in
Fabrino, Italy, to a general audience.]

In substance it is a question of two realities: the family and work, not two realities which are distinct, but which are rather connected to one another in a close, mutual relationship.

The Family and Work

The family and work! In the light of the Gospel and the Church's tradition, which are expressed not only in the continuity of her teaching but also in the Christian practice of life and morality, these two important human realities shed light on the proper hierarchy of values; they emphasize the primacy that belongs to the human being as a person and as a community of persons, in the first place, therefore, to the family. All work, and especially physical labor, binds the person to the world of things, to the whole "order" of things. The world has been given to mankind as a task by the Creator, as an earthly job: "Subdue the earth!" The words from the Book of Genesis indicate precisely this subordination of things to the person.[108] The visible world is "for man." Things are for people.

Consumerism

May this order be understood and respected! May it never be violated, and even less so upset! Modern progress, as can be clearly seen, has such a danger in itself. The "progressive" culture, with the exception of those projects which have the person as their true reference, all too easily becomes a culture of things rather than of people. There are so many things that can be done, the calls of advertising and publicity are so insistent, that there is the risk of being overcome. People can end up being, even against their will, slaves of things and of the desire for possessions. Does not perhaps the so-called consumerism represent the expression of "order" (or rather of "disorder") in which "having" is more important than "being"? Is it perhaps not symptomatic that this line of culture is sometimes hostile to the beginning of life, almost as if that human being who is just beginning its existence were an impediment to the possession and use of things?

There is great risk of seeing the very dignity of the person offended, having its autonomy and deepest freedom jeopardized.

Servants of Sharing

Subdue the earth!

Dear brothers and sisters, accept the message offered to you by today's liturgy and open your heart to the strength of the love which knocks down the barriers of selfishness and indifference. You are not slaves to selfish possession, but servants of sharing in solidarity! Fix the eyes of your spirit on the holy family and through the intercession of St. Joseph draw the determination that is enlightened by faith, courage and perseverance in goodness!

How much more easily society could find solutions to the problems that affect it were it to accept the humble though eloquent witness of life offered in the home at Nazareth! With what concrete trust we would be able to look at others if our daily activity were seen as a valuable way of giving praise to the Creator and service to others!

Obedience

The family of Nazareth and, in a special way, the person of St. Joseph, have a profound relation to this vast problem which is affecting mankind and which shows the order in which everyone must work. It is an order which concerns persons, families, and society, the world of labor and legislation. It involves the principal problem for mankind and its future.

In replying to Mary and Joseph, "I must be about my Father's business," Jesus shows that the human order in the family-labor field is established on a divine basis: the Father's concern. For this reason, returning to Nazareth he lived in filial "obedience."

This is one of the elements which are part of the life and work of every human family: the Father's concern, confident trust in divine Providence.

After 30 years the time will come for Christ's messianic mission, and from that moment to the end he will reveal the meaning of the words spoken when he was 12 years old.

The obedience of the youth of Nazareth will be revealed as the redemptive "obedience" of the Son of God to the Father: obedience unto death.

Obedience to God, from whom "all fatherhood in heaven and on earth" has its origin and model.[109] Work also has its origin and model in this obedience.

The Father "works" unceasingly with the Son.[110] God gives ultimate meaning and full dignity to all human activity, to all human activity on the earth.

The image of this meaning and dignity is the Son of God.

It is Christ who worked with Joseph the carpenter.

At the same work bench, he worked in the home at Nazareth.

Amen!

88. The Free Market Cannot Satisfy All Human Needs[111]

Common Good, Dialogue and Cooperation, Economic Laws and Profits, Human Rights/Dignity, Justice, Meaning of Work, Private Property/Co-ownership, Service, Solidarity, Universal Destination of Goods, Work and Society.

[An address on April 1, 1991
in Rome, to a general audience.]

One event seems to dominate the difficult period in which we are living: the conclusion of a cycle in the history of Europe and the world.

The Marxist system has failed, and precisely for the very reasons which *Rerum Novarum* had already acutely and almost prophetically indicated. In this failure of an ideological and economic power which seemed destined to prevail over and even to root out the religious sense in human consciences, the Church sees – beyond all sociological and political factors – the intervention of God's Providence, which alone guides and governs history.

The liberation of so many peoples, of distinguished Churches and of individual persons, should not, however, be transformed into an inappropriate sense of satisfaction or unjustified triumphalism.

Problems Remain

That system has, at least in part, been overcome; but in various areas of the world the most extreme poverty continues to prevail, entire populations are deprived of the most elementary rights and lack the necessary means to satisfy basic human needs. In the wealthiest countries one frequently observes a sort of existential confusion, an inability to live and to experience properly the meaning of life, even though surrounded by an abundance of material possessions. A sense of alienation and loss of their own humanity has made people feel reduced to the role of cogs in the machinery of production and consumption, and they find no way to affirm their own dignity as persons made in the image and likeness of God.

Justice, Solidarity and Human Dignity

Yes, a system is finished; but the problems and situations of injustice and human suffering on which it fed have not, unfortunately, been overcome. It has failed to provide a satisfactory answer, but the question to which that answer had been given continues to remain current and urgent.

With the new encyclical *(Centesimus Annus)* the Church not only presents this question to the whole of humanity, but she also proposes adequate solutions. This means a renewed question about social justice, about solidarity among working people, about the dignity of the human person; it means not to be resigned to exploitation and poverty, never to abandon the transcendent dimension of the person, who wants to and who must place his own work at the heart of building society.

Right to Private Property and Entrepreneurial Activity

The social doctrine of the Church has always recognized the individual's right to private ownership of the means of production and has seen in this right a defense of freedom against every possible oppression. Furthermore, the division of property into the hands of many entails that each person must count on the cooperation of others to satisfy his needs, while the indispensable social exchange must be regulated by contracts in which the free will of one encounters that of another. In contrast to the overbureaucratic and centralized command economy, the free and socially inspired economy presupposes truly free subjects who assume precise responsibilities upon themselves, loyally respect their duties to their co-workers and constantly take the common good into account.

It is right, therefore, to recognize the ethical value of the free market and of entrepreneurial activity within it, of the ability to "arrange the meeting" between consumer needs and the adequate resources to meet them by free bargaining. On this point Leo XIII, in opposition to collectivist theories, vindicated the rights of individual initiative in the context of service required to be given to the community.

The Market Is Not the Model of Social Life

The Catholic Church, however, has always refused and today continues to refuse to make the market the supreme rule and almost the model, or the summation, of social life. There is something that is due to the human person because he is a person, by reason of his dignity and his likeness to God, independently of his presence or not in the market, of what he possesses and therefore can sell, and of the means to buy what he needs. This something must never be disregarded, but rather demands respect and solidarity, the social expression of love which is the only attitude appropriate to the human person. There are human needs that are not accessible to the market, due to natural and social impediments, but which must be equally satisfied.

It is, in fact, the duty of the national and international community to answer these needs, either by giving direct assistance when, for example, an obstacle is insuperable, or by opening the way to proper access to the market, to the world of production and consumption, when that is possible.

Economic freedom is an aspect of human freedom which cannot be separated from its other aspects and which must contribute to the full realization of people in order to construct an authentic human community.

Universal Purpose of the World's Resources

Without a doubt, along with individual ownership, one must affirm the universal purpose of the world's resources. The owner of these resources must always remember their purpose and the fact that, while they guarantee his liberty, they also serve to defend and develop the freedom of others. When, on the other hand, he removes them from this complementary and co-essential function, he consequently removes them from the common good, betraying the purpose for which they were entrusted to him. No free economy can function for long and respond to the conditions of a life more worthy of the human person, unless it is framed in solid legal and political structures, and above all, unless it is supported and "enlivened" by a strong ethical and religious conscience.

This outline, ideal and real at the same time, is rooted in human nature itself. Man, in fact, is a being who "can fully discover his true self only in a sincere giving of himself."[112] He is a unique and unrepeatable subject who can never be absorbed into an undifferentiated human mass, and who truly fulfills his destiny when he is able to transcend his limited individual interests and to join himself to other human beings with many ties. This is the way the family is born; this is the way society is born.

Work Promotes the Person and the Human Community

Work, too, by its essential nature, promotes the autonomy of the person and the necessity of being joined with the work of others. Man works together with others, and through his work he enters into relationship with them: a relationship which can be one of opposition, competition or oppression, but also one of co-operation and membership in a community of solidarity.

Moreover, the human person does not work only for himself, but also for others, beginning with his own family and including the local community, the nation and all of humanity. This is the reality which work must serve. The free and fruitful gift of self is expressed even through work. By confirming the close connection between private property and the universal purpose of the earth's resources, the social doctrine of the Church is merely putting economic activity in the loftiest and broadest context of the general vocation of the human person.

Need for Grace and Personal Commitment

History has always known new attempts to construct a better and more just society, one marked by unity, understanding and solidarity. Many of these attempts have failed, while others were directed against the human person himself.

Human nature, which is ordered toward social existence, also seems to reveal signs of division, dishonesty and hatred. But this is why God, the Father of all, has sent his only Son, Jesus Christ, into the world, in order to overcome these constantly threatening dangers and to change the heart and mind of man by the gift of his grace.

Dear brothers and sisters!

A great commitment at the political, economic, social and cultural level is necessary to build a society that is more just and worthy of the human person. But this is not enough! A decisive commitment must be made in the very heart of man, in the intimacy of his conscience, where he makes his personal decisions. Only on this level can the human person effect a true, deep, and positive change in himself, and that is the undeniable premise of contributing to change and the improvement of all society.

89. Free Time Should Promote Authentic Humanism and Contemplation[113]

Human Rights/Dignity, Leisure, Spirituality, Work and the Worker.

[A Homily on May 13, 1991 in Madeira, Portugal, to Catholics of the Diocese of Funchal.]

A tourist center, universally known as the "Pearl of the Atlantic" because of the great beauty with which the creator has endowed the scenery of these islands, because of the hospitable hearts of their inhabitants and the gift of the rest and health which can be found here, your land is the goal of a great number of men and women of different countries, traditions and creeds. This offers you the opportunity to give to your lives, through your use of free time, the Absolute of God, with the "things that are above, where Christ is seated at the right hand of God."[114] Indeed, Christians have a fundamental role to play in it, in that they contribute an authentic ethical and spiritual context to the use of free time: a time that is propitious for the development of human values and the search for and contemplation of God.

It is certainly not without meaning that the Lord of History has allowed this century's humanity to enter into the "civilization of rest," offering many people the opportunity for a new space in their life which is parallel to their working hours, or rather, of free time which, because of the technological era, in many countries now surpasses working hours in length and importance.

Action and Rest

People are created in God's image, and called to fulfill in their lives both the Creator's active dimension as well as the Lord's tranquil, joyous and festive encounter with his works: "God saw what he had made, and it was very good. . . . Then on the seventh day God finished the work which he had done and on the seventh day he rested from all work."[115] We could say that our century has shown itself memorable in the former dimension, but quite lacking in the latter. As a consequence, the progress created by technology has thus been limited almost exclusively to "dominating" nature and its products, but it has not progressed in the same manner to that dominion which people are called to exercise over their destiny. To the contrary, there is a marked loss of the awareness of their real self and their dignity.

Technical Efficiency Versus the Human Dimension

Unfortunately, certain types of production work tend to deprive work of its human dimension and favor technical efficiency, thus becoming an arid experience, reduced to automatic acts and mechanical movements, marked by an obligatory pace, deprived of human relationships and amid which it is difficult to express one's own identity. It is indispensable that free time regain the dimensions of humanity which work has lost.

Authentic Humanism

In particular free time should allow people to find the opportunity to achieve authentic humanism, which is that of the "Easter Person which the Church proclaims and bears witness to, shining with new life, which liberates people from sin and opens to them the horizons of eternity, finding in God the rest for which hearts yearn."[116] Truly the Lord, in that he is absolutely good, rests in himself, in his fullness: the human person, the image of God, can rest only in God, in whom he or she finds meaning and holiness.

Easter Peace

"Easter People" do not need false infinities, or the most beautiful, the greatest, the most exciting, because they know that their unlimited freedom is enclosed and contained in the celebration of the Paschal event: Easter possesses and confers the freedom which makes our free time a most intimate principle. From this Paschal freedom is born the supremacy of the Christian life which spreads and gives peace, which leads the person to rest and even causes it. "Redeemed by Christ, and having become a new creature in the Holy Spirit, people in fact, can and must also love the things which God created. From God they receive them; they look upon them as coming from God's hands, and they respect them. They thank the divine benefactor for them, and using and enjoying creatures in a spirit of poverty and freedom, they are taught the true possession of the world, as someone who has nothing and yet possesses everything: 'Everything, in fact, is yours; but you are Christ's and Christ is God's.' "[117]

Celebration of the Goodness of God's World

Thus in dignity, contemplation, and adoration the new person confidently submits to the Lord in a great festival of the whole renewed creation. There is a celebration of the renewed splendor and the full goodness of the world in God; the risen Christ, in his infinite grace, frees people from their limits. Easter is the new creation of the world and of mankind. We celebrate all this in the Sunday Eucharist: that which is new, that which is creative, that which is restful, until "the coming of our Lord Jesus Christ."[118]

---

90. We Are Called to Share the Table of Creation[119]

Universal Destination of Goods.

[A Lenten Message in 1992 from the Vatican, marking the fifth centenary of the evangelization of the American continent.]

Creation belongs to everyone. Yes, as Lent draws near, when our Lord Jesus Christ calls us in a particular way to conversion, I wish to address each one of you and invite you to think about this truth and to do good deeds which will show your sincerity of heart.

This same Lord, whose supreme proof of love we celebrate at Easter, was with the Father from the beginning, preparing the wonderful table of creation, to which he meant to invite all without exception.[120] The Church has understood this truth, made known since the dawn of revelation, and she sees it as an objective to be proposed to people as a way of life.[121] In more recent times she has repeatedly preached the universal destination of the goods of creation, both material and spiritual, as a central theme of her social teaching. Continuing this long standing tradition, the encyclical *Centesimus Annus*, published on the occasion of the centenary of my predecessor Leo XIII's *Rerum Novarum*, is meant to encourage reflection on this universal destination of goods, which comes before all particular forms of private property and which should give them their true meaning.

The Failure of Distributing Goods

However, it is sad to see how, in spite of the frequency with which these clearly expressed truths have been proclaimed, the earth with all its goods – which we have compared to a great banquet to which all the men and women who have lived or will live have been invited – is unfortunately in many ways still in the hands of a few minorities. Wonderful are the goods of the earth, both those which come directly from the generous hands of the creator and those which are the result of the activity of human beings, called to cooperate in the work of creation through their intelligence and labor. Moreover, all human beings need a share in those goods in order to reach their fullness. It is thus all the more painful to note how many millions of people are excluded from the table of creation.

For this reason I earnestly invite you to concentrate your attention on this year commemorating the fifth centenary of the evangelization of the American continent, which in no way should remain a mere historical anniversary. Our vision of the past must be complemented by a look around us and toward the future.[122] We must try to discern the mysterious presence of God in history, where he engages us and calls us to give him definite responses. Five centuries of the Gospel's presence on that continent have still not produced a fair distribution of the goods of the earth. And this is all the more painful when we think of the poorest of the poor: the indigenous groups, and together with them many campesinos, offended in their dignity by being excluded from the exercise of even their most fundamental rights, which also are a part of the goods destined for all. The situation of these brothers and sisters of ours cries out for justice from the Lord. Consequently, a generous and bold reform of economic structures and agrarian policies needs to be fostered, so as to ensure well-being and the conditions required for the rightful exercise of their human rights by the indigenous groups and the great masses of the poor who have so often been unjustly treated.

For those people and for all the dispossessed of the world – for we are all children of God, brothers and sisters to each other, and the goods of creation are meant for us all – we must work hard and without delay so that they can occupy their proper place at the table of creation. In the season of Lent and also during campaigns of solidarity – Advent campaigns and weeks for the poor – a clear awareness that it is the Creator's will to place the goods of creation at the service of everyone should inspire work for the genuine and complete development of the person and of all people.

In a spirit of prayer and commitment we must listen carefully to the words: "Behold, I am at the door and knock."[123] Yes, it is the Lord himself who knocks gently at the heart of each one of us, without forcing us, waiting patiently for us to open so that he can come in and sit down at the table with us. But, again, we must never forget that – according to the central message of the Gospel – Jesus calls us through each of our brothers and sisters, and our personal response will serve as the criterion for being put at his right hand with the blessed or at his left with the accursed: "I was hungry ... I was thirsty ... I was a stranger ... I was naked ... sick ... in prison."[124]

Praying fervently that the Lord will enlighten the efforts of all on behalf of the poorest and most needy, I bless you with all my heart, in the name of the Father and of the Son and of the Holy Spirit. Amen.

Notes

1 The translation was taken from *Origins*, June 21, 1979, pp. 76-77.
2 Gen 3:19.
3 Jn 1:12.
4 This text was taken from *Origins*, October 25, 1979, pp. 293-294.
5 Gen 3:7.
6 Gen 1:26.
7 Jn 15:1.
8 Gen 1:28.
9 Address to the World Food Conference, Nov. 9, 1974, n. 4.
10 Phil 2:5.
11 Mt 6:26.
12 Mt 6:28.
13 Mt 13:4ff.
14 Jn 15:1.
15 Jn 10:14.
16 *Gaudium et Spes*, n. 69.
17 Address to the World Food Conference, Nov. 9, 1974, n. 9.
18 Mt 14:16.
19 *Confessions* I,1.
20 The translation was taken from *L'Osservatore Romano*, November 17, 1980, pp. 3, 20.
21 Jn 4:19-24.
22 1 Pt 2:4-9.

23 Ps 95:1-2.
24 1 Thess 5:18.
25 Eph 5:18-20.
26 1 Thess 5:15.
27 The translation was taken from *L'Osservatore Romano*, September 28, 1981, p. 2.
28 Mt 20:1.
29 2 Thess 3:10.
30 Address to farmers of Legazpi City, February 21, 1981.
31 The translation was taken from *L'Osservatore Romano*, November 2, 1981, p. 2.
32 May 31, 1980.
33 The translation was taken from *L'Osservatore Romano*, December 14, 1981, p. 7.
34 *Pacem in Terris*, n. 10.
35 Address in Guadalajara, Mexico, January 10, 1979.
36 *Laborem Exercens*, n. 15.
37 *Laborem Exercens*, n. 19.
38 *Laborem Exercens*, n. 19.
39 Address to the XIX National Congress of CIF, n. 2, December 7, 1979.
40 Address to the XIX National Congress of CIF, n. 2, December 7, 1979.
41 The translation was taken from *L'Osservatore Romano*, May 10, 1982, p. 19.
42 Col 3:23f.
43 Mt 25:40.
44 The translation was taken from *L'Osservatore Romano*, March 20, 1984, p. 9.
45 Gen 1:28.
46 *Insegnamenti*, II, 1979, p. 281 and *L'Osservatore Romano* in English, February 12, 1979, p. 11.
47 *Gaudium et Spes*, n. 67.
48 *Lumen Gentuim*, n. 36.
49 Mt 20:28; Mk 10:45.
50 Pius XII, Message of September 1, 1944.
51 *Laborem Exercens*, n. 27.
52 Gen 1:28.
53 *Gaudium et Spes*, n. 67.
54 The translation was taken from *Origins*, February 20, 1986, p. 593.
55 *Laborem Exercens*, n. 6.
56 Gen 1:26-28.

57 Gen 1:28.
58 Gen 3:16-19.
59 *Laborem Exercens*, n. 27.
60 *Laborem Exercens*, n. 19.
61 Jn 14:6.
62 Mt 5:14.
63 Mt 5:13.
64 The translation was taken from *L'Osservatore Romano*, August 11, 1986, p. 2.
65 Mt 4:4.
66 The translation was taken from *L'Osservatore Romano*, August 8-15, 1988, pp. 9-10.
67 *Sollicitudo Rei Socialis*, n. 38.
68 *Sollicitudo Rei Socialis*, n. 38.
69 Lk 12:12-21.
70 *Gaudium et Spes*, n. 65.
71 *Sollicitudo Rei Socialis*, n. 32.
72 Lk 11:33.
73 The translation was taken from *L'Osservatore Romano*, August 8-15, 1988, p. 11.
74 *Sollicitudo Rei Socialis*, n. 38.
75 Gal 5:22.
76 The translation was taken from *L'Osservatore Romano*, August 8-15, pp. 14-15.
77 The translation was taken from *L'Osservatore Romano*, May 22, 1989, pp. 4-5.
78 *Gaudium et Spes*, n. 34.
79 *Gaudium et Spes*, n. 34.
80 *Gaudium et Spes*, n. 35.
81 Gen 1:26, 28.
82 Ps 127:1.
83 Ps 127:2.
84 The translation was taken from *L'Osservatore Romano*, September 4, 1989, p. 5
85 Acts 17:28.
86 Gen 1:28-31.
87 *Laborem Exercens*, n. 6.
88 Ps 127:1.
89 Mt 25:21, 23.
90 Col 3:23, 17.

91 Col 3:14.
92 Col 3:24.
93 The translation was taken from *L'Osservatore Romano*, May 21, 1990, pp. 8-9.
94 Mt 6:35-36; 28.
95 Mt 6:26, 28.
96 Mt 6:33.
97 Mt 13:44,45.
98 Mt 6:24.
99 Mt 6:24.
100 Mt 6:33.
101 Acts 2:44.
102 Mk 12:34.
103 Acts 2:45-46.
104 *Laborem Exercens*, n. 5.
105 *Laborem Exercens*, n. 11.
106 The translation was taken from *L'Osservatore Romano*, March 25, 1991, p. 7.
107 The translation was taken from *L'Osservatore Romano*, April 2, 1991, p. 10.
108 Gen 1:28.
109 Eph 3:15.
110 Jn 5:17.
111 The text was taken from *L'Osservatore Romano*, May 6, 1991, p. 3.
112 *Gaudium et Spes*, n. 24.
113 The translation was taken from *L'Osservatore Romano*, May 20, 1991, p. 9.
114 Col 3:1.
115 Gen 1:31; 2:2.
116 *Confessions*, I,1.
117 1 Cor 3:22-23; *Gaudium et Spes*, n. 37.
118 From the Ordinary of the Mass, after the Our Father.
119 The translation was taken from *Origins*, March 5, 1992, p. 634.
120 Jn 1.1-3.
121 Acts 2:44-45; 4:32-35.
122 *Centesimus Annus*, n. 3.
123 Rev 3:20.
124 Mt 25:34f.

GLOSSARY

Note: The definitions of terms in the glossary are drawn from the way John Paul uses these terms in his talks. Hence, they often contain an exhortation to do or be something, as well as a definition of the term.

1. ***Christian Witness/Mission***
   It is indispensable for Christians to see themselves as apostles in their daily work: "always be prepared to make a defence to anyone who calls you to account for the hope that is in you." (1Pt 3:15)

2. ***Collaboration with God***
   Human work expresses a sharing in the divine work of creation. By putting to use the wealth of spiritual and material resources given them by their Creator, human persons contribute to the progress of society and their own sanctification.

3. ***Common Good***
   The set of conditions of social living whereby human beings are enabled more fully and more readily to achieve their own perfection.

4. ***Community of Persons***
   Every business must become a true community of work where everyone's rights and duties receive recognition and are properly coordinated and harmonized with regard to the common good.

5. ***Culture of Work***
   We need to rediscover a "culture of work" which is not dictated simply by productive demand but in which businesses become genuine working communities of collaboration and service.

6. ***Dialogue and Cooperation***
Through the contribution of each person, the workplace can take on the characteristics of participation and solidarity where management and workers live together in harmony, committed to generous cooperation aimed at improving relations among them.

7. ***Dignity of Work***
The dignity of work derives fundamentally from God's revelation of himself as a worker and from the revelation that we are made "in the image and likeness of God." Therefore, human work, carried out by beings in the image of God who are imitating God, has a fundamental dignity.

8. ***Dominion over the Earth***
Human beings, created in God's image, have received the command to subject the earth and govern it in justice and holiness so as to lead themselves and the whole universe to God.

9. ***Economic Laws and Profits***
Search for legitimate profits must not have a detrimental effect on the respect for and true development of the human person.

10. ***Entrepreneurship***
Entrepreneurs require a breadth of vision to recognize that their responsibilities extend beyond the purely managerial and financial fields to use technological progress for personal growth and a greater solidarity with their neighbor.

11. ***Environment***
Accomplish your work by correctly using the resources God has given you. Transform nature's wealth with the help of science and technology, but do not abuse it or be usurpers or exploiters without concern for the goods of creation. Remember your neighbor and the poor. Think about future generations.

12. ***Fair Wage***
Central to securing a just relation between worker and employer is a just remuneration for work.

13. ***Gospel of Work***
The role of work in the mystery of creation and redemption, including what insight the revelation of God as a worker can give us into designing and running workplaces.

14. *Human Development/Progress*
True human progress requires a single development for all peoples that respects the dignity of the person and is open to the fundamental values of the spirit.

15. *Human Rights/Dignity*
There is something, often described as a 'right' or as 'dignity,' due to human persons because they are persons, by reason of their likeness to God, independently of economic or market factors. This dignity must never be disregarded but demands respect and solidarity, the social expression of love, which is the only attitude appropriate to the human person.

16. *Humanization/Dehumanization*
It is through work that man's humanity is actualized. It is through the proper conditions of work that life becomes more human for individuals and for society.

17. *Justice*
Just as the "structures of sin" exist, there can and must be a "structure of good," of justice, solidarity, mutual respect and peace which results from the activities of individual persons.

18. *Leisure*
Christians have a fundamental responsibility of providing an ethical and spiritual dimension to free time, one that furthers the development of human values and the search for and contemplation of God.

19. *Materialism and Consumerism*
We must never forget that the riches of this world are transient and cannot be our ultimate goal: the human person is more important than things and the soul more important than the body.

20. *Meaning of Work*
One must know the why and the wherefore of work beyond the immediate benefits which derive from it. By means of human work, one commits oneself not only for one's own sake but also for others and with others, working to provide for the needs of one's family, community, nation, and ultimately all humanity.

21. *Private Property/Co-ownership*
The ownership of private property receives its moral justification by creation of opportunities for work and human growth for all.

22. *Professional Training/Responsibility*
Business leaders have a responsibility to increase their knowledge of Christian social principles and to make human and Christian virtues shine forth in the complex world of economic activity the virtues that respect the dignity of the person and are open to mutual solidarity.

23. *Saint Joseph*
Saint Joseph the Worker is the model to remind us that individual and collective activity to improve the circumstances of the world is an essential feature of God's plan for the human race.

24. *Selfishness*
Learn to develop those social virtues of solidarity and service without which one will fall inexorably into selfish individualism, alienation and exploitation.

25. *Service*
Never think of others merely as people who use your talents but as brothers and sisters to be respected and served.

26. *Solidarity*
The virtue by which we promote a professional ethic that respects human rights and seeks to bring about fraternal understanding and cooperation among all peoples.

27. *Spirituality*
Work provides a constant opportunity to meet people in whom we may recognize God's image, and in this way to make of work a real process of our sanctification.

28. *Technology*
Christians appreciate technological innovation, but they know they must not make it an "idol" but must assure that it is used for the common good under the control of all elements of society.

29. *Unemployment*
More than an economic loss, unemployment is an evil because it deprives those unemployed of the human development and dignity that is derived from work.

30. *Universal Destination of Goods*
The right to private property is not absolute but depends on the prior gift of all creation to all human beings. Private property

exists only so that God's good creation can be better shared with all.

31. Work and Family
Work and the family are closely related because in both the human person is called to cooperate with God in fulfilling his plan of love.

32. Work and Prayer
Christian believers should endow their work with a real dimension of sanctification, making their work a liturgy, an act of worship which they joyously offer to God.

33. Work and Society
The responsible performance of work does not isolate the job from society but rather consists in social improvement, laboring in the vineyard of one's own nation and that of the whole world.

34. Work and Women/Mothers
Work must never take away from the woman, as wife and mother, the social and familial functions which are proper to her and which constitute her particular dignity.

35. Work and the Worker
Before considering human work in its objective aspect, we should see it first in its subjectivity. It is the human person who gives meaning to work. Work is for the worker, not the worker for work.

36. Worker Participation
In economic enterprises it is human persons who work together, free and independent human beings created in the image of God. Therefore, the active participation of everyone in running an enterprise should be promoted.

37. World Community
Solidarity must pass over political borders in order to be open to a proper respect for the dignity of each member of the human family.

SUGGESTIONS FOR ADDITIONAL READING

Books and Collections of Essays

Charles E Curran, and Richard A McCormick, SJ, eds, *Readings in Moral Theology No. 5: Official Catholic Social Teaching*. New York: Paulist Press, 1986.

John W Houck and Oliver F Williams, CSC, *Co-Creation and Capitalism: John Paul II's* Laborem Exercens. Lanham, MD: University Press of America, 1983.

Michael Naughton, *The Good Stewards*. Lanham, MD: University Press of America, 1992.

Richard John Neuhaus, *Doing Well and Doing Good*. New York: Doubleday, 1992.

Michael Novak, *The Spirit of Democratic Capitalism*. New York: Simon and Schuster, 1982. (Reprinted by University Press of America.)

Michael Novak, *Catholic Social Thought and Liberal Institutions*, 2nd edition. New Brunswick, NJ: Transaction Publishers, nd. (Originally published as *Freedom with Justice* by Harper & Row in 1984.)

Michael Novak, *The Catholic Ethic and the Spirit of Capitalism.* New York: The Free Press, 1993.

George Weigel, ed, *A New Worldly Order.* Washington: Ethics and Public Policy Center, 1992.

Recent Articles

Rocco Buttiglione, "Behind *Centesimus Annus*," Crisis (July-August 1991) pp 8-9.

Rocco Buttiglione, "Christian Economics 101," *Crisis* (July-August 1992) pp 32-36.

Matthew Habiger, "Reflections on Centesimus Annus," *Social Justice Review* (September/October 1991) pp 139-142.

Bryan J Hehir, "Reordering the World," *Commonweal* (14 June 1991) pp 393-394.

David Hollenbach, "The Pope and Capitalism," *America* (1 June 1991) pp 590-591.

James V Schall, SJ, "The Unexpected Encyclical," *Social Justice Review* (September/October 1991) pp 143-147.

Frank Turner, "John Paul II's Social Analysis," *The Month* (August 1991) pp 344-349.

Documentary Sources

L'Osservatore Romano, the official newspaper (and newspaper of record) of the Vatican, is published weekly in an English edition. It may be ordered from their Editorial and Management Offices, Via del Pellegrino, 00120 Vatican City.

Origins is a weekly documentary newsletter published by the Catholic News Service of the United States Catholic Conference. It may be ordered from CNS, 3211 4th Street NE, Washington, DC 20017-1100.

The Pope Speaks is published bi-monthly by Our Sunday Visitor, 200 Noll Plaza, Huntington, IN 46750.

INDEX

Note: The numbers below refer to the talks, not pages.